THREE CAPITALS

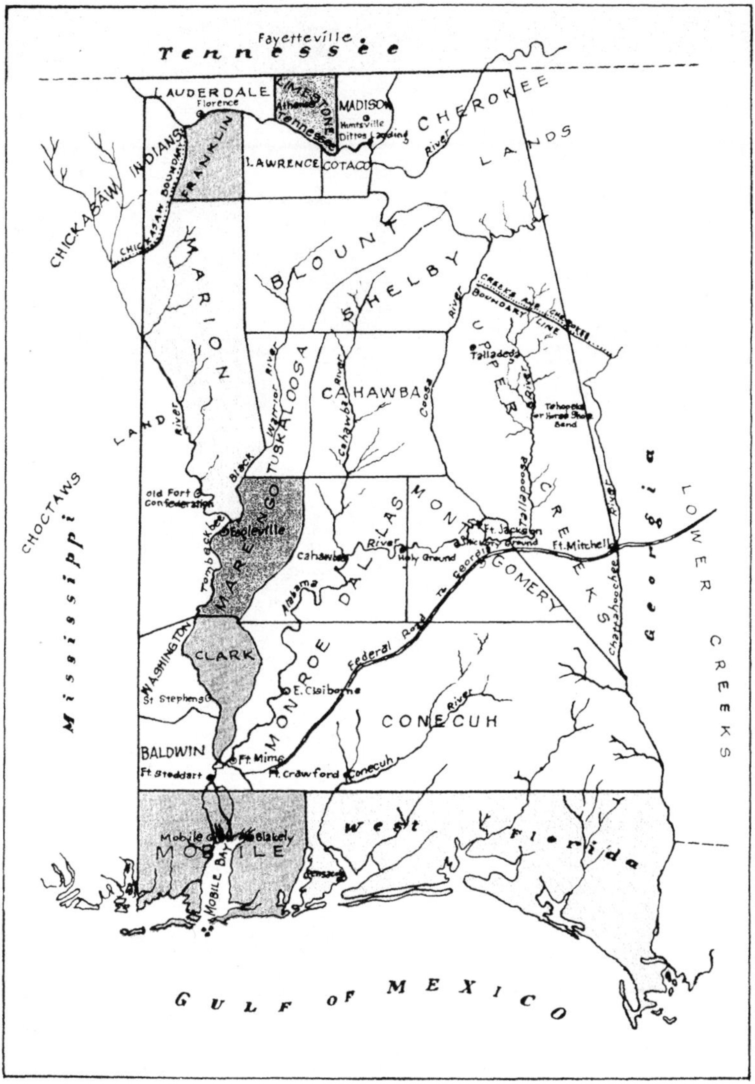

Map of Alabama
1818

THREE CAPITALS

A Book About the First Three Capitals of Alabama

ST. STEPHENS, HUNTSVILLE & CAHAWBA

Including Information About the Politics, Laws, and Men of

THE TERRITORY AND STATE OF ALABAMA

1818 TO 1826

ALSO SIGNIFICANT HISTORICAL DOCUMENTS AND RECORDS

BY WILLIAM H. BRANTLEY

The University of Alabama Press

LIBRARY OF CONGRESS CATALOGING IN PUBLICATION DATA

Brantley, William Henderson, 1896-1964
Three capitals.

Reprint of the priv. print. 1947 ed.
Includes index.
1. Alabama—Capital and capitol. 2. St. Stephens, Ala.—History. 3. Huntsville, Ala.—History. 4. Cahawba, Ala.—History. 5. Alabama—Politics and government—To 1865. I. Title.
F326.B826 1976 976.1 76-28483
0-8173-1249-8 (pbk: alk. paper)

To

ANN, WILLIAM and KIRVEN

Acknowledgments

The author is grateful for the assistance given him by friends in producing this book. Miss Frances Hails, of the Alabama Department of Archives and History, furnished the photographs of the portraits of Governor William Wyatt Bibb, Acting Governor Thomas Bibb, and Henry Hitchcock. The sketch of the State House at Cahawba was prepared by Mr. Hugh Martin, distinguished Birmingham architect. The map of Alabama in 1818 and the maps showing the vote on the removal of the seat of government were executed by Walter Schoel, civil engineer, of Birmingham, from drafts prepared by the author. Mr. Robbie Sturdivant, noted citizen of Dallas County and enthusiastic historian, walked over the site of Cahawba with the author and gave freely of his vast knowledge of the vanished town. John Lapsley, able lawyer of Selma, assisted in searching and checking the official records of Dallas County. Miss Julia Robertson and Mrs. George Griffin, of Birmingham, typed the manuscript and aided in the verification of citations.

Contents

Illustrations

Introduction

TO THE 1976 EDITION

William Henderson Brantley, Jr. was born September 17, 1896 in Pike County, Alabama, and died June 19, 1964 in Birmingham. Brantley, a professional lawyer and amateur historian, had a deep love for the State of Alabama, and a continuing interest in her history. His book, *Three Capitals: A Book About the First Three Capitals of Alabama,* brings this love and interest into focus to a greater extent than any of his other works. Brantley's *Three Capitals* remains his most popular book and deserves republication after being out of print for some years. It is a meticulous, scholarly, and thorough work.

In 1946 Mr. Brantley was one of the founders of the Alabama Historical Association, and remained one of its continuing counsellors and guides until his death. A Phi Beta Kappa at The University of Alabama, a graduate of Harvard University Law School, and a long-time trustee of Howard (now Samford University), he compiled many personal historical records including a diary, 1948-1956, all of which he donated to Samford University in 1963. These, along with his collection of rare books, manuscripts, and photographs, are available in the Brantley Room at Samford University Law Library.

Alabama, like other frontier states, had a "capital on wheels" in the antebellum period, as population shifted and transportation needs changed. Five towns—St. Stephens, Huntsville, Cahawba, Tuscaloosa, and Montgomery (where the capital finally came to rest)—were capitals of Alabama between 1818 and 1846. But Brantley chose to study thoroughly only the first three: the territorial capital at St. Stephens (1818-1819); the temporary capital at Huntsville, where Alabama's first constitution was written in 1819; and the first semipermanent capital of the state at

Cahawba, 1820-1826. These three capitals cover a time span of only eight years, but Brantley wrote that it was "within this short span that government was born, put into operation, and made to function under the merciless decrees of suffrage." He concluded his book with the words: "the annals of Tuskaloosa and Montgomery are for others to tell—this of St. Stephens, Huntsville and Cahawba is finished."

Brantley's *Three Capitals* is divided into three chapters. The first two chapters, about one-fourth of the book, are devoted to St. Stephens and Huntsville. Significant insights into Alabama's early history are found in chapter two, in which Brantley, a student of legal history, features the writing of Alabama's first constitution.

It is in the last chapter on Cahawba, however, that the author makes his chief contribution. Here he presents significant and interesting details of one of Alabama's most thriving early towns. Cahawba was a wealthy cotton center and Alabama's capital. History preserves the memory of its former greatness. Brantley details a chronological narrative of the accomplishments of the annual sessions of the legislature (1819-1825) and presents interesting personalities during the administrations of Governors William Wyatt Bibb, Thomas Bibb, Israel Pickens, and John Murphy. Such issues as early State finances, the State Bank, and the location of The University of Alabama are featured. State leaders such as Arthur Bagby, Seth Barton, Clement C. Clay, and Marmaduke Williams, as well as national leaders such as Henry Clay, William H. Crawford, and Andrew Jackson, come to life in the narrative.

This book is a must for all readers and collectors of Alabamiana, because of its thorough research, interesting details about the State's early history, handsome format, and excellent maps and illustrations.

Brantley's other publications include *Chief Justice Stone of Alabama,* 1943. Volume I of his magnum opus, *Banking in Alabama, 1816-1860* was printed by the Birmingham Printing Company in 1961. The second volume was published posthumously in 1967.

MALCOLM C. MCMILLAN
Hollifield Professor and
Head, History Department,
Auburn University

THREE CAPITALS

Three Capitals

ST. STEPHENS

The First Capital

THE TOMBIGBE is a moody and treacherous river. Gathering its waters from the uplands of Northern Alabama and Mississippi, this least-known of Alabama's mighty streams gains in strength and volume as it alternately surges and glides down to Mobile Bay. Thus was the Tombigbe when the French, the first European settlers on Mobile Bay, cautiously ascended its waters, almost as somber and forbidding as the name[1] suggests, and claimed the stream and surrounding lands for France.

These new masters of the country built fortifications at strategic points on the river and made some use of it for transportation, but if they gained much knowledge about this almost secretive stream it was not preserved for posterity. Certainly they did not evidence the quality of permanent sovereignty so noticeable in the practical British, who succeeded them in ownership of the country. Taking it for granted that they would rule this land forever, the English, with characteristic foresight and before spending any considerable sums for developments, sought to inform themselves about their newly acquired territory. An expedition was sent out to explore the Tombigbe country and report the details of what was found. The experienced Bernard Romans was in charge of the party.

The explorers traveled north from Mobile on land and returned by water—down the Tombigbe. On January 14, 1772, Romans reached the last rapids in the river, which swirled and foamed and shoaled at the foot of a limestone bluff rising sheer and high on the western bank. Below these rapids was deep water to the Gulf, so Romans re-

[1] "Tombigbe" is a Choctaw word meaning "coffin makers."

corded in his journal a practical observation coupled with a prediction:

> Stout sloops and schooners may come up to this rapid: therefore, I judge some considerable settlement will take place.

The prophecy made by Romans was not to go unfulfilled. His keen judgment had selected and identified the place where, more than a quarter of a century later, would be the pioneer town, St. Stephens, marked for fame and doomed to oblivion. Eventually the Congress of the United States would choose this remote village for the seat of government of the newly created Alabama Territory, but before that momentous day St. Stephens, nurtured and protected by the Tombigbe, builded for herself a lusty and picturesque personality every bit worthy to wear the laurels of a frontier capital.

When the French explorers and traders pushed up the Tombigbe they, too, looked appraisingly upon the great limestone bluff which Romans afterward noted and which the Choctaw Indians called Hobuckintoopa. Evidently the French thought the place too near Mobile for a fort, so they went higher up the river and deeper into the Indian Country to erect Fort Tombeckbe. The French, however, did not fail to make some use of this magnificent natural fortification. They had a sort of outpost here, for it was at this point, just below the shoals,[1] that their ocean-going ships ended their upstream journeys[2] and surrendered their cargoes to barges waiting above the rapids; and so on to Fort Tombeckbe. But the French in America were victims of French failure in Europe. The treaty of Paris gave this vast undeveloped section to Britain.

During the seventeen years of British dominion over the

[1] McGrew Shoals. Named for John McGrew, who acquired the site from Choctaw Indians in 1799.

[2] "The Schooner Experience out of New Orleans for St. Stephens with two hogsheads of sugar, met tempestuous weather. . . ." (Channing v. Caskaden —I Minor, p. 73)

land which is now Alabama no fort was built on the high stone bluff Hobuckintoopa. The land around it, however, was considered by the King as Crown land and not as a part of the Colony of Georgia. There were more Englishmen living in the section than the usual number of traders and a scattering of Indian Countrymen, for many Tory-minded men, who also had a distaste for war, had left the eastern seaboard when the American revolution began and migrated into this wild and undeveloped section, where they lived as well as they could and did as they pleased.

But even the stout land-loving English failed to hold the country. The thirteen rebelling American colonies won their independence, and in the peace-table shuffle, the British Colonies of East and West Florida, which had not participated in the Revolution, went to Spain, who promptly claimed to own as far north as the present city of Montgomery. The new Spanish Governor, Estevan Miro, knowing Spain was claiming too much, moved quickly to hold it if he could. He put a garrison in Fort Confederation,[1] and then in the year 1789 built a new fortification atop Hobuckintoopa which was named Fort St. Stephens.[2] The Spanish were digging in deep and fast. They knew from many unhappy experiences what to expect from Englishmen, and to them an American was only a particularly tough breed of Englishman.

Lieutenant Joseph DeVille Degoutin was made Commandant at Fort St. Stephens in 1790. He was succeeded the following year by Captain Fernando Lisora, who garrisoned the fort with one company. The Spanish were industrious, for soon they had an outer system of earthen works thrown up around the stout blockhouse. A church was erected and a special house was built for the Commandant. These three buildings were plastered. Smaller and

[1] This was the name the British had given to the old French Fort Tombeckbe.

[2] Perhaps the fort was named for Miro, whose first name was Estevan.

less substantial buildings were located near the main fort building. This display of permanence encouraged Spanish citizens in the Mobile district to apply for land grants in the St. Stephens locality, with the result that numbers of Spanish families moved up the river and settled in the community.

But Spain's title to this region was insecure and the Spanish authorities knew it. Finally they yielded to the aggressive assertion of the Americans that the line between the United States and Florida was the 31° of latitude. Where was this line? No one knew! There was long delay in getting the line established but finally, in 1799, Andrew Ellicott finished the survey and set up the stone to mark the boundary. Fort St. Stephens, to the great disappointment of the Spanish, fell to the United States. The port of Mobile, of course, was south of the line and remained a possession of his Catholic Majesty Charles IV of Spain.

The Americans had been as aggressive and alert to the developing situation as had the Spanish. Even before Ellicott had approached near enough to indicate who would rule at Fort St. Stephens, United States soldiers had been busy cutting a trace from Natchez to the west bank of the Tombigbe which hit the river some distance upstream from Fort St. Stephens. The American detachment was in charge of Lieutenant John McClary, who made no attempt to keep secret the presence of his military unit in the neighborhood.

The Spanish acknowledged the American rights as established by Ellicott's survey without any contest, and on May 5, 1799, the Commandant, Antonio Palaas, struck his colors from Fort St. Stephens and led his Spanish garrison out. Lieutenant John McClary marched his troops in and raised the American flag over the place which was to become the first Alabama capital.[1]

[1] Hamilton's *Colonial Mobile* (1910). But see affidavit of John Brewer and Richard Brashear made before Judge Harry Toulmin on December 16, 1806, in which they state that on February 5, 1799, Lieutenant Lasoral, Commandant at Fort St. Stephens, summoned them and others to the Fort to witness

This "Change of Colors" on high Hobuckintoopa was more than a compliance with the terms of a boundary treaty. Here in the isolated Tombigbe valley occurred the first step of the United States in territorial expansion. The occupation of Fort St. Stephens did not merely decide that this section would be Anglo-Saxon instead of Latin, but from this Spanish recession, begun when McClary expelled Palaas, the world was given notice that the new nation—this United States—would dare assert her rights. And those "Southwestern" men who took over at Fort St. Stephens were the fathers of the same breed who expanded this nation by Florida, by Louisiana, by the battle of New Orleans, by Texas, and by the tremendous country beyond the Rockies to the shores of the Pacific.

The Saxon is a land-loving man, and the lower Tombigbe-Alabama basin was lush country, inviting occupation and cultivation. Mr. Whitney's cotton engine was a success, so that the last barrier to the extensive use of cotton was down. From the eastern seaboard states the settlers poured southwest to raise cotton and get rich. As is usual, the pioneers were not the first citizens in the communities from which they came. Those who are successful and established stay at home while the man who has less to risk blazes the trail. These first settlers were for the most part a stout and rough set of men. Lorenzo Dow, the famous itinerant preacher who visited the Tombigbe settlement in the St. Stephens locality above the "cut-off" in 1803, recorded in his journal:

> The inhabitants are mostly English but are like sheep without a shepherd. Whilst under the Spanish Government it was a place of refuge for bad men, but of late, since it fell to us, seems

its surrender by officers of his Catholic Majesty and giving the keys to Richard Brashear for delivery to the American officer when he should come. The affidavit further states that the Spanish troops evacuated the Fort that day, February 5, 1799, "and removed into the old church near said fort where they continued two or three days, and then took water in order to remove out of the territory." (Territorial Papers by Carter, Vol. v, p. 482)

to be in a hopeful way, but there is still room for great amendment.[1]

Dow was back again in 1805, when he wrote that Fort St. Stephens would "be a place of fame in time."[2]

The Reverend Mr. Dow was right in his prediction. The river valley was teeming with new people. The United States Government put a "factory" at Fort St. Stephens in 1803 with Joseph Chambers[3] in charge, assisted by Thomas M. Williams. In 1805 George Gaines became assistant and the following year succeeded Chambers. Trade was brisk at the factory, for the Choctaws liked the American, and Gaines was bringing in merchandise overland from Nashville and down the Tombigbe River in order to escape the heavy duties which the Spanish levied on all merchandise that came up by Mobile.

A treaty was made with the Choctaws at Fort St. Stephens which ended all fear of the Indians. The Mississippi Territory[4] Government, in order to take care of the growing settlement on the Tombigbe, in 1804 made a separate Court district out of Washington County[5] and Ephraim Kirby[6] was appointed Judge thereof on April 6, 1804, be-

[1] *History of Cosmopolite or Lorenzo's Journal.* (6th Ed., 1849, p. 163)

[2] *Lorenzo's Journal*, p. 220. In January 1805, the Postmaster General had already established a post office at Fort St. Stephens (Carter, Vol. v, p. 370) and in December of the same year Thomas W. Maury was made Receiver for the lands east of the Pearl River with his office at Fort St. Stephens. (Carter Vol. v, p. 425) He resigned in February, 1807, being afraid of another summer at St. Stephens. (Carter, Vol. v, p. 515)

[3] Ephraim Kirby, named by President Jefferson as U. S. Commissioner to Washington County to determine the rights of persons claiming lands in the Mississippi Territory east of the Pearl River, selected Chambers for Register of the U. S. Land Office in Washington County, and wrote Jefferson on February 5, 1804, from Fort Stoddert: "Fort St. Stephens is more in the center of population, and will be a more convenient place for the permanent establishment of the Register's Office." (Carter, Vol. v, p. 304)

[4] Organized by Congress on May 10, 1798.

[5] Washington County at that time was of tremendous size, stretching eastward all the way to the Chattahoochee River.

[6] Kirby was a graduate of Yale College, a lawyer, and editor and publisher of the State Reports of the State of Connecticut—the first of the kind in the

coming thereby the first Common Law Judge to function as such within the boundaries of what is now the State of Alabama. Upon his death Harry Toulmin succeeded to the office.[1]

The inhabitants of Washington County near Fort St. Stephens wanted an organized town in which to live. They therefore prepared and presented a petition to the Legislature of the Mississippi Territory in which it was stated:

> . . . that it would be expedient and of great utility to themselves and to the inhabitants in general to have a town laid out on the lands of Edwin Lewis on the Tombigby River near Fort Saint Stephens.

The Legislature was agreeable—the law was quickly passed and John Baker, James Morgan and John F. McGrew were named in the Act as Commissioners to lay out the town, "the streets of which shall not be less than one hundred feet wide," and to reserve for the *public use* in the town so laid out so much land as the Commissioners thought necessary —subject to the future disposal of the Legislature of the Mississippi Territory. The Commissioners were further required to deliver a "plan of the town" to the Clerk of the County Court for recording within one month after laying out same.[2]

Very probably the surveyors were at work laying out the town when an event occurred near by which excited the

United States. (Carter, Vol. v, p. 222) Kirby died October 20, 1804. (Carter, Vol. v, p. 356)

[1] Harry Toulmin, English-born, politician, author, Judge, and the most prolific letter-writer of his day, compared the cost of living of the time (December, 1805) between Kentucky and the Mississippi Territory: ". . . in Kentucky—wheat is 50 cents,—flour 4$—Ind. corn 20 cents,—pork 2.25 to 2.50 —bacon 8 cents p^r lb.—whiskey 50 cents,—brown sugar 12½. In Washington County, wheat is 1.50—flour 12$—Ind. corn 50 to 75 cents—pork 5 to 6$ bacon 20 cents (as I have been informed, for I have seen none for sale) whiskey 2$,—brown sugar 25 cents,—and imported articles generally 50 per cent: higher than in Kentucky. I cannot hire a common negro man to cut fire wood for less than 100$ a year, nor a woman for less than 60." (Carter, Vol. v, p. 437)

[2] Toulmin's *Mississippi Territory Statutes* (1807), pp. 407–408, January 8, 1807.

whole nation and interested the whole world. Aaron Burr was arrested just a few miles from Fort St. Stephens and taken down the river to Fort Stoddert near the Spanish line, from which place he was carried overland to Richmond, Virginia, tried for treason, and acquitted. Strange fate that ended Burr's career at the very place where the nation's territorial expansion began and which Burr alone had visualized and realized must be, and later was, at Spain's cost!

The Burr arrest only temporarily diverted the settlers. They were too busy opening up a new country by assaulting its forests and struggling with its mighty rivers. The flow of immigrants into the Tombigbe basin had been increased by the advertisement given the southwest when President Thomas Jefferson purchased Louisiana. Settlers on their way to the fabulous land turned aside to inspect the lands in the vicinity of Fort St. Stephens and on down to the Spanish boundary.

Evidently the incorporation of St. Stephens in 1807 was unsatisfactory for the law was amended in 1811 and the town was named "Saint Stephens."[1] This law was amended again in 1815 when "St. Stephens" was the name given the town by the law which incorporated "the President and Trustees of the town of 'St. Stephens.'"[2] This was the final birth rite. Under this legal status St. Stephens was to bloom, fade, perish and disappear.

The year 1811 was a time of activity and excitement for St. Stephens. In addition to the law amending the town's charter, the Assembly acknowledged the progress of that section by establishing Washington Academy, Alabama's first chartered school, in Washington County on December 17, 1811, and at the same time authorized a lottery to the extent of $5,000 for its benefit. This law was amended in 1812 and again in 1814, and Lewis Sewall, James Caller,

[1] Turner's *Digest of the Laws of the Mississippi Territory*, p. 106, Dec. 18, 1811.

[2] Turner's *Digest* (1816), p. 113, etc.

George S. Gaines, Joseph Phillips, Thomas Malone, Joseph Carson, Thomas B. Creagh, Benjamin S. Smoot, Reuben Saffold, Benjamin J. Biddill, and John Dean, all leading citizens of the county, were made trustees. The Academy was located in St. Stephens and must have become known as St. Stephens Academy, for the Assembly appropriated $500 to St. Stephens' Academy in 1816[1] and there is no record of any Academy by that name having been chartered in or before the year 1816.

That same year, 1811, Lemuel Henry, who had been appointed Receiver, wrote to the Secretary of the Treasury of the St. Stephens Land Office that "the public buildings at St. Stephen are in such a state of decay as to make the public records unsafe," and inquired if "by the President's proclamation establishing the land office at St. Stephens, we are confined to the walls of that place. . . ." If not, Henry advised that he would move the land office to a building on a lot he had purchased in the town of St. Stephens.[2] The first land office must have been housed in the old Fort, or at least within the enclosure of the old walls of Fort St. Stephens.

The greatest excitement of the year came, however, when a Grand Jury in Baldwin County indicted its presiding judge, Harry Toulmin, charging him with nine offenses.[3] The matter swelled to large proportions and divided the leaders of this section of the Mississippi Territory into two hostile camps. Each side invoked all the political pressure and appeal to public sentiment which it could, but in the end Toulmin's enemies failed in their purpose, for the charges were dismissed and the defendant commended for his attention to the duties of his office. From this time until his death Harry Toulmin's position as an officer and citizen was secure.

While relations between the settlers in the lower Ala-

[1] Toulmin (1823), p. 543.

[2] Carter, Vol. VI, pp. 208–209.

[3] Carter, Vol. VI, p. 245.

bama and Tombigbe Rivers and the Creek Indians had been steadily deteriorating for several years, it is likely that the big land sales in St. Stephens in September 1811, upon which the Creeks looked with great apprehension, coupled with a propagated animosity emanating from, paid for, and encouraged by British leadership in Pensacola, brought about a condition which alarmed Harry Toulmin sufficiently for him to write on March 10, 1812, to his friend, Harry Graham, in the State Department at Washington, that he had just returned to Fort Stoddert from a court trip up the country and:

> I find that a considerable consternation pervades the upper settlements,—particularly in the forks of the Tombigby and Alabama, of an immediate attack upon them from the Creek Indians, founded as it is said, on information communicated from a person in the Creek Nation to Col. Callier. The Col. has accordingly,—secured,—as I am informed, all the ammunition and arms at the Choctaw factory,—with the consent of Mr. Gaines,—(who I am sure would not have given that consent but on the best of principles) and proposes employing a company of spies to pass round the frontiers. The next step will probably be to call out the militia. . . .

Toulmin further expressed the opinion that a troublesome chief called Cap^{n} Isaacs, if supported by the Creek Nation, would endeavor to exterminate settlements in that section. He expressed the belief that a council or talk had been fixed upon by the Creeks and that war measures against the whites would be proposed. Toulmin counseled care and preparation.[1]

Judge Toulmin was closer to the truth than even he thought, for the hatred of the settlers by the Creeks, which Toulmin reported, was to rise to such a fury that St. Stephens, the town which was to become Alabama's first capital, was soon to witness an unparalleled orgy of fear, blood, and death. Tecumseh, the magnificent Indian leader from the Northern Lakes, swung through the South urging up-

[1] Carter, Vol. VI, pp. 283–284.

rising and slaughter and destruction of the white man. He was heard with eager ears by the young bloods in the warlike Creek Nation because he promised British aid and British gold. The young nation—the United States—was again at war with Britain. While actively campaigning with her troops and fleet on the eastern seaboard, the British were also stirring the Creeks in the Southwest to insurrection and murder. The enemy did not merely burn our public buildings at Washington as a spiteful gesture, they were in the war for keeps and saw in the angry Creeks a useful and powerful ally.

By July, 1813, the incitation efforts of Tecumseh and the British had brought confusion and fear into the lower Alabama-Tombigbe basin. The settlers were fleeing to the forts and stockades all over that section. The Creeks were known to be in Pensacola getting arms through the Spanish, which actually were being furnished by the British. On July 25, 1813, Colonel James Caller, with three small companies, crossed the Tombigbe at St. Stephens. He was on his way to intercept the Indians returning to Alabama from Pensacola. The affair at Burnt Corn followed and it was a victory for the Indians. Consternation prevailed over the whole country, and the fortified places were soon overflowing with refugees.

In the center of St. Stephens on a knoll Fort Republic was built. It was filled with frightened people who there heard the news of the terrible slaughter at Fort Mims on August 30th—the bloodiest massacre of the white man by the Indians ever to occur on the soil of the United States. This mass slaughter served to rouse the settlers to unity and grim determination. Fear and disorganization disappeared as the white men rallied to the cry: "Remember Fort Mims!" The Creek War was now on with all the fury which goes with an Indian's hatred and a white man's resentment and lust for revenge.

The organization of military units from the west and

south centered at St. Stephens. Here was the crossroads for Mobile and Fort Stoddert, and Natchez and South Mississippi, in sending forces to punish the Creeks. George S. Gaines, with his friend McKee, induced the great Choctaw Chief, Pushmataha, to throw his warriors in with the whites against William Weatherford, the Red Eagle and now leader of the Creek war party. The great Choctaw Chief was at St. Stephens when word reached him that General Flournoy accepted his services. The Chief at once went to Mobile, where he was given the rank of Brigadier General and a resplendent blue-and-gold uniform costing over three hundred dollars. This proved a good investment, for the Choctaws fought with Flournoy and his white soldiers through the battle of the Holy Ground, leaving to General Andrew Jackson the finishing of the war with his great victory at Horseshoe Bend on the Tallapoosa, March 19, 1814.

The British lost their war with the United States, but the Creeks did not merely lose—they were forever crushed. The Spanish were cowed. General Jackson required the Creeks to cede to the United States all their lands west of the Coosa. The Americans had already appropriated Mobile from Spain.[1] These acquisitions of new terrritory were followed by a tremendous influx of settlers to the Tennessee Valley, along the Mississippi River, and now not only in the lower basin of the Tombigbe, but along the Alabama, the Cahawba, the Sipsey, and the Warrior.[2]

The tremendous increase in population in the Tennessee Valley, particularly in Madison County, and the substantial increase in all that part of the Mississippi Territory east of the Pearl River emphasized more than ever before the heated question of division of the Mississippi Territory.

[1] In Caldwell v. The State, Vol. 1, Stewart and Porter at p. 341, Chief Justice Lipscomb said: "The United States took forcible possession of Mobile." (See Act of Congress, February 12, 1812.)

[2] A treaty with the Chickasaw Indians opened up that section to the white men.

This controversial matter was of long standing. It had developed naturally and steadily because there had never been any binding common interest or feeling of comradeship between the settlers on the Mississippi River and those on the Tombigbe-Alabama. In the beginning it was the settlers in the eastern section of the Territory who demanded separation, but in the end the situation was reversed with the Mississippi River men demanding division of the Territory.

The first determined effort to procure a division of the Mississippi Territory was made by the 'Bigbe settlers in 1803. Lawyer Nicholas Perkins must have written the petition to Congress for his name heads the list of signers. They prayed "a division of the Territory and that a Separate Government be established within the now District of Washington, independent of that of the Mississippi Territory." Along with other reasons given for wanting division the petition stated: "That part of the Territory on the Mississippi and the settlements on the Mobile, Tombeckbee and Alabama Rivers are composed of people different in their manners and customs, different in their interests, and nature appears never to have designed the two countries to be under the same government."[1]

This petition was presented long before Madison County in the "Big Bend" of the Tennessee was settled, and eleven years before the treaty of Fort Jackson, which took from the Creeks all their lands west of the Coosa; but the difference in people and lack of common interests between the two sections continued to be the enduring reason for division.

Nothing came of the 1803 petition, but the desire of the Alabama-Tombigbe folk for separation from the Mississippi River settlements did not die out. In 1809 it revealed itself again in a convention held at the Court of Washington County on November 11, 1809. This petition was signed by the Delegates of the People of the several settle-

[1] Carter, Vol. v, p. 290.

ments of the district east of the Pearl River in the Mississippi Territory.[1]

This document is one of the most impassioned and picturesque in the history of the Republic. At times the reader hears echoes of Patrick Henry and Thomas Paine. Addressed to the Congress of the United States, this, one of its many paragraphs, was perfectly fitting:

> Representatives of the American People! We have Petitioned for a Government.—At present we have only the name of one. We know nothing of our Executive Officers:—we know nothing of our Delegates in Congress.—They know nothing of us. We covet not the honour of being a part of a State on the Mississippi.—A change of names will not bring us nearer to the Seat of Government;—it will not bring our Public Officers nearer to us:—it will not give to the Mississippi Legislature any greater knowledge of us,—any greater sympathy with us,—any greater zeal for our security, for our interests, or for our rights.

And again:

> But it is not only future evils that we dread. We feel present grievances. We have frequent collisions with the Indians and Spaniards. We not only pay taxes to the Spanish Government, but our runaway negroes find protection under it. It would be unreasonable indeed, to expect from a Governor residing on the Mississippi a steady and prompt attention to our interests, whilst he cannot know when they are violated, or an adequate protection against the arbitrary and oppressive conduct of foreign powers, holding provinces in our neighborhood, or against the plundering spirit of the savages, or the artful machinations or daring outrages of the worthless & proscribed citizens of other states,—whilst the chief magistrate is remote from us, and unconnected with us, and a stranger to our sorrows, and our sufferings.

The conclusion is lengthy but worth recording:

> Representatives of America! Give us a Government of our own: and you will give us respectability; you will give us population: you will give us strength.—Nor ought we to leave out of our calculations the probability of our obtaining possession of West Florida, which is too poor, and too thinly Peopled, and

[1] Carter, Vol. VI, pp. 26–30.

too much broken into settlements totally unconnected with each other, to form a Territorial District by itself,— and would most inconveniently add to the extent of the projected state of Mississippi, already too unwieldy for the purposes of good Government. One half of West Florida naturally belongs to the District East of Pearl River, and can never conveniently be united with any other Territory.

A regard to the improvement of the Public finances, we humbly conceive strongly recommends an attention to our Petitions for a new Territorial District.—It would scarcely be believed in any other part of America, that the best Lands on the tide water within 40 miles of the bay of Mobile, can be purchased at the rate of Two dollars per acre: yet such is the truth, and such may we not say, is the natural consequence of the degraded situation of the Mobile country?

And what will be the additional expence of a new Territorial Government?—Trifling indeed, when it is considered that a fourth Judge of the Mississippi Territory has been appointed for this district,—that a fifth must be appointed for the county of Madison, and that 800 or a thousand dollars a year, are expended on a mail in Order to keep up an artificial connection between the Mobile and the Mississippi.

We fear that your Honourable body will too justly conceive, that we trespass too much upon your indulgence: but we trust that it will be some apology—that we are an unrepresented portion of the American nation.—In this way therefore we are compelled to make known to the National Council, our grievances, and our wants: and we petition, we entreat, we pray that they may meet with your paternal attention, and that you will at once give us a Government adapted to our situation, and deliver us from the heavy burthen of foreign oppression.—We pay to the Spanish Monarchy, Twenty four per centum on our active capital.—We cultivate crops calculated for Exportation, and we import some of the main necessaries of life, as well as foreign manufactures.—We pay on what we sell, 12 per centum, and on the proceeds of our sales, another 12 per centum before we can bring them home. Hence we often pay for the flour of Kentucky and Pennsylvania, four times the price that is paid by our fellow citizens at Natchez,—but neither they, nor their delegate know any thing of this,—and it is to you, and not to them, that we look for relief.—Are we Americans or Spaniards? —Shall we support the Republic of the United States, or the

Spanish Monarchy?—Our principles,—our habits,—our affections,—our hearts, drive us to you,—but you,—shall we say it, dare we pronounce the dreadful curse,—drive us back again to the Spaniards!—No: you do not:—we will not believe it:—we will not indulge the idea that you are aware that we pay taxes to an European Monarchy.—We have seen,—we have read,—we have admired,—we have been enraptured with your discussions, your discourses,—your reports,—your resolves,—all breathing the spirit of independence,—of patriotism, and of indignant scorn at foreign oppression;—and we will not believe that you will coolly, passively, and complacently look on, and see a member of the great American body politic, trampled in the dust!—It has been done,—and it is done: but you do not know it.—and because you do not know it, even the tawny Indian himself, has thought his nation superior to the American Republic,—and the Creeks, and their Big Warrior have felt themselves secure in interrupting, in seizing, in confiscating cargoes, peaceably and harmlessly proceeding from the people of Tennessee to your oppressed and suffering citizens on the Mobile.

—We do not ask for your relief:—for we know it will be granted. We confide in it,—we anticipate it,—we rejoice in its consequences, and even now we are thankful for it.—

Court of Washington County, Novr 11th 1809.

JOHN JOHNSTON *President of the Convshon*
JNO CALLER *Representative from the Fork Settlement*
FRANCIS STRINGER *Represente of the St. Stephens District*
WM McGREW *Representative of Tallow District*
WM D. FELPS *Representative of the Pasegola District*

This petition, warm as it was, did not produce any immediate results, and since there was not entire satisfaction with what had been included in it, another convention was held a short time later on December 26, 1809, with almost the same delegates present but served this time by that daring lawyer-leader, Joseph Pulaski Kennedy, as clerk of the convention. Now new and specific demands for government of their section of the Territory were set forth in detail. It was proposed that the eastern section be called "The Mobile Territory of the United States." The petition concluded with the statement that if division could not be had on the terms set out, then "We declare as the Representatives of the People that we do not want a division but be made a State with the rest of the Territory."[1]

Such an ardent appeal should have produced at least a promise of success but such was not yet to be the reward of the people "east of the Pearl." It is likely, however, that these impassioned appeals and demands did aid in inducing the State of Georgia to grant the request made by Congress for the right to form *one* or *more* State Governments out of the Mississippi Territory.[2] At the time Georgia ceded her rights in this territory to the Federal Government she had included a provision that only one state could be formed from it. This limitation had to be removed before a division of the Territory could be legally had.

The first bill in Congress to divide the Mississippi Territory was introduced on November 18, 1812.[3] About this time, by a memorial not identified, the majority of the Legislature of the Mississippi Territory prayed Congress for admission of the entire Territory as a state. The minority protested vigorously by addressing their own separate memorial to Congress asking that no law for admission be passed until the Territory had 60,000 free persons, according to the agreement between Georgia and the United States. All the minority objectors were from the Mississippi section of the Mississippi Territory.[4] Citizens from the counties whose representatives had composed the minority bloc in the Legislature joined the fight with their

[1] Carter, Vol. VI, pp. 36–39.

[2] Carter, Vol. VI, p. 337. The Georgia Act was passed December 5, 1812. The Legislature of the Mississippi Territory presented a memorial to Congress protesting a division of the Territory in which they stated that they had urged the State of Georgia in the strongest terms not to agree to a division of the Mississippi Territory. (Carter, Vol. VI, p. 331)

[3] Carter, Vol. VI, p. 332. [4] Carter, Vol. VI, p. 339.

own petition, praying Congress "That all proceedings in your Honorable Body relative to the admission of the Mississippi Territory into the Union as an Independent State may be for the present postponed."[1] The Senate Committee in Congress favored postponement and the surge toward division and statehood both came to nought.[2]

The election of William Lattimore as the Territory's delegate to the House of Representatives gave added strength to the Mississippi River contingent who at this time wanted admission of the entire Mississippi Territory as one state. The Senate would not, however, concur in a House bill which provided for one state only to be formed from the Territory. One is constrained to believe that the Southern Senators, sensing the rising tide of the free-soil movement, saw both the opportunity for and the need of two additional Senators to be had from an extra state from the Mississippi Territory. Eventually the House yielded to the Senate, leaving open only the troublesome question of the location of the division line.

But before the matter was finally settled the citizenry, especially of the section east of the Pearl, continued to press hard for their desires. In December, 1815, they addressed a memorial to Congress in which they claimed a greater population than the country west of the Pearl and yet declared they had only *eight* members of the Territorial Legislature, while the Mississippi River Section had *sixteen.*[3] The legislators from the counties east of the Pearl supported the citizens by another petition of their own reciting the same facts and making known their fears that if Congress were to make the Mississippi Territory a state, the same inequality might persist in the convention which would be

[1] Carter, Vol. vi, pp. 347–351.

[2] Carter, Vol. vi, pp. 358–359. These delaying tactics were aided to success by differences as to where the line of division, if one, should be. Residents of the upper Tombigbe section wanted the division line to run east and west, but this proposal seems never to have had any chance of succeeding.

[3] Carter, Vol. vi, pp. 601–602.

created for this purpose. The legislators wanted Congress to provide by law that in such a convention the delegates be apportioned according to free white population.[1]

These various petitions had their effect at home as well as in Washington. Observing the definite trend toward division, a group led by Cowles Mead and supporting the policy of forming only one state from the entire Territory called a convention at John Ford's, on the Pearl River, which met there on October 29, 1816.[2] The avowed purpose was to counteract the influence and impression that a majority of the citizens desired that the Territory be divided. Present at Ford's were:

Daniel Williams, Jr.	Wilkinson County
Cowles Mead and Jos. E. Davis	Jefferson County
Bailey E. Chaney and J. F. Weatherspoon	Franklin County
David Dickson	Pike County
Samuel H. Garrow	Mobile County
Sterling Dupree	Jackson County
Samuel Dale	Monroe County
Harmon Runnels	Lawrence County
Henry B. Slade	Baldwin County
Benjamin S. Smoot	Washington County
Geo. H. Nixon	Marion County
Thos. Anderson	Hancock County
Jacob J. H. Morris	Greene County
John G. Creagh	Clarke County
James Patton	Wayne County

Cowles Mead, from Jefferson County, was elected President of the Convention, and James Phillips, Secretary. This Cowles Mead was long experienced in the affairs and politics of the Mississippi Territory. In January, 1807, while he was Secretary of the Territory, he also had exercised for a

[1] Carter, Vol. VI, pp. 655–656. (Feb. 15, 1816)

[2] Carter, Vol. VI, p. 708, *et seq.* John Ford's home was a large and comfortable plantation house on the Pearl River.

time the powers and performed the duties of Governor of the Territory.[1] Regardless of whether Cowles Mead was a voluntary leader or was selected for the job, the position of President of the Convention was in able hands. He was well-known, firm and sagacious.

Mr. Davis, also of Jefferson County, appointed on the committee to draft a memorial to Congress, produced a masterpiece arguing for and asking admission *without division*. Mr. Runnels, delegate from Lawrence County, proposed an amendment dividing the Mississippi Territory by a line running up the middle of Mobile Bay and Mobile River to the confluence of the Tombigbe and Alabama Rivers, thence along the ridge dividing the waters of the said rivers to the Tennessee line, so as to leave Madison County in the eastern section of the divided Territory. The motion to amend lost 11 to 4. The memorial prepared by Mr. Davis was then adopted by the same vote—the same four delegates opposing it. The Convention then voted 10 to 5 to elect a special delegate "to promote the objects of this Convention." Harry Toulmin was chosen as the special envoy to go before Congress and urge admission of the entire Territory *without division*. James Phillips resigned as Secretary of the Convention, and John Ford was elected in his place.

An address to the electors of the Counties of Amite, Adams, Claiborne, Warren, and Madison, who were not represented in the Convention, was drawn up praying that they join in the object of the Convention by organizing meetings in their respective Counties, "for the purpose of preventing that evil resulting from a division of the Territory, a measure which, if adopted, will destroy our future prospects of greatness as a State."

A similar memorial was addressed to the Council and House of the Mississippi Territory and to the Honorable W. Lattimore, the Territory's delegate in Congress, asking

[1] Toulmin, 1807, pp. 408–416. This of course is Jefferson County, Mississippi.

them to join in the plea for admission of the entire Territory as a single state.[1]

Another address by the Convention was directed to Harry Toulmin advising him of his appointment as special delegate, and arranging for the delivery to him of the memorial to lay before Congress. Five hundred dollars was appropriated to pay the expenses of Delegate Toulmin. It was contributed pro rata by those who voted in favor of the memorial and put in the hands of Henry B. Slade for delivery to Toulmin. The Convention adjourned on October 31, 1816.[2]

In 1816 a census was taken of the Mississippi Territory which revealed a population of free inhabitants in excess of 45,000, and over 30,000 slaves.[3] When the totals were known the Legislature of the Mississippi Territory memorialized Congress for a law authorizing a convention to form a constitution for its admission into the Union on an equal footing with the original states.[4] The memorial does not mention a division and the language is so couched that it is clear that a division was not contemplated nor asked for.

This petition by the Assembly was followed on January 8, 1817, by another—this time by the members of the Legislature.[5] This paper disclosed that the pressure for division was now from a strong group from Adams County, which county was in turn controlled by the city of Natchez. The petition further revealed that Adams County had more than double the number of representatives to which it was entitled by its free population, compared with other counties, and called attention to the fact by way of comparison that in Monroe County the people were unanimous for admission of the Territory without division, yet under the law they were without any representation in the Mississippi Territory Legislature.

Among the signers from the section which is now Ala-

[1] Carter, Vol. VI, pp. 715–716.

[2] Carter, Vol. VI, p. 717.

[3] Carter, Vol. VI, p. 730.

[4] Carter, Vol. VI, p. 731. (Dec. 16, 1816)

[5] Carter, Vol. VI, pp. 744–746.

bama were James Titus and Robert Beaty, of Madison County, Joseph Carson, of Washington County, Gabriel Moore and Hugh McVay, of Madison County, Reuben Saffold, of Clarke County, John Bond, of Lawrence County, and J. D. Lister, of Washington County. From the allegations of the petition and an analysis of the names, it appears that Natchez foresaw her doom as the dominant town of the new state should the Territory not be divided. Madison County had already passed Adams in population and it was likely that Huntsville had exceeded or would soon exceed Natchez. The only way that Natchez could save her political power and prestige was by division. She had some strong friends in Washington, but her trump card, which was never openly or publicly mentioned, was simply that if two states were made from the Territory instead of one there would be two more Southern Senators in Washington. They would be needed to offset free-soil states which even now were knocking loudly at the doors of the United States for admission.

The great strength of the group now pressing for division, which strangely enough was the section which had opposed division in the beginning, was soon discovered by the special envoy of the "No division" group, Harry Toulmin, who wrote about it to his friend, Henry B. Slade, from Washington City on January 16, 1817.[1] He reported to Slade that when he reached Washington it appeared that the Dr. Lattimore bills for two states from the Territory would pass and that "if I had not come there would be no doubt about it." Toulmin then related in detail his efforts against division and his various appearances before committees, opposing Dr. Lattimore. He reported a conversation which he had with General Desha, a Representative from Kentucky, and no doubt an old friend of the Special Delegate, since Toulmin had formerly lived in Kentucky and there held the office of Secretary of State. Said Desha:

[1] Carter, Vol. VI, p. 748.

I have always voted for one State out of the whole, but I never shall again. You may by great exertion put off the division now, but it is impossible to erect a new State out of the whole Territory.

Toulmin, however, continued to fight the "division act," even spending twenty dollars to print his statement of the reasons why the Territory should not be divided, but he must have realized that the Senate would prevail and the House eventually yield.

This understanding no doubt led Toulmin to draft a petition of his own on the matter, which he presented to the United States Senate.[1] In this paper he urged that "the whole territory should be admitted into the Union as one State," and declared that at least three fourths of the people of the Territory desired that this be done. He also suggested that if division be inevitable, a division line different from the one proposed in the bill be selected. The Senate was unmoved by Toulmin's facts and logic, but one cannot say that he did not earn his compensation as Special Delegate.

The inhabitants "west of the Pearl" had the last word. They filed a petition on February 14, 1817, with Congress, opposing admission of the whole Territory as one state.[2] They wanted the Territory divided and both sections admitted as states as soon as possible. This is what eventually came to pass. Congress passed the Enabling Act on March 1, 1817, and on August 15, 1817, the Convention at the Town of Washington, in the State of Mississippi, adopted a Constitution for the people in the Western part of the Mississippi Territory.[3] On December 10, 1817, Mississippi became one of the states of the United States by joint resolution of Congress, and at the same time the Alabama Territory, with St. Stephens as its seat of government, became a separate Territory.[4]

[1] Carter, Vol. VI, p. 763. (January 28, 1817)

[2] Carter, Vol. VI, pp. 765–766. [3] Carter, Vol. VI, p. 798.

[4] 3 Statutes at Large, pp. 472, 473, 413. The Act establishing the Alabama Territory was passed March 3, 1817. Code of Alabama 1923, Vol. I, p. 29.

The long controversy was over. At last the 'Bigbe-Alabama people were free from the Mississippi River domination. Now they had their own polity, with the numbers and wealth most concentrated in Madison County but with the seat of government—their capital—atop high Hobuckintoopa in the town of St. Stephens.

The Act of Congress creating the Alabama Territory gave the Governor power to convoke as a Legislature for the Territory those members of the Mississippi Territory Assembly from that part of the Territory now Alabama, as Representatives and Councillors. Because this arrangement provided only three Councillors—Joseph Carson, of Washington County, Robert Beatty, Esq., and James Titus, of Madison County—the Congress further provided for the Alabama Assembly to nominate six persons to the President of the United States, who would select three of the six nominees to serve as Councillors, thus increasing the number of Councillors to six. William Wyatt Bibb was appointed Governor of the Alabama Territory and, as directed by Congress, he called the Territorial Legislature together at St. Stephens, the seat of government,[1] on January 19, 1818.

At this first session of an Alabama General Assembly twelve Representatives were present, representing seven counties. They were A. S. Lipscomb and John F. Everitt, from the County of Washington; Gabriel Moore, Hugh McVay, John W. Walker, and Clement C. Clay, from the County of Madison; John McGrew and Neil Smith, from the County of Clarke; Henry B. Slade, from the County of Baldwin; Alvan Robishow, from the County of Mobile; Sam Dale, from the County of Monroe; and Phillip Fitzpatrick, from the County of Montgomery. The House

[1] Section 8 of the Act provides "that the town of St. Stephens shall be the Seat of Government for the said Alabama Territory until it shall be otherwise ordered by the Legislature thereof." The town of St. Stephens was growing and the commerce there increasing in December, 1816, when its merchants and traders petitioned Congress to establish St. Stephens as a Port of Delivery. (Carter, Vol. VI, p. 743)

William Wyatt Bibb

elected Gabriel Moore, of Madison, Speaker of the House, and chose Isaac Nicholson as Clerk, Samuel Smith, Sergeant at Arms, and Matthew Lasoy, Doorkeeper.

The Council convened with only one member present—James Titus, of Madison. Robert Beatty, Esq., also Councillor from Madison, resigned his office, and Joseph Carson, Councillor from Washington County, died. But Titus was equal to the occasion. He elected himself President of the Council, appointed Curtis Hooks, Secretary, and John Pearson, Doorkeeper. Thus organized, Titus conducted the proceedings of the Council with studied formality. He called the Council to order, answered the roll call, voted on bills, moved for adjournment, voted on his motion, and declared the Council adjourned.

Governor Bibb did not appear in person before the Assembly but delivered his message in writing by his private secretary, Joseph Noble, Esq. They received the message at one o'clock in the afternoon on February 20, 1818, and promptly gave it their sober consideration.

In joint session the Assembly nominated George Phillips, Joseph Howard, Matthew Wilson, Joseph P. Kennedy, John Gayle, and Reuben Saffold, from whose number the President was to choose the three new Councillors. In another joint session the Assembly exercised the authority given them by Congress by electing John Crowell as Alabama's delegate to Congress—her first Congressman.

Most of the time the Assembly was occupied with the business of creating new counties, establishing boundaries and writing laws concerning bridges, ferries, and roads, but time was found to reincorporate St. Stephens Academy with leading citizens as trustees.[1] The St. Stephens Steamboat

[1] Acts 1st Session—Ala. Ter., p. 22 (Feb. 7, 1818). Silas Dinsmore, Samuel Smith, George Buchanan, Benjamin S. Smoot, Lemuel J. Allston, Davis H. Mayhew, D. Wilson, and Abner S. Lipscomb were the trustees. They were authorized by the Assembly (Acts Ala. Ter. 1818, Feb. Session, p. 101) to raise a fund for the Academy by a lottery. The drawing was held in the spring of 1819, and one Horatio Dade won $5,000. The trustees failed to pay him

Company was chartered.[1] The need for banking facilities was urgent, so the Assembly chartered the Tombeckbe Bank with a capital of $500,000.[2]

At this session occurred Alabama's first manumission of a slave. It is a singular coincidence that the owner and master was a negro—Honoré Colin, a free man of colour of the town of Mobile, who emancipated his female slave, Rozetta.[3] The first Alabama divorce was granted to Elizabeth Bennett from James Bennett.[4] A law providing for taking the census of Alabama Territory was enacted.[5] This was an important and necessary law. It was needed to guide the Assembly in writing a law apportioning representatives in the Assembly and to furnish proof that Alabama had sufficient population to qualify for statehood. The Federal law required a minimum population of 60,000 *free* inhabitants.

The Assembly enacted a law authorizing Clement C. Clay, Samuel Taylor, Samuel Dale, James Titus, and William L. Adams as Commissioners "to examine and report to the Governor the most eligible scite for the Seat of Territorial Government."[6] This law, by which the Assembly itself selected and named the members of the Commission,

and he sued Buchanan, Smoot, and Wilson as Managers of the St. Stephens Academy Lottery. (Minor, p. 415)

1 Acts 1st Session—Ala. Ter., p. 50. James Pickens, David Files, Silas Dinsmoore, Henry Bright, Benjamin S. Smoot, and Daniel B. Ripley were the incorporators. They asked the Assembly to grant them the *exclusive* privilege of navigating the Alabama and Tombeckbe Rivers by steam. The Assembly refused. (H. J. Ala. Ter., 1st Session, p. 71)

2 Acts 1st Session—Ala. Ter., p. 62. Superintendents of subscription were David Files, James A. Torbet, Dennison Darling, Thomas I. Strong, Israel Pickens, James G. Lyon, Jack F. Ross, William Crawford, Abner Smith Lipscomb, William D. Gaines, Thomas Crowell, and George Buchanan.

3 Acts 1818, p. 57. 4 Acts 1818, p. 7. 5 Acts 1818, p. 24.

6 Acts 1818, p. 94. Among other things the Act provided that "the Commissioners examine and report to the Governor the most eligible site for the Territorial Government, as near the centre of the Territory as may be, having due regard to commercial advantages, and the nature and situation of the country; and if said Commissioners believe on examination that two or more places have equal or *nearly* equal advantages, they shall report the same with a correct description of each."

was by far the most important business of the session. Even before the first move was made to select a "scite for the Seat of Government," these pioneer Assemblymen seemed to realize instinctively that the location of the capital would carry the trend of the state's political life along with it. There were two contending factions which may be roughly classified as the Alabama-Cahawba River basins group and the Warrior-Tombigbe River system group. The powerful Tennessee Valley section leaned toward an alliance with the Warrior-Tombigbe faction, because of kinship among its peoples and better natural conditions for communication and transportation. Its political power was courted by both contenders because the Valley never voted as a solid bloc.

The Warrior-Tombigbe faction had considerably more than a majority of the votes in the Assembly because at the time they had with them the numerous and powerful Madison County delegation led by Clement C. Clay, Gabriel Moore, and John Walker. They had the only vote present in the Council and a majority in the House of Representatives. It was, therefore, a simple matter for them to place four[1] of their men on the Commission to find an eligible "scite" for the seat of government. Clement C. Clay, being the Commissioner first named in the Act, was Chairman of the body. When the Assembly adjourned and thus freed the Commissioners to go about the business of finding the most eligible "scite" for the capital, the Warrior-Tombigbe men were well satisfied with the situation. They were confident that the Commissioners would find the best location on the Warrior-Tombigbe system at a place convenient to the Tennessee Valley and that the next Assembly would write

[1] C. C. Clay and James Titus were from Madison County, Adams and Taylor were from the "second district," which was composed of Tuskaloosa, Blount, and Marion Counties. Their exact addresses have not been discovered although there is cause to believe that Adams lived in Tuskaloosa County. Sam Dale, the South Alabama representative on the Commission, was a resident of Monroe County.

a law making that place the seat of government. They reckoned without an understanding of the resourcefulness of their Governor.

On February 14, 1818, the first session of the first Assembly adjourned, having been in session twenty-six days. Alexander B. Meek, the historian, says the body met in the Douglass Hotel, which was kept by Thomas H. Douglass. The Assembly appropriated two hundred eight dollars to pay him for "house rent and furniture, furnished the General Assembly at the present Session."[1] This amount for twenty-six days would be at the rate of $8 per day. It is fair to assume that the House and the Council each had a separate room, which would make each legislative chamber cost the Territory $4 per day. The stationery used by the Assembly during the session cost $52.37½. Government was not very costly in those pioneer days.

Before the Assembly adjourned the Seminole War was already under way along Alabama's southern border. That seasoned and trusted warrior, General Andrew Jackson, was sent by the War Department to restore order. On May 28, 1818, while the United States was still at peace with Spain, the aggressive Jackson occupied Pensacola and thereby precipitated a political controversy which quickly became a national issue. The attack made on General Jackson by Speaker of the House Henry Clay so stirred the people of Alabama to partisan allegiance to Jackson that the hero of Horseshoe Bend and New Orleans became their political champion as well as military hero. As such he cast a long shadow over Alabama politics for many years to come. The immediate effect of Jackson's action in invading West Florida, however, was salutary in that the hostile Creeks living in South Alabama lost all confidence in the ability of the Spanish to protect them and migrated across the state, crossing the Warrior River in the neighborhood

[1] Acts 1st Session, 1st General Assembly of Alabama Territory, p. 112. (Feb. 13, 1818)

of the Falls of Tuskaloosa and passing out of the state on their way toward Mississippi.[1]

The excitement which arose from the American invasion of Spanish Florida and the Indian unrest, together with the urgent and important business of finding a site for the permanent seat of government and sequestering the land upon which to found it, which authority the Governor appropriated to himself, no doubt caused Governor Bibb to miss the visit of the French emigrants, the most spectacular event in the history of St. Stephens, the ejectment of Palaas by McClary and the arrest of Aaron Burr not excepted. The French refugees, on their way up the Tombeckbe to found the "Vine and Olive Colony," visited briefly in the Territorial capital in June, 1818. These Bonapartists, fleeing to escape the wrath of the Bourbons, arrived at St. Stephens on a United States Government barge. The rapids in the river made it necessary to change barges at this head of sloop navigation on the river, and while this was being accomplished the people of St. Stephens looked upon a vivid scene and a most extraordinary group of people.

Most distinguished was Count Lefebvre Desnoettes, one of Napoleon's Lieutenant Generals, who was so close to the Emperor that he rode with Napoleon in his carriage in the bitter and dismal retreat from Moscow. Count Desnoettes was a handsome military man and the most splendid rider of the age in which he lived. No wonder the backwoodsmen on the Tombigbe marveled at his presence!

Beside him was the dapper M. Peniers, famous in French Civil Government. He was a member of the National Assembly and had voted for the death of Louis XVI.

Perhaps the most striking figure of all was Colonel Nicholas Rooul, who had accompanied Napoleon to Elba dur-

[1] Governor Bibb's Message to Second Session of Assembly, Journal of House, p. 10. Bibb says that in September, 1818, the gallant Colonel Dale commanded an expedition against the Creeks, but that "this very extraordinary movement may be justly ascribed to the occupation of Pensacola by American forces."

ing his banishment. Upon Napoleon's return to France Rooul commanded the Emperor's advance guard of grenadiers on the march from Cannes to Paris. Rooul's wife had been Marchioness of Sinabaldi and maid of honor to Queen Caroline when Murat was King.

J. J. Cluis, another colonist, had been an aide to Marshal Lefebvre, the Duke of Rivigo, who was later the head of the police department of Paris. Cluis served him as secretary and Napoleon had placed in the custody of Cluis the royal prisoner, His Majesty Ferdinand VII, King of Spain.

General Count Bertrand Clausel had served Napoleon faithfully in many ways. It was he who commanded at Bordeaux during the "Hundred Days." The General did not like his land grant, so he returned to Mobile and, being without funds, he earned his living raising vegetables and selling them in the town. Later he returned to France and was made Governor and Marshal of Algeria.

Henry L'Allemand, a Lieutenant General and Commander of the Artillery of Napoleon's Imperial Guard, was with the colonists for a short time but left for broader and more exciting fields. M. Lackanal, one of the settlers, was a member of the French Academy. He too had voted for the death of King Louis XVI. With these Frenchmen was General Juan Rico, a native of Valencia, Spain, who had been proscribed in his homeland when Ferdinand VII returned to the throne. He was a man of extraordinary appearance and marvelous experiences but adjusted himself to the hardships of a life in frontier country with skill and good humor.

These and many other men of fame and women of beauty and elegance rested for a day at the capital of the Territory on their journey up the swirling, muddy Tombigbe toward a new life. After many struggles with misfortune the colony failed, and many of its members traveled down that same river to Mobile and beyond, still seeking a better life. When they passed through St. Stephens the second time, it too had failed and was disintegrating. The seat of government had been moved away and St. Stephens, unknown to herself, was marked for disappearance from the face of the earth.

During the interim between the adjournment of the first session of the Assembly and the convening of the second session which met in St. Stephens on November 2, 1818, the politically powerful men of the Territory had been steadily and quietly at work. The main objective was, of course, to direct the location of the seat of government. The two major contending forces were led respectively by C. C. Clay, of Huntsville, Chairman of the Commission, and Governor Bibb, a South Alabama man living on his large plantation in Autauga County. Clay's commission, after viewing several sites, selected Tuskaloosa as the place for the capital and so reported[1] to the Governor as the law required them to do. But Governor Bibb had other plans for the location of Alabama's capital. The Governor, single-handed, on his own authority, and without the collaboration of the Commissioners named by the Assembly, selected the site where he desired to locate the seat of government. Then, through his influence and connections in Washington, he had the land chosen by him for the site of the capital set aside for a free grant to Alabama for public use and exempted from public sale until after the Alabama Assembly should have acted on the matter. What Governor Bibb was doing and how he did it was not disclosed until the Governor delivered his message to the November Session of the Territorial Assembly.

The Legislators assembled for the second and last session at St. Stephens on November 2, 1818. John W. Walker, of Madison County, succeeded Gabriel Moore as Speaker of the House,[2] but James Titus held over as President of the

[1] Senate Journal 1826, p. 32. Governor Bibb ignored and did what he could to suppress this report, which probably accounts for Owen's error (Owen, Vol. 1, p. 186) in stating that the Commissioners chose Cahawba.

[2] Gabriel Moore was not even a representative at this session. This temporary

Council.[1] Both Houses organized on the opening day of the session. The first business before the Assembly was to find shelter—a place in which to hold its session.

As soon as the Assembly was organized they appointed Committees to advise the Governor of the fact and that they were ready to receive any communications His Excellency might desire to make. The Governor sent word to the Assembly that he would make his communication in writing at noon.[2] Promptly at 12 o'clock Mr. Lyons, the Governor's private secretary, delivered to the Speaker a written communication addressed to both Houses. In this message Governor Bibb for the first time revealed his method and reasons for locating the capital at the junction of the Cahawba and Alabama Rivers. He said:

The National Government by Act authorized an entire township of land for the support of a Seminary of Learning, and

retirement of one of the Territory's leading public men may have been occasioned by Moore's wife divorcing him. (Acts 2nd Session, Alabama Territory, p. 10)

[1] There is no known printed copy of the Journal of the 2nd Session of the Legislative Council and the manuscript has never been found. The Acts of the 2nd Session show that James Titus was again President of the Council. Certain references in the Journal of the House for the 2nd Session disclose that Peter Martin was Secretary of the Council, and Matthew Lasoy, Doorkeeper, and that George Phillips, John Gayle, Jr., Matthew D. Wilson, Lemuel Meade, Henry Chambers and, of course, James Titus, constituted the entire membership of that body. The members of the House for the 2nd Session were:

Henry B. Slade—Baldwin County
Isaac Brown—Blount County
Littlepage Syms—Cahawba County
Neal Smith and William Walton—Clarke County
Richard Warren—Conecuh County
Melcajah Vaughan—Cotaco County
Edwin D. King—Dallas County
Benj. Murrell—Limestone County
Sam Dale—Monroe County
Clement C. Clay, John Walker, and Samuel Walker—Madison County
Wm. Anderson—Marengo County
Alvan Robishow—Mobile County
Charles Hudspeth—Marion County
Phillip Fitzpatrick—Montgomery County
Jesse Wilson—Shelby County
Julius H. Sims—Tuskaloosa County
John F. Everitt and Abner S. Lipscomb—Washington County

Littleberry Vaughan was elected Doorkeeper of the House.

Note: The only known complete copy of this House Journal is in the Archives of the Historical Society of Pennsylvania.

[2] Tuesday, November 8, 1818.

also of "any one entire section" to be located under the direction of the Governor, *for the Seat of Government.* Fully aware of the public sensibility which the selection of the scite of Government always excites and the influence of local feeling in the determination of the question, I could not expect, by any choice however judicious to afford universal satisfaction. And the delicate task assigned to the Executive has been rendered the more embarrassing by a combination of accidental circumstances. A copy of the Act did not reach me until the month of June when the town of Cahawba, which among other scites was offered for sale on the first Monday of October.[1] Should that place be considered most eligible, not to have examined its claims in due season would have deprived the territory of their choice—while on the other hand, it was possible that the selection made by the Executive might not be approved by the Legislature. That I should endeavor to prevent the former appeared to me an imperative duty; while at the same time, to avoid the injurious consequences of a collision of opinion between public functionaries was so much desired. In this dilemma I was disposed to confer with the Commissioners appointed at the last session of the General Assembly to report the situation they might deem most eligible; and without delay addressed a letter on the subject to the gentleman first named in the Act. Owing to circumstances beyond their control, they were unable to meet me, and I lost the benefit of their views.

Anxious only to promote the general interests of the Territory, and guided by an impartial judgment, I was persuaded that the scite which might present the best prospect of permanency and of avoiding, hereafter, those unpleasant discussions which have so much disturbed the repose, and distracted the councils of our sister states, ought to be selected. Considerations resulting from our future prospects, and connected with the general convenience, were not to be overlooked; nor the grati-

[1] Wm. H. Crawford, of Georgia, Secretary of the Treasury and a close friend of Governor Bibb, had written Josiah Meigs, Commissioner of the General Land Office, on June 6, 1817—a year previous—that although the present law did not apply to the Alabama district, ". . . it was deemed proper to make reservations *there also* for the purpose of laying off and establishing towns when authority shall be given for that purpose. . . ."—"The falls of the Coosa, Tallapoosa, and Cahawba, and the junction of the latter river with the Alabama river are points to which his [the Surveyor's of the District] attention will necessarily be directed." (Carter, Vol. VI, pp. 794, 795) It is submitted that Bibb, who was constantly in touch with Crawford, knew of this order long prior to June, 1818.

fication of a part of our population to be regarded in opposition to the rights and interests of the whole. The experience of other states had shewn, that to consult as far as practicable in the choice of position, the convenience of every portion of the Country, is the surest method of rendering that choice permanent. In pursuing that principle the nearest eligible scite to the center of the Territory, presented the highest claim, while the probable future population of the different parts was also to be considered. The latter, however, being necessarily matter of conjecture only and liable to be estimated according to various impressions, furnished a criterion altogether uncertain; and therefore was entitled to less attention. With such views, I proceeded to examine the junction of Cahawba and Alabama. The bluff on the west side of those rivers presents a beautiful scite, with springs of good water and the prospect of health. Situated on a river capable of being navigated by boats of great burthen and supported as it will be, by the abundant production of an extensive and fertile back Country on the Alabama and Cahawba and their tributary streams the town of Cahawba promises to vie with the largest inland towns in the Country, possessing in my judgment the necessary advantages, approaching certainly nearer to the center of the Territory, and probably of its future permanent population than any other place otherwise equally eligible. I communicated the result of my examination to the President of the United States, with the request that such parts of sections as I thought best calculated for the Seat of Government might be reserved from sale. The request has been granted and I herewith transmit a copy of the correspondence, together with a letter from the Commissioner of the General Land Office to the Register and Receiver and a report signed by three of the Commissioners appointed at the last session of the General Assembly "to examine and report to the Governor the most eligible scite for the Seat of the Territorial Government." It is possible that the geographical views presented in my communication to the Secretary of the Treasury may not be entirely accurate, but should there be any error, your liberality will find an apology in the very limited means of information which were within my reach.

In submitting the further disposition of the subject to the wisdom of the Legislature, I feel no other solicitude, than that the course may be pursued, which shall best promote the welfare of the Country and the happiness of our fellow-citizens, and I have the fullest confidence that such will be, the object of your deliberations.

Wm. W. Bibb

St. Stephens 3d November—1818.

There is no doubt that Bibb prepared this part of his message with great care. He discloses the fact that he chose to locate the capital at Cahawba without even conferring with the Commissioners appointed by the Assembly. He refuses to mention Mr. Clay by name, referring to him as "the gentleman first named in the Act." There was certainly some deep feeling about the matter between the men and between the sections. Bibb realized and mentioned the possibility that the selection made by him might not be approved for he said, "While on the other hand, it was possible that the selection made by the Executive might not be approved." He also stated that he transmitted to the Assembly "a report signed by three of the Commissioners appointed at the last session of the General Assembly to examine and report to the Governor the most eligible scite for the Seat of the Territorial Government." This is the report of the Commission which selected and recommended Tuskaloosa, but Governor Bibb does not disclose what recommendation the report made nor which three of the five Commissioners signed it.[1]

Clement Clay listened intently to the Governor's message and particularly to that part dealing with the location of the seat of government. As he listened he no doubt realized that the Governor would prevail, that the Assembly would approve his selection, for Clay was a realist

[1] This report must have been a strong and interesting document. It is evident that Bibb was doing all he could to suppress the report and its contents. There is no known copy of the report. Its findings were not disclosed by the Governor nor printed in the Journal, and the fact that the Commission selected Tuskaloosa would have been buried and lost forever except for the efforts of disappointed lot-buyers to recover for their losses when the capital was moved from Cahawba. During that investigation (Journal Senate 1826) it was disclosed that the Commissioners had recommended Tuskaloosa for the "Seat of Government."

as well as a very intelligent man. But if the Governor for one moment thought the seat-of-government issue was settled, he misjudged his man. Right now Clay was a chagrined and circumvented Commissioner, but he was a fighter and even before the Assembly acted on the Governor's selection Clay was planning for the future and intending to use to his advantage, if he could, another public issue of present pressing importance. This was the matter of apportionment of representation now before the Assembly. If the Governor appropriated the capital for the Alabama River basin section, then Clay concluded that North Alabama was entitled to demand that apportionment of representation in the Assembly be according to population. Of course, this was an advantage to the more thickly populated counties.

Since the census had proven what everyone already knew to be a fact—that the North and Northwest Alabama counties possessed a large preponderance of the population of the Territory and could therefore control the Assembly—the Alabama-Cahawba River section citizens demanded that the apportionment law provide that no county could have more than a fixed number of representatives. By this means they hoped to maintain approximate equality in the Assembly. The fact that, in the Assembly as it now was, the Tennessee Valley counties and the western section of the state together had a clear majority and could pass any apportionment law they chose, was not a sufficient answer to the problem of apportionment. There were two reasons why this was true.

The law which now controlled apportionment provided: "... the number and proportion of representatives shall be regulated by the legislature."[1] This language left it wide open for the Assembly to pass any law they pleased, and of course the Tennessee Valley Assemblymen, when allied

[1] Ordinance of 1787 (Code Alabama 1923, Vol. 1, pp. 15 and 16, and Vol. 1, p. 29, Section 2) inherited from the Mississippi Territory.

with the West Alabama men, controlled that body. But it would profit them nothing to use their strength injudiciously because of the extreme veto power held by the Governor—which was: "No bill or legislative act whatever shall be of any force without his assent."[1]

Thus Governor Bibb had two powerful influences with which to control the action of the Assembly in fixing the site of the seat of government. In one hand he held a fat dowry of valuable land for the maiden Alabama whose treasury chest was empty; in the other hand a big stick, the power of withholding by veto the apportionment law so much and so justly wanted by the North Alabamians.

No wonder Clement Clay, James Titus, and John W. Walker agreed to dispense with the rules and yielded to the passage of the law locating the seat of government without a recorded battle. No wonder the report of the Commissioners recommending Tuskaloosa was thrown aside. Wisdom here was the better part of valor. The Alabama River system section gained the seat of government but the opposition got their apportionment law based on population and with it certainty of control of the Assembly, and tagged onto the tail end of the apportionment law, as a rider, was the seat-of-government provision:

> Section 3. And be it further enacted that from and after the adjournment of the present session of the Legislature, the Seat of Government shall be established permanently at the town of Cahawba.[2]

There is cause to believe that Governor Bibb was well pleased with the words "*established permanently at the town*

[1] Ordinance of 1787. (Code Alabama 1923, Vol. 1, p. 16) This law, of course, applied to the Mississippi Territory and was inherited by the Alabama Territory.

[2] Acts 1818, Second Session Alabama Territory Assembly, p. 4. Governor Bibb approved the Act November 16, 1818. John F. Everitt, one of the members of the House from Washington County, had the honor of making the motion which amended the apportionment bill to include Section 3 and thus locate the capital at Cahawba. (House Journal, November Session 1818, p. 46)

of Cahawba," but the Governor was not permitted to rest on his laurels. The Tombigbe-Warrior River basins group, aided by their friends in the Tennessee Valley, were not long in advising him that the seat-of-government issue was not to be looked upon as being finally settled.

The capital having been located and the apportionment dispute settled, the Assembly soon passed an Act providing for the *temporary* and *permanent* seats of government.[1] This law gave the Governor power to locate the site of the seat of government at the confluence of the Alabama and Cahawba Rivers and to carry into effect the Act of Congress in that behalf, passed at its last session. The Governor was appointed Commissioner and given the power to lay off, on such plan as he might deem most suitable, a town at the place now called and known as the town of Cahawba. He was authorized to survey the site into lots and sell them to the highest bidder on ninety days' notice, to deposit the money in the treasury, and out of the proceeds of the sale of said lots to contract for and cause to be erected a building suitable for the *temporary* accommodation of the General Assembly of the Territory or State (until permanent buildings should be thereafter provided). The Act provided that the Governor could not spend in excess of $10,000 to erect the State House building at Cahawba. It was provided in the Act:

> . . . that the temporary Seat of Government shall be and remain at Huntsville, until suitable buildings and accommodations can be provided in the town of Cahawba.

Public officers who were required by law to keep their offices at the seat of government were given until the meeting of the convention or next Legislature to remove the same to Huntsville.

Sections 9 and 10 of this Act were evidently the work of Clement C. Clay. The State House was to be a "*temporary*

[1] Acts of November Session 1818, p. 46.

accommodation"; and Huntsville was to be the temporary seat of government. Those facts, together with the apparent certainty that the approaching Constitutional Convention would be held in Huntsville, would provide Clay and his friends with a golden opportunity to move the seat of government from Cahawba. Unless a provision for removal of the seat of government *without the approval of the Governor* could be written into the forthcoming Constitution, it seemed certain that the capital would remain at Cahawba.

The passage of the Act which provided for a State House at Cahawba and a temporary capital at Huntsville was the final curtain for St. Stephens.[1] The small hopes which the loyal group at St. Stephens had of holding the seat of government at that place vanished. They saw their dreams of a metropolis moving from the Tombigbe to the banks of the Alabama.

Right now, though, the Assembly was concluding its affairs and soon St. Stephens would have only its memories and its small but sure place in history. On the last day of the session, November 21, 1818, the Assembly provided for the payment of the expenses of a Convention—"in case a convention should be authorized by Act of Congress to meet and form a Constitution and State Government before the next meeting of the Legislature."[2]

The quarters for the second and final session of the Alabama Territory Assembly were not rented from the same landlord who provided them for the February session. It seems fair to assume that there were two different "Capitols" at St. Stephens. The cost of the quarters rented from Lemuel and William Alston for the November session was $228 for "house rent, fuel and furniture during the present

[1] Aside from the strength of the contending political factions, a practical argument for abandoning St. Stephens as a capital might well have been the fever of a severe and malignant type which visited the place in the summer of 1818. (*Medical History of Alabama*, by D. H. Lewis, 1846)

[2] Acts, Nov. Session, p. 78. (November 21, 1818)

session."[1] The stationery used by both houses during the session cost $46.12½.

On November 21, 1818, the second session of the Territorial Assembly adjourned. So ended St. Stephens, the capital. The archives were packed for removal to the temporary seat of government at Huntsville, and the democratic process, which had put aside St. Stephens for Huntsville and Cahawba, had prevailed. But before leaving St. Stephens, one brief look at her men and their town now so alive, so soon to be only a memory.

If the instructions of the "Mississippi Territory Legislature" that the plan of St. Stephens be made and recorded were carried out, it seems to have been irrecoverably lost, for such a diligent and learned student as Peter Hamilton was never able to find it. Failing to discover the plat, Hamilton, from his own store of knowledge and careful study, has recorded much of St. Stephens, the capital, and her people, which otherwise might have been forever lost.

The landing on the river was kept by Reuben Chamberlain and Dennison Darling. There were two hotels, one kept by Douglass and the other by the Alstons. A public square was reserved for use of the people. A market place existed and a theatre prospered,[2] for St. Stephens was a churchless and godless place, with a prevailing indifference to anything that savored of religion.[3] The conditions noted by the Reverend Mr. Dow in 1805 seem to have continued.

High Street ran east and west along a ridge below the old fort. Parallel to it were Front and Madison Streets toward the river, with Jackson and Monroe on the other side. At right angles with High Street were Chambers, Orange, Spring, and Lime Streets, one of which later became the

[1] Acts, Nov. Session, p. 77.

[2] Vol. III, *Alabama Historical Society*, note 4, p. 210.

[3] Vol. III, *Alabama Historical Society*, p. 210, "Reminiscences of Miss Mary Welch."

highway to Mobile. The streets were paved with brick or stone. At the northwest corner of the intersection of High and Lime Streets was the famous Tombeckbe Bank, and facing it were the buildings in which sat the Assemblies of the Alabama Territory. Here, too, were located the Receivers of the public lands: Thomas Maury, Lemuel Henry, William Crawford, John H. Owen, and Elijah H. Gordy. On this high bluff where the honeybees found homes in the deep crevices of the rock, amid the crepe myrtle and plum bloom, these pioneers did their work well. They took Andrew Ellicott's line and from it, with the aid of Josiah Meigs, Commissioner of the General Land Office, and Seth Pease and Thomas Freeman, Surveyors General of the Mississippi Territory, settled the title to all the lands in South Alabama.

Among the leading St. Stephens citizens of note were Henry Hitchcock, lawyer, who was also first Attorney General of Alabama and later Chief Justice of her Supreme Court; Thomas Eastin, publisher of *The Halcyon and Tombecke Advertiser*, which newspaper he established in 1815; George Fisher, who as late as 1817 had the contract to carry the mail between St. Stephens and Mobile; and Jack F. Ross, Legislator and State Treasurer. The leading business men and firms were James Lyon, Coolidge and Bright, David Files, George Buchanan, Davis and Patton, John Mayers, R. Chamberlain & Company, Jno. Crowell, Pleasant May, Wm. McDonald, G. C. Russell, Robert Miller, Lem^{l} Espy, and Samuel Pickens, Jr. Ptolemy T. Harris was also engaged in trade and was successful in politics for a period. John Meeker was the foremost physician of the town. There was Lewis Sewall, Alabama's first poet, James Caller, the military man who commanded at Burnt Corn, George S. Gaines, factor for the Government, Thomas Malone, who escorted the captive Aaron Burr all the way to Virginia, Benjamin S. Smoot, active in all kinds of public and business undertakings, Reuben S. Saffold, lawyer, judge, and later Chief Justice of the Supreme Court of Alabama, James Pickens, member of the Constitutional Convention, and Israel Pickens, later Governor of the State for two terms. Silas Dinsmoor, one of the most active and public-spirited citizens of St. Stephens, was unsuccessful in business and also failed in politics because of his wit. He lost his job in the Collector's office because when his superiors in Washington wrote and inquired: "How far does the Tombigbe River run up the Country?", Dinsmoor replied, "It doesn't run up, it runs down."

So ends the story of St. Stephens, first and only capital of the Territory of Alabama. Though vanished from the eminence of Hobuckintoopa even as the stalwart Choctaws who once owned this rock are gone, she is not dead, but proudly lives on in her great-great-grandchild, Montgomery, capital home of Alabama.

HUNTSVILLE[1]

The Second Capital

The Year 1819

The General Assembly—Annual Session of 1819

The *Alabama Republican*, a newspaper published in Huntsville, in its issue of June 26, 1819, contained this brief statement:

> His Excellency Governor Bibb arrived in Huntsville on Monday last. The Secretary of the Territory is daily expected and the public records, etc., have already arrived here, where they will remain while this place continues to be the Seat of Government.[2]

The State officials had hardly settled in their quarters[3] when the Alabama Constitutional Convention assembled in the town. The Congress, by Act of March 2, 1819, directed that the election of delegates to the Convention be held on the first Monday and Tuesday in May, and authorized them to meet in Huntsville on the first Monday in July to form a Constitution and State government for the people within the Territory.[4]

The government officials of the Territory, including Governor Bibb, did not move to Huntsville until after the election of the Convention delegates. They were busy at their homes, participating in the choice of the delegates. This Convention was a political event of major importance. A

[1] See note on Madison County and Huntsville prior to 1819—Appendix, p. 211.

[2] *Alabama Historical Society*, Vol. I, p. 87. (Monday last was June 20.) Governor Bibb was only twenty days behind the President of the United States, James Monroe, who visited Huntsville on June 1, when Clement Comer Clay was selected to invite the President to a dinner, presided over by Col. LeRoy Pope as President, assisted by C. C. Clay and Henry Minor, Esqs., as Vice-Presidents. After the cloth was removed twenty-four toasts were drunk, accompanied by the discharge of cannon and appropriate songs. (*Trans. Ala. Hist. Soc.*, Vol. III, p. 154)

[3] It is not known where the State Offices were housed.

[4] Code of Alabama 1923, Vol. I, pp. 33 and 34. The first Monday in July was July 5.

lot would depend on the Constitution which was to be written, so the delegates were selected with great care.[1]

As directed by Congress, the Convention met and organized in Huntsville on July 5.[2] They chose John W. Walker, of Madison County, President of the Convention and John Campbell, Secretary. The work of drafting the Constitution was, by the vote of the Convention, placed in the hands of a Committee of Fifteen. The remarkable thing about this Committee is that there were seven members from counties definitely North Alabama, and seven from counties just as certainly South Alabama. The fifteenth member was from the border county of Shelby. The best brains in the Territory were on this Committee. The members were:

North Alabama

C. C. Clay, Madison County
Thomas Bibb, Limestone County

[1] There were 44 delegates, representing 22 counties, as follows:

Madison County
J. W. Walker, *President of the Convention*
Clement C. Clay
John Leigh Townes
Henry Chambers
Lemuel Mead
Henry Minor
Gabriel Moore
John M. Taylor

Monroe County
John Murphy
John Watkins
James Pickens
Thomas Wiggins

Blount County
Isaac Brown
John Brown
Gabriel Hanby

Shelby County
George Philips
Thomas Amis Rogers

Limestone County
Thomas Bibb
Beverley Hughes
Nicholas Davis

Montgomery County
John Dandridge Bibb
James W. Armstrong

Washington County
Israel Pickens
Henry Hitchock

Tuskaloosa County
Marmaduke Williams
John L. Tindall

Lawrence County
Arthur F. Hopkins
Daniel Wright

Franklin County
William Metcalf
Richard Ellis

Cotaco County
Thomas D. Crabb
Melcajah Vaughan

Clarke County
Reuben Saffold
James Magoffin

Cahawba County
Littlepage Sims

Conecuh County
Samuel Cook

Dallas County
William R. King

Marengo County
Washington Thompson

Marion County
John D. Terrill

Lauderdale County
Hugh McVay

St. Clair County
David Conner

Autauga County
James Jackson

Baldwin County
Harry Toulmin

Mobile County
S. H. Garrow

[2] The Daughters of the American Revolution placed a bronze tablet at the southwest corner of the intersection of Franklin and Gates Streets as the site of the "Assembly Hall" where the Constitutional Convention held its sessions.

Clement Comer Clay

John M. Taylor, Madison County
Henry Chambers, Madison County
Arthur F. Hopkins, Lawrence County
Beverley Hughes, Limestone County
Richard Ellis, Franklin County

South Alabama

Israel Pickens, Washington County
William R. King, Dallas County
Henry Hitchcock, Washington County
John Murphy, Monroe County
Reuben Saffold, Clarke County
John Watkins, Monroe County
John Dandridge Bibb, Montgomery County

Shelby County

George Philips, Shelby County

This Committee actually wrote Alabama's first Constitution, C. C. Clay being the member who prepared the draft which contained the main features of the Constitution which was adopted by the Convention with only minor changes. Henry Hitchcock, assisted by William R. King and John M. Taylor, did the actual work of reducing the Clay outline to form.[1]

The Committee of Fifteen evidently did not keep any minutes or journal of their meetings and discussions, and no memoirs or recollections of members are known, but in view of the Constitution which they wrote and which the Convention accepted almost without change, it seems probable that George Philips voted with the Tennessee Valley group. Otherwise, it is unlikely that the Constitution would have contained that singular provision for a change of the capital, which reads:

> The first session of the General Assembly shall commence on the fourth Monday in October next, and be held in the town of Huntsville, and all subsequent sessions at the town of Cahawba, until the end of the first session of the General Assembly to be held in the year one thousand eight hundred and twenty-five;

[1] Pickett, Vol. II, pp. 419 and 412.

during that session the General Assembly shall have the power to designate by law (to which the executive concurrence shall not be required) the permanent Seat of Government, which shall not thereafter be changed; PROVIDED, HOWEVER, that unless such designation be then made by law, the government shall continue permanently at the town of Cahawba; AND PROVIDED ALSO, that the General Assembly shall make no appropriations previous to the year one thousand eight hundred and twenty-five for the building of any other State House than that now provided by law.[1]

Governor Bibb, of course, was not a member of the Convention which wrote this section into the Constitution, but he was in Huntsville at the time. He was also the most influential public man in the state and no doubt had a strong influence in the framing of the Constitution, though not enough to prevent the combination of delegates from the Tennessee Valley and the Warrior-Tombigbe from inserting the section requiring a reconsideration of the location of the seat of government by the Assembly in the year 1825.

The writing of Section 29 into the Constitution was a distinct victory for C. C. Clay—it was Clay's answer to Governor Bibb's action in ignoring and circumventing the Commissioners named by the Assembly at St. Stephens to select a suitable site for the seat of government. And while Clay, aided by J. W. Walker, Marmaduke Williams, John L. Tindall, and Nicholas Davis, was able to write Section 29, so that the Governor did not have to approve a law to remove the capital from Cahawba—which was a sweet revenge in itself—the victory was not absolute, for the Tennessee Valley and Warrior-Tombigbe Rivers system combination was taking a chance on being able to have a majority in *both* the Senate and House in the 1825 General Assembly. If the change was not made in the year 1825, then the capital was to remain at Cahawba.

Immigration was a fickle and uncertain thing in the early

[1] Alabama Constitution of 1819, Article III, Section 29. See Code of Alabama 1923, Vol. 1, p. 68.

eighteen-hundreds. The Tennessee Valley, already pretty densely settled, might slow down enough for the Alabama River basin to overtake her by the time the elections of the 1825 Assemblymen would take place.

It was even more than a possibility that the Alabama River section might gain a majority in the 1825 Senate. A majority of one or a stalemate would be sufficient to prevent a removal since, under the law, in order to remove the seat of government from Cahawba both Houses would have to vote a majority in favor of the change.

The political situation thus presented was intriguing and fascinating. Political men in the state never lost sight of the stalking shadow of "removal" through the years from 1819 to 1825. It was Alabama's foremost political problem of the time, and was to continue for many years yet to come to be an issue which refused to be permanently settled.

The Alabama Constitution was adopted by the Convention on August 2, 1819. It was not submitted to the people for ratification. The first exercise of rights of the people under the Constitution was to vote for the election of their Representatives and Senators in a general election held on the third Monday and Tuesday of September, 1819.[1] Under the schedule attached to and made a part of the Constitution each county was given one Senator; and the Representatives, pending a new census, were apportioned exactly, a fixed number being given to each county, there being fifty in all.[2]

Marmaduke Williams, Esq., of Tuskaloosa, was a candidate for the office of Governor. He ran against Governor Bibb as a protest candidate on account of Bibb's high-handed action in locating the seat of government at Cahawba. The group who felt that Bibb had gone too far in his autocratic action in inducing the rejection of Tuskaloosa by substituting Cahawba saw to it that Bibb had opposi-

[1] Section 28 of Article III, Alabama Constitution of 1819.

[2] Schedule, Section 7, Alabama 1923 Code, Vol. 1, p. 80.

tion. There were no real political parties, and the location of the capital was almost the only issue. Personal political strength elected Bibb.

The Huntsville session of the Alabama Assembly was one of the most vital and interesting in the history of our state. This was the real beginning of Alabama's functioning as an equal state under the Federal Constitution. United States Senators were chosen, a Supreme Court elected, and precedents for the unknown future were instituted. The political functions of the Assembly were important and exciting. The debut of a sovereign state is no ordinary matter.

This famous first Assembly[1] convened on October 25 and adjourned December 17, 1819, three days after Alabama was formally received into the sisterhood of States—and in time for members who lived at great distances from Huntsville to reach their homes in time for Christmas, if they did not linger too long at wayside taverns.

William Wyatt Bibb was Governor, and Henry Hitchcock, Esq., Secretary of State; the latter was succeeded by Thomas A. Rogers, and was thereupon elected Alabama's first Attorney General. The Treasurer was Jack F. Ross, and Samuel Pickens, Esq., was Auditor of Public Accounts. During the session the Assembly elected Carter B. Harrison Adjutant General, and William Peacock Quartermaster General. The militia was an important department of the state government—there were still thousands of resentful Indians within the borders of Alabama, and the militia was frequently in action.

The Governor's written message was delivered to each House by his private secretary, Mr. James S. Walker.[2] These prophetic words were part of it: "Your present meeting will form a memorable epoch in our history." A large part of what the Governor had to say was in the nature of

[1] Members of this Assembly, and all others through the year 1825, are given in the Appendix.

[2] Senate Journal 1819, p. 7, *et seq.*

Henry Hitchcock

a report on the sale of lots[1] at Cahawba, and the building of the State House at that place:

> Reporting on the sales of lots at Cahawba to the highest bidder—182 lots sold in the 4th week of May for the sum of $123,-856, of which $30,964 (being one fourth part) was received at the time of sale, together with $51.25, being the second installment of lot 53, total $31,015.25. The expenses of surveying and sale as appears by the receipts of Willis Roberts and Benjamin Clements were $730.00, leaving, $30,285.25, of which $20,405 were paid over to the Territorial Treasurer. . . . $10,000 was deposited in the Planters and Merchants Bank of Huntsville and will be expended in the erection of a temporary State House at the town of Cahawba, for which a contract was made in the month of May last. Of that sum $3,000 have been drawn and placed in the hands of an agent in Cahawba to be advanced to the contractor in conformity with the terms of the agreement. The principal parts of the buildings are to be finished on or before the first day of August next for $9,000, and the remainder of the sum appropriated will be required and is sufficient to complete the whole, and to provide the necessary accommodations for the two branches of the Legislature. I learn that the building has been commenced and that no doubt is entertained of its completion within the time specified in the contract.

Governor Bibb advised that in lieu of the section of land for the Territorial seat of government, "We got 1620 acres for the same object at the junction of the Cahawba and Alabama Rivers." The Governor expressed the belief that from this grant the State would realize at least $300,000—a sum amply sufficient to provide permanent buildings and accommodations for several departments of government and to defray the expense of erecting other works of public convenience. He advised laying off and selling additional lots in Cahawba.

The first practical business of the Assembly was to find accommodations within which to hold its sessions. This was not an easy task in such a thriving town.[2] A joint commit-

[1] The lots were auctioned off. Governor Bibb was present, and his presence encouraged the bidders.

[2] Ebenezer H. Cummins wrote a *Summary Geography of Alabama, One of the*

tee composed of House and Senate was appointed to "find rooms and report the price, etc. to the Assembly." But the lack of a hall which it could call its own did not delay the election of two United States Senators. The need of the infant State for representation in the United States Senate was too important to be postponed for any reason. By mutual understanding one Senator was chosen from South Alabama and the other from North Alabama. William R. King,[1] of Dallas County, was the selection of the down-State men, while John W. Walker was so honored by North Alabama.[2]

United States, which was published in Philadelphia on August 16, 1819. In it he said (p. 19):

"Huntsville is the principal and oldest town in the valley of Tennessee, and is the capital of Madison County. The United States have here a land office which, since its establishment, has done more business than any two others. It has a bank with a capital of 500,000 dollars; two printing offices, and 2,500 inhabitants. It is a most flourishing town, in the midst of one of the finest counties on earth. Here met the Convention in July, 1819, to frame the Constitution for the government of the State."

Anne Royal, in her *Letters from Alabama*, wrote on January 1, 1818 (p. 44), that Huntsville had:

"260 houses principally built of brick, has a bank, a court house and a market house. There is a large square in the centre of the town, like the towns in Ohio, facing this are the stores, twelve in number. The buildings form a solid wall, though divided into apartments. The workmanship is the best I have seen in all the State; and several of the houses are three stories high and very large. There is no church. The people assemble in the Court House to worship. Huntsville is settled by people mostly from Georgia and the Carolinas—though there are a few from almost every part of the world;—and the town displays much activity. The citizens are gay, polite, and hospitable, and live in great splendor. Nothing like it in our county."

[1] Charles Tait, former U. S. Senator from Georgia but at this time a resident of Claiborne, Monroe County, desired greatly to be one of Alabama's first Senators. He made the statement that he had done more to create the Alabama Territory and later the State of Alabama than any other person in Congress. Governor Wm. W. Bibb wrote Tait on being informed of Tait's wishes: "Major Walker will be one of the Senators in Congress and I am desirous that you should be the other. It is, however, prudent that the public mind be sounded on this subject with caution and delicacy. Your short residence here, and the jealousy of Georgia influence, which the idea of the Governor and both Senators may create, make this caution proper. I shall be able to ascertain the prospect during the present session, and will then write you." Of course, Tait failed to get the senatorship but he was appointed Federal Judge, being Alabama's first officer in that capacity.

[2] Senate Journal 1819, pp. 24–25. House Journal 1819, p. 29.

The quarters used by the two Houses at this time were in different locations. The Committee reported to the Senate that the "room now occupied by the representative branch can be retained only a few days at $10.00 per day."[1] It was further reported that:

> Two rooms sufficiently spacious, having one chimney place each within the Huntsville Inn have been examined neither of which will be rented unless both are taken, at $16.00 per day, chairs and fuel included.
>
> Two large sheet iron stoves with a small one (if necessary) for the use of the Speaker can be procured in this place, fitted up for use by Monday next on the lower floor of the Court House, for sixty dollars.
>
> A large cast iron stove is prepared for the Senatorial Chamber now occupied and which on the suggestion of the representative house can be exchanged for one of sheet iron.
>
> Your committee therefore can have no hesitancy in reporting the *lower floor* of the Court House to be the most proper apartment for the reception of the Representative branch, and the *room now occupied* by the Senate to be the most convenient for the accommodation of that body.[2]

After receiving the report of the Committee the House, on Monday, November 1, 1819, by resolution in which it asked the Senate to concur, resolved: "That when it adjourns on Monday next . . . it will adjourn to the Court House of this town, and that Daniel Rather be empowered to have said house fitted for that purpose."[3]

Before moving to the lower floor of the Court House, the House of Representatives held its sessions in the house of one Irby Jones. He was paid "one hundred and fifty dollars for the use of his house whilst occupied by the House of Representatives."[4]

The Senate, of course, did not move but remained in "*the room now occupied.*" It is believed that this room was in

[1] Senate Journal 1819, pp. 29–30.

[2] House Journal 1819, p. 30.

[3] House Journal 1819, p. 34. The Senate concurred. House Journal 1819, p. 34.

[4] Acts 1819, p. 136.

the house of John K. Dunn. The Assembly appropriated "to John K. Dunn One Hundred fifty-one dollars ninety three and three-fourths cents for preparing and furnishing the Senate Chamber with chairs and other articles."[1]

Joint sessions were occasionally held by the two Houses. When these were held, the Assembly gathered in the quarters of the House of Representatives. One of the first and most interesting of the joint sessions was that to open and publish the vote for Governor. The incumbent, William W. Bibb, received 8,342 votes, and Marmaduke Williams, Esq., received 7,140. The vote by counties[2] discloses how the people felt about the capital matter, and about the candidates.

County	*Bibb*	*Williams*
Shelby	278	96
Conecuh	460	39
Monroe	650	534
Mobile	172	83
Baldwin	126	11
Marengo	184	405
Franklin	161	387
Lawrence	493	297
St. Clair	350	178
Blount	111	722
Cotaco	195	454
Cahawba	350	73
Marion	83	225
Autauga	440	6
Washington	257	322

[1] Acts 1819, p. 136. It is submitted that by these words the Assembly intended to say that Dunn was paid for providing the Senate Chamber furnished with chairs and other articles. This interpretation becomes the more convincing when it is noted that no other appropriation was made by the Assembly to pay for the quarters of the Senate. Moreover, it is to be observed that the Assembly paid Pleasant Willis only twenty-five dollars for the rent of *fifty* chairs for the House (Acts 1819, p. 136), which had fifty members during most of the Session, whereas the Senate at no time had present over twenty-one members. The appropriation of $151.93¾ to John K. Dunn cannot be considered as reasonable unless it paid for use of the *room* as well as the "chairs and other articles."

[2] Senate Journal 1819, p. 38. House Journal 1819, p. 37.

Limestone	906	191
Lauderdale	142	355
Dallas	647	115
Clarke	543	274
Tuskaloosa	123	824
Madison	1,225	1,244
Montgomery	440	350
	8,342	7,140[1]

Whereupon, Mr. Speaker declared that W. W. Bibb, Esq., was duly elected Governor and Commander-in-Chief of the State of Alabama by a majority of 1,202 votes.

Following his election, the Speaker of the House administered to him the oath of office prescribed by the Constitution, after which His Excellency the Governor arose and addressed both houses as follows:[2]

GENTLEMEN: I avail myself of this occasion to express my acknowledgments, for the proof which has been afforded me, of the public confidence. Called by the voice of our fellow citizens to the Chief Magistracy of the State, I proceed to the station with a full conviction of its high responsibility and with a sincere desire to promote the welfare of the country, and the happiness of the people.

We have entered on the exercise of the rights of self-government, and I am persuaded that no one has stronger inducements to rejoice, at the change in our political condition, than the individual who now addresses you. A territorial government can never be acceptable to any portion of the American Community, and such is the nature, and extent of the powers delegated to the Executive that his acts are always viewed with suspicion and jealousy. His best deeds are seldom correctly esti-

[1] An examination of the vote discloses that Williams' strength follows the Tombigbe-Warrior River system, while Bibb carried the counties drained by the Alabama and Cahawba Rivers. The Tennessee River Valley divided on a mixture of protest and personal following. Limestone, where Governor Bibb's brother resided and was well liked, went heavily for Bibb, while he lost Madison because of the capital issue, in spite of his support there by the "Georgia men" who were politically in control in that county at that time. It appears that an error in addition gave Bibb 6 more votes than the detail shows him to be entitled to, and deprived Williams of 45 votes, so that the correct majority received by Bibb should be shown as 1,151 votes.

[2] Senate Journal 1819, p. 55, *et seq.*

mated; and his unintentional errors are often ascribed to unworthy motives.[1]

Happily for all concerned, these sources of collision and distrust, are now removed, and we behold the gratifying spectacle of the representatives of a free people erecting and establishing the Temple of Liberty.

United to the great family of American States; possessing ample resources for the advancement of learning and the diffusion of knowledge; blessed with a country abounding in navigable waters and rich in the advantages of soil and climate, we surely cannot contemplate the high destiny which awaits us without sentiments of profound gratitude and without a firm determination to cherish and support the government of our choice under which alone such distinguished blessings can be enjoyed.

On my part, I solemnly declare, that my best exertions shall be devoted to the promotion of virtue and intelligence, the only sure basis of free institutions; to the encouragement of obedience to the laws, to the cultivation of harmony, and good will among ourselves, and with public functionaries of our sister states, and of the United States; to the improvement of those natural advantages with which we are so bountifully supplied; and to the accomplishment of every object which according to my deliberate judgment may tend to elevate the character of our State and to establish its true and permanent interests.

Whereupon His Excellency retired.

Perhaps the most exciting event to occur during the Huntsville session was the visit there of General Andrew Jackson. The General came down to race his horses and also to maintain first-hand contact with the yeomanry of the county. He was quite aware that he was politically important as well as war famous. At this time the General was the most heroic and at the same time the most controversial public man in the country. His star was in the ascendancy —a man from west of the mountains who challenged the entrenched power of the eastern seaboard states. There were those who feared Jackson's popularity and were con-

[1] Bibb was referring to the criticisms made of him for circumventing the Commission appointed by the Assembly to find a site for the capital and his own dictatorial action in locating the capital at Cahawba.

stantly working to check his rise to power and thwart his ambitions. The Whigs, led by the indomitable Henry Clay, disagreed with the policies of Jackson and disliked his supporters. These influences were present in the remote frontier village of Huntsville, where a pioneer Legislature was laying the foundations of a commonwealth.

The first move of the Jackson men was a resolution in the Senate inviting the General to take a seat within the bar of the Senate.[1] But this was only the beginning. Howell Rose, Senator from Autauga, on Tuesday, November 2, 1819, offered the following resolution:

> Resolved by the Senate and the House of Representatives of the State of Alabama in General Assembly convened: That the thanks of the General Assembly be and the same are hereby presented to Major General Andrew Jackson for his valor, patriotism and meritorious conduct in the late war; but particularly for the decisive and glorious victory obtained over the British forces at New Orleans.[2]

The words "late war" referred to the war against the Seminole Indians, in which campaign Jackson had marched over most of West Florida and occupied Pensacola while the United States was at peace with Spain. The anti-Jackson men had seized upon this incident as a means of discrediting Jackson and ending his surge toward the Presidency. Senator Joseph Farmer, of Lauderdale, thought the wording of the resolution too mild, so he proposed the following amendment:

> Resolved that this General Assembly do highly disapprove of the late attempt made by some members of the Congress of the United States at the last session to censure the military course of this invaluable officer, from motives (as we believe) other than patriotic.

The amendment was adopted and the resolution sent to the House for concurrence. The House at first voted concurrence, but the next day, on a reconsideration vote, they

[1] Senate Journal 1819, p. 38. [2] Senate Journal 1819, p. 42.

declined Mr. Farmer's amendment as too violent by the close vote of 25 to 24.[1] In lieu of the refused paragraph the House offered the following substitute:

2. And be it further resolved, that he is more particularly entitled to the admiration and affection of the citizens of this State because by his military skill and indefatigable exertions our exposed frontiers have been saved from savage inroads and the inhabitants from indiscriminate slaughter.

3. Resolved that his whole conduct during his military career receives our entire approbation.

4. Resolved that his visit to this place at this time affords us the liveliest satisfaction; as it enables us to express to him the high sense which was entertained of his services, and our perfect confidence in his talents, integrity and patriotism.

5. Resolved that a joint committee be appointed to wait on Maj. General Jackson and present to him the foregoing resolution.[2]

The Senate accepted the amendment proposed by the House and Senator Howell Rose was chosen as its representative to serve on the committee to wait on General Jackson. The House appointed Griffin Lamkin to serve with Mr. Rose. A letter was drafted and handed the General with the resolutions:

Major General Jackson: The General Assembly of the State of Alabama have instructed us to present you with these resolutions as a testimony of their high respect and gratitude for the important service you have rendered to the United States of America, and particularly to this State.

Permit us to add, sir, as individuals, our best wishes for your prosperity and happiness.

(*Signed*) by the Committee[3]

Jackson's letter acknowledging the honor extended him is a complete answer to those historians who have said that "Old Hickory" was a soldier only, without gentlemanly grace or learning. Moreover, his answer carries the mark of genius—a genius for politics:

[1] House Journal 1819, pp. 45 and 50.

[2] Senate Journal 1819, pp. 47 *et seq.*

[3] Senate Journal 1819, p. 59.

Madison County, Nov. 9, 1819

GENTLEMEN: I have received with the highest satisfaction the resolutions of the General Assembly of the State of Alabama; the honor conferred on me by that body is accepted with feelings of warmest sensibility.

The first pride of a soldier should be to discharge the duties of the field with zeal and fidelity, and the first reward, the approbation of his countrymen; and it is a source of peculiar satisfaction to have received the manifestation of the confidence of those who have gloriously participated in the fatigues and dangers of the camp.

As a testimony of my gratitude for the high sense of my public services which you have been pleased to express; permit me, gentlemen, to present to you and through you, to the honorable body of which you are a committee, the assurance of my high consideration and regards.

I am, gentlemen, very respectfully,

Your obedient servant,

ANDREW JACKSON

MAJOR HOWELL ROSE, *Chairman of Committee.*[1]

Near the close of the session came the important elections. For Attorney General, Henry Hitchcock received 45 votes; his opponent, Dunklin Sullivan, received 14 votes, and John N. S. Jones, 10 votes.

The election of the Circuit Judges was a matter of first importance for, under the Constitution, Alabama's Supreme Court was composed of the Circuit Judges sitting together as the highest judicial power of the state. For Judge of the First Circuit Abner Lipscomb won over Harry Toulmin 63 to 5. Reuben Saffold was the only person nominated for Judge of the Second Circuit, and Henry Y. Webb had no opposition for Judge of the Third Circuit. The only real contest arose concerning the Judgeship in the Fourth Circuit. There were three candidates—John McKinley, Richard Ellis, and Beverley Hughes. Election was not achieved until the fourth ballot, when Ellis won with 37 votes to 31 for McKinley. The Fifth Circuit produced only

[1] Senate Journal 1819, pp. 59 *et seq.*

one nominee—Clement Comer Clay. These were all good sound men, well suited to administer justice in a pioneer state. They were satisfactory Circuit Judges, and they made a good Supreme Court.

The business men of early Huntsville were willing to profit what they could from this windfall session of the Assembly in their town. Some of them attempted to make inflated charges for services and goods furnished the State, but when it came to appropriations to pay for them, the House was "close." John Boardman charged $91 for printing. The House decided that this was too much and cut it to $73. But they paid William Leech $10 without challenge for making a railing for the lobby of the House. For Samuel K. McGraw they appropriated $30 for two sheet-iron stoves furnished the House. McGraw rendered a bill of $50 but the House thought it unreasonable and recommended that $20 be deducted. The Senate was softer, and induced the House to cut off only $10, so McGraw was eventually paid $40 for his stoves.

Glass and Hudnall rendered their bill in the amount of $185.25 for making tables and benches, etc. The House found this unreasonable and recommended a deduction of $45. The Assembly finally agreed on $150.25, and this sum was appropriated to pay their bill. William K. Dunn (evidently the brother of John K. Dunn who furnished quarters for the Senate) rendered a bill for the hire of a stove for use of the Senate. The House found the "account unreasonable and ought not to be granted."[1]

Alabama's first Assembly, in their efforts to protect the State's Treasury, were probably regarded by the Huntsville tradesmen as a stingy lot.

Before ending their Huntsville session the Assembly authorized the Governor to rent a suitable building in the town of Cahawba for the reception and safekeeping of State papers, and provided the funds to pay for same "until

[1] House Journal 1819, p. 175, and Acts 1819, pp. 135–136.

a proper apartment shall have been completed within the temporary State building for the reception of the State papers." The Governor was authorized to draw on the contingent fund "for that sum of money which will be sufficient to pay for office rent at Huntsville."

The days which that beautiful and pleasant city was the "Seat of Government" were not many, but they were memorable. The foundations of a commonwealth were laid with care and patience. The first rules of legislative procedure were conceived and adopted here. That they were wise rules is attested by the fact that many of them are in service today. The first elected Governor here took the oath and delivered the first inaugural address. The original Supreme Court was elected at Huntsville, reserving its organization as such to a later time at Cahawba.

Amid these stirring events, Andrew Jackson, no stranger within Alabama's borders, came to visit the young commonwealth even as statehood began, and here cemented a friendship with her people which was to endure to the end of his days.

On December 16, 1819, by joint resolution, Daniel Rather was authorized, "As soon as may be after the rising of the General Assembly, to sell at public outcry the tables and stoves and other furniture which have been procured for the use of both Houses," and, after deducting the expense thereon, to pay over the balance into the treasury. Next day, the Assembly adjourned.

The capital days of Huntsville were over.

CAHAWBA[1]

The Third Capital

WILLIAM WYATT BIBB had need of his broad experience in public affairs, personal determination, and legal power in order to force the location of the seat of government at Cahawba. That he succeeded without a revolt against his authority is a high compliment to the political genius of the man. But many of the members of the Assembly who had yielded to the Governor's demand that the capital be at Cahawba had done so grudgingly and with a subdued resentment against the combination of forces which they realized had deprived them of their free choice in selecting the site. The opportunity for striking back was not long in coming to the offended Assemblymen. The Governor had to have funds with which to build the State House.

When the bill for an appropriation to erect the State House came up the recently coerced Assemblymen became pinchfisted and silent. This was a matter entirely within their power and no outside influence could now intimidate or control them. With a fixed purpose in mind and a firm hand on the public purse, they authorized a building suitable for a *temporary* accommodation of the General Assembly—not to cost more than $10,000.[2]

Considering that Alabama, thanks to the astuteness of Governor Bibb, now had a valuable land grant for her capital and no debts, this niggardly expenditure for a State House could mean but one thing—that a majority in the Assembly were convinced that the seat of government would be moved from Cahawba in 1825. In the event of removal the loss occasioned by abandonment of this modest structure would not be great. Moreover, if an expensive building were erected it could well be offered as a reason

[1] See note on Cahawba prior to 1818—Appendix, p. 224.

[2] Acts November 1818, Alabama Territory, p. 46 at p. 49.

for retaining the capital at Cahawba. Those in favor of removal were careful not to provide the opposition with effective argument against removal.

That Governor Bibb was disappointed with the small grant given him to erect a "temporary accommodation" for the General Assembly cannot be doubted. The language used in the law making the appropriation for the State House, if not a repudiation, was certainly an insult to the seat-of-government law which read: "The Seat of Government shall be established *permanently* at the town of Cahawba."

But Bibb was not easily discouraged. He believed in the wisdom of his choice and now with the advantage of having the seat of government at Cahawba, he was determined to keep it there. To him this was more than a partisan political contest. The Governor envisioned a metropolis arising at the junction of the Alabama and the Cahawba. In his message to the Assembly on November 8, 1818, he had said:

> The bluff on the west side of those rivers presents a beautiful scite, with springs of good water and the prospect of health. Situated on a river capable of being navigated by boates of great burthen, and supported as it will be by the abundant production of an extensive and fertile back country on the Alabama and Cahawba and their tributary streams the town of Cahawba promises to vie with the largest inland towns in the country.

The next year at Huntsville Governor Bibb had informed the Assembly that he had induced the Federal Government to increase the "Seat of Government" land grant from a mere section of land to 1,620 acres. From this liberal donation Bibb expected to realize at least $300,000—a sum in his opinion "amply sufficient to provide *permanent* buildings and accommodations for the several departments of government, and to defray the expenses of erecting other works of public convenience."[1]

[1] Governor Bibb's Message to Assembly, October 26, 1819, Senate Journal, p. 18.

The enthusiastic Governor had the Assembly place the entire 1,620 acres within the corporate limits of the town of Cahawba.[1] Great numbers of people were moving southwest, and Alabama was getting her share of the immigrants. The steamboat was a reality now and the winding, unruly Alabama awaited its coming. Maybe the Governor's vision would become a fact and a metropolis would arise on the high bluff below which the clear Cahawba made junction with the muddy Alabama.

The Governor proceeded as rapidly as possible with his building program, considering the handicaps of the day. Mails were slow and irregular, and there were no public transportation agencies. For transport a man was limited to what he could supply himself. Contractors to build a State House were not excepted from obstacles which interfered with the construction of any considerable building.

Within view of the site of the proposed State House, nature had disposed with a lavish hand most of the raw materials needed; yet reducing the forests to building lumber and burning the clay into bricks were no easy accomplishments. There were few contractors available capable of building a State House and none of these could finance the undertaking. The whole nation was going through a period of pecuniary distress. Credit, where available, was limited in amount and the rates of interest very high. The State of Alabama would have to provide the cash to build its State House.

The farsighted Governor had foreseen these difficulties before they became actualities. As soon as he had received the warrant of authority from the Territorial Assembly Bibb had concentrated his efforts on completing the survey of the town of Cahawba into lots in order that they could be sold at public outcry to the highest bidder. By this method the Governor could acquire the cash needed to pay for Alabama's first State building.

[1] Acts 1819, p. 118.

Messrs. Willis Roberts and Benjamin Clements were engaged by the Governor to make the survey of Cahawba and to conduct the sale of lots. Their map of the Town of Cahawba shows a well-designed city said to have been modeled after the plan of Philadelphia. That Roberts and Clements conducted the sale of the lots with skill and enthusiasm is attested by the huge success of the auction.

The sales were made in the fourth week of May, 1819. Governor Bibb had timed this move after reflection. There is no lovelier place on the globe than Dallas County in Maytime. Under the influence of a beautiful and delightful spring and the prospects of a capital which would also be an inland metropolis, the eager buyers purchased one hundred eighty-two lots for a sum of $123,856, of which $30,964 was paid in cash. Roberts and Clements earned their fee of $730 for their services, which the Governor cheerfully paid them.[1]

The funds needed to build the State House were now in hand, together with a comfortable surplus in the State Treasury. Considering the hard times of that day, the infant State of Alabama was in excellent financial condition.

While Bibb had delayed the sale of the Cahawba lots until after the freshets, so that it might take place during the pleasant part of springtime, he had with his usual forethought previously had the specifications for the State House drawn and advertised for bids for its construction. The following notice, dated March 1, 1819, was published in the *Halcyon and Tombeckbe Advertiser* and printed at St. Stephens April 5, 1819:

NOTICE

The Governor having been directed by the Territorial Legislature to contract for building a house for their accommodation at the town of Cahawba, will be prepared to receive proposals at that place from the third to the fourth Monday of May next, for furnishing the materials and erecting a brick house of the

[1] Governor Bibb's Message to Assembly, Senate Journal 1819, pp. 7 *et seq.*

following description: The building to be two story, fifty-eight feet long, and forty-three feet wide; each story to be twelve feet in the clear. The interior to be divided above and below stairs by a passage fourteen feet wide, on one side of which shall be one room the whole width of the house, and on the other, two rooms. Two chimnies and eight windows are to be provided at each end and twelve windows on each front of the building; each window to be twenty-four lights, 8 x 10. The outer walls to be commenced two feet below the surface of the earth, and to be two brick and a half thick to the first floor (which must be three feet above the surface of the earth), and from thence two brick. The inner wall dividing the apartments to be one brick and a half thick, and each apartment to be plastered and white-washed. The shingles are to be of cypress or heart pine. Doors, stairs and the like to be included in the contract.

A sufficient obligation will be required of the contractors to construct the house of good materials, and in a proper manner; and to complete it on or before the first Monday of June, 1820.

WM. BIBB

Coosada, 1st March, 1819.[1]

The successful bidders for the contract to erect the State House were David and Nicholas Crocheron, of Dallas County. The contract was entered into in May, 1819—very probably just after the completion of the sale of the lots. The exact date on which the Crocherons began construction is not known, but the work was well under way before the Assembly convened in Huntsville in the autumn of 1819. At that time Governor Bibb informed the Assembly concerning the State House as follows:

The principal parts of the building are to be completed on or before the first day of August next, for nine thousand dollars; and the remainder of the sum appropriated will be required, and is sufficient to complete the whole, and to provide the necessary accommodations for the two branches of the legislature. I learn that the building has been commenced, and that no doubt is entertained of its completion within the time specified in the contract.[2]

[1] Owen, Thomas McAdory, *History of Alabama and Dictionary of Alabama Biography*, Vol. 1, p. 203.

[2] Governor Bibb's Message to the Assembly, Huntsville, October 26, 1819, Senate Journal 1819, p. 18.

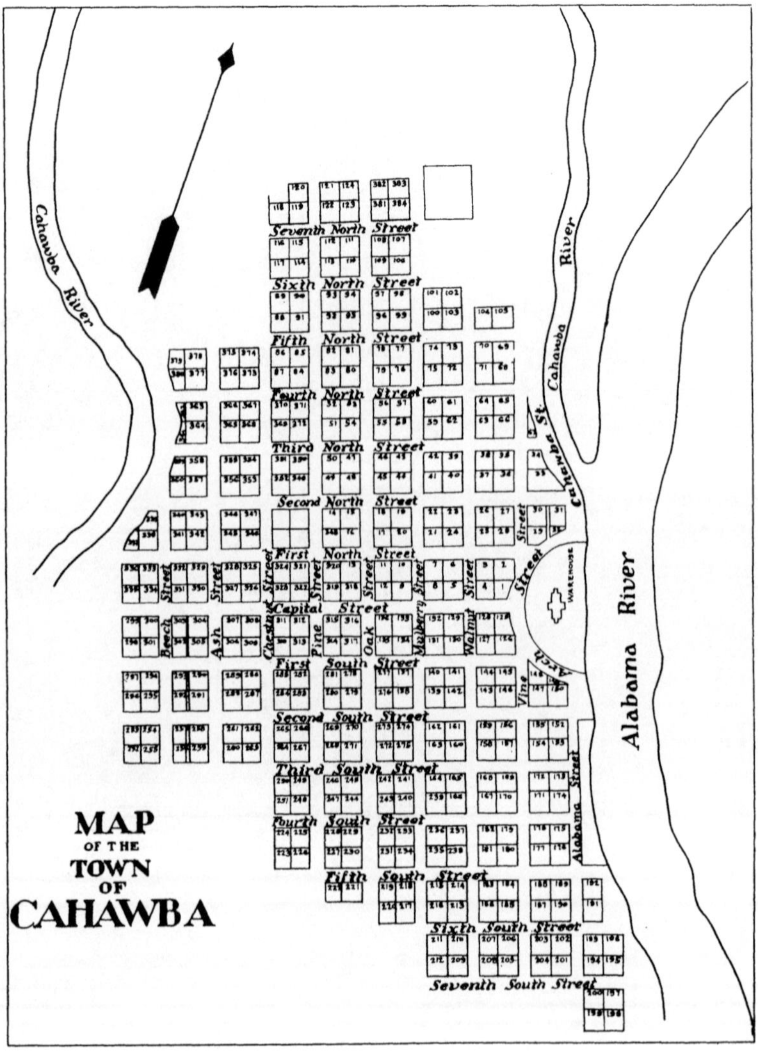
MAP
OF THE
TOWN
OF
CAHAWBA
Cahawba River
Cahawba River
Alabama River
Seventh North Street
Sixth North Street
Fifth North Street
Fourth North Street
Third North Street
Second North Street
First North Street
Capital Street
First South Street
Second South Street
Third South Street
Fourth South Street
Fifth South Street
Sixth South Street
Seventh South Street
Beech Street
Ash Street
Chestnut Street
Pine Street
Oak Street
Mulberry Street
Walnut Street
Vine Street
Arch Street
Cahawba St.
Alabama Street
WAREHOUSE

The map of the Town of Cahawba reproduced herein was made before the sale of lots at the first auction during the fourth week of May, 1819. The conveyancing records on file in Dallas County all refer to it as "the original plan of the Town of Cahawba."

The arrangement of the streets and avenues as pictured by "the original plan of the Town of Cahawba" suggests the idea that the parcel of land lying between Arch Street and the Alabama River was set apart for a State House which would face down Capitol Avenue. This was not the fact. Moreover, an examination of the original records discloses that Arch Street was not shown on the original plan of the Town of Cahawba, and that the plot of ground enclosed by it was originally, at least in part, surveyed into lots. Arch Street was drawn into the original map immediately after the first sale of lots and enclosed a section of the bluff which was not offered for sale, but was set aside for warehouses.

The reason becomes apparent upon an examination of the terrain of the place. Arch Street got its name from its shape; it rose from the river's edge up the steep river bank in the form of an arch and thus afforded a means of travel from the river to the town on the top of the bluff. The ferry across the Alabama landed at the northern end of Arch Street. A team could not pull a loaded wagon straight up the bluff, but could do it by progressing at a gradual angle around the curve on the bluff to the top level. Arch Street was an afterthought arising from a practical necessity. It was first mentioned in the records when the Assembly directed the Commissioners of Cahawba "to open and make a good and sufficient ferry landing on the Alabama River where *Arch Street* strikes said river."[1]

Since the State House was not located within the half

[1] Acts 1820, p. 84. This was not the only Arch Street in Alabama rising from the river to the town on top of the bluff above. The original map of Demopolis Town Company in 1819 had such an Arch Street (Webb v. Demopolis, 95 Ala. 123–125).

circle made by Arch Street and did not face westward down Capitol Avenue, and since it ceased to exist over one hundred years ago, the question at once arises: Where was the State House at Cahawba erected? Which lot of the "original plan of the Town of Cahawba" was chosen for the honor of bearing the State House? Alabama's State House, its first public building, was built on Lot No. 125 at the southwest corner of the intersection of Capitol Avenue and Vine Street. The building faced Vine Street and the Alabama River.[1]

Men of authority on Alabama historical matters have expressed the opinion that the State House was built on Lot No. 151. This is incorrect. The error very probably arises from the fact that certain copies of the original maps of Cahawba are so blurred that the lot numbers cannot be made out. It was evidently believed that Lot No. 151 and not Lot No. 125 was located at the southwest corner of Capitol Avenue and Vine Street, because it is an established and undisputed fact that the State House was built on this corner. The erroneous conclusion that Lot No. 151 was the site of the State House could have been reached because of a misunderstanding of the language of an act of the General Assembly passed at Huntsville in 1819, which said:

> SEC. 4. That the lot or parcel of land numbered one hundred fifty-one in the plan of Cahawba as now laid off be and the same is hereby appropriated and set apart, for the erection of such buildings for the accommodation of the Executive as the General Assembly may hereafter deem necessary and proper.[2]

In construing this language, if it is remembered that at

[1] This is the opinion of R. D. Sturdivant, elderly citizen and native of Dallas County, who is well versed in her history and who many years ago carefully examined the ruins of the foundation of the State House. There is a stone marker erected on the site where the State House stood. Unfortunately the inscription contains an error. The law removing the capital to Tuskaloosa was passed Dec. 13, 1825, and not in January, 1825. The old State House served as a courthouse for Dallas County until 1834.

[2] Acts 1819, p. 84, passed December 4, 1819.

the time the act was passed the State House had been under construction since prior to October, 1819,[1] then it could not possibly be inferred that Lot No. 151 was being set aside for the State House. Moreover it is noted that Lot No. 151 was by the Assembly "set apart for the erection of such buildings . . . as the General Assembly may *hereafter* deem necessary and proper." These Assemblymen certainly were not thinking about using the lot *hereafter* for a State House which had already been under construction for months.

Since the "original plan of Cahawba" does not show a lot numbered 151, recourse was had to the conveyancing records of Dallas County in an effort to identify this lot which has been said to have borne the State House. These records disclose that the long, narrow plot reaching from Fifth South Street to Second South Street and between the easterly line of Alabama Street and the Alabama River was Lot No. 151.[2] The shape and location of Lot No. 151 make it inconceivable that it should be used for the State House.

Since the State of Alabama owned all the lots in Cahawba before the auction sale, there is no deed of the lot upon which the State House was built to the State. The lot No. 125 was merely selected and withheld from sale. The lot adjoining No. 125 on the Capitol Avenue side, No. 128, was also withheld from sale by the State and probably was used as a wagon-and-carriage yard and a place to hitch saddle horses. During the sessions of the Assembly there were many visitors to the State House, and most of them used horses for transportation. Around Lot No. 125 was

[1] Governor Bibb's Message to Assembly at Huntsville.

[2] Book T, p. 35, Deed Record, Probate Court of Dallas County, shows deed from Edward T. Watts and wife, Louisa M. Watts, to James L. Evans conveying: "Those certain lots or parcels of land situated in the Town of Cahawba, Alabama, and known and designated on the original plan of said town as lots numbered 150–152–153–154–155 and *also lot numbered 151 excepting that portion of last named lot lying south of 4th South Street* in said town of Cahawba."

built a picket fence. The enclosed area was called the State House grounds.

When the General Assembly of 1825 after a fierce fight finally did enact a law removing the seat of government to Tuskaloosa, they then passed a resolution authorizing the State Treasurer "to sell the State House and the lot on which it is situated in the town of Cahawba, either for cash, or on such reasonable credit as he may think proper, provided however that the State House shall *not be sold for less than three thousand dollars*."[1] But Cahawba, her growth already arrested by the threat of removal of the seat of government, drooped and shriveled when the removal actually occurred. There were no buyers for the old State House. The same act which had authorized the State Treasurer to sell the State House empowered him to appoint a fit and suitable person to take charge of the building for such terms and on such conditions as he thought expedient.

This last provision made the abandoned State House available as a courthouse for Dallas County while the State Treasurer was looking for a buyer. Finally, in 1829, the State, not having found a purchaser, capitulated and made a gift of the old State House in the town of Cahawba, together with the lot of land on which it stood, to the County of Dallas. The Act provided:

> That it shall be the duty of the Governor to make out and execute a deed of conveyance for the old State House and the lot of land on which said House stands in the town of Cahawba, together with appurtenances thereunto belonging, to the judge of the County Court of Dallas County and his successors in office, for the use and benefit of said County, and that said deed shall be recorded in the books of the County Court of said County.[2]

[1] Acts 1825, p. 74, Section 4.

[2] Acts 1829, p. 11. The Governor approved the Act January 13, 1830. Since the Act instructed the Governor to execute the deed *forthwith* he no doubt did so, but if the deed is recorded in the books of the County Court a careful search by the author and John W. Lapsley, Esq., leading member of the bar of Dallas County, failed to discover it. All the court records of the County

The County of Dallas continued to use the old State House as a courthouse until 1834, when, with a new courthouse erected within the enclosure of Arch Street at the corner of Vine and First North Streets available for use, the Commissioners' Court of Dallas County at the December term, 1834, authorized Joseph Babcock, James D. Craig, and Thomas M. Jackson to sell at public auction "the following named lots, namely: The lot on which the old Courthouse stood and the one adjoining to the highest bidder on a credit of 12 months first giving 30 days notice by advertisement."

Under this authority the Commissioners did sell said lots, being "lots numbered 125 and 128 in the original plan of the town of Cahawba to Matthew Gayle at public auction for $349.50." The deed was executed on August 11, 1837, and attested by subscribing witnesses Joseph P. Saffold and J. W. Outlaw.[1]

The language used by the Commissioners' Court in authorizing Babcock, Craig, and Jackson to make the sale suggests that at the time the State House was no longer on Lot No. 125. "The lot on which the old Court House *stood*" is definitely in the past tense, indicating that at that time, 1834, the old courthouse (State House) was no longer standing. The low price of $349.50 for the two lots seems to confirm this idea. It must be remembered that only nine years before the Assembly had placed a minimum price on the State House and the lot on which it stood (No. 125) of $3,000. It is suggested arguendo that Dallas County tore down the building and used the brick and other usable material in constructing the new courthouse.

Court were available and inspected. All the minute books of the County Court, except the first one, which is missing, were also checked. It is most likely that if the deed were in fact recorded it would be in the missing minute book.

[1] This deed is recorded in Book F, p. 95, in the Deed Records of Dallas County. Subsequent conveyances of these two lots refer to them as the "Gayle lots."

The Year 1820

While the State House was in the early stages of construction, several important men from various sections of the State assembled in Cahawba and there, incidentally, observed first-hand what progress the Crocherons were making in the way of building Alabama's capitol. But these men were not gathered in Cahawba for the purpose of inspecting the work; they were there this second Monday in May, 1820, to organize the Supreme Court of Alabama and to hold its first term. The men were Abner S. Lipscomb, Reuben Saffold, Henry Y. Webb, Richard Ellis, and Clement C. Clay. Having been elected to their high office at Huntsville in December, 1819, they now met in Cahawba as they were required to do by law.[1]

The Court's organization meeting and its sessions were held in the house of William Pye, who was paid the magnificent sum of $20 for the use of his house and for "other accommodations."[2] This plain and humble house was the first courtroom of the Supreme Court of Alabama. Here the Court adopted its rules for practice in the Supreme Court;[3] chose its youngest member, Clement C. Clay, as Chief Justice; and gave its considerate attention to the several arguments of learned counsel. Nine opinions in writing were the fruit of this first term—the foundation stones of the case law of Alabama.[4]

The Crocherons had agreed to finish the principal parts of the State House by August 1, 1820, and to have the entire building completed in time for the accommodation of

[1] "Supreme Court . . . shall hold the sessions of said Court at Cahawba, twice each and every year, the first session to begin on the second Monday in May, and the second session on the second Monday in November." Acts 1819, p. 10.

[2] Acts 1820, p. 33.

[3] A copy of this rare document is in the Library of the Supreme Court at Montgomery, Alabama.

[4] Minor, pp. 1–9, inc.

the Assembly when it convened in November. In a determined effort to fulfill their agreement, the brothers worked faithfully and industriously, but unexpected difficulties, together with extra work which had to be done, delayed the completion of the Capitol. While the struggle to get the building on schedule was going on, and while the Crocherons from time to time were consulting with Bibb at his home in an adjoining county, fate took a hand and decreed that William Wyatt Bibb, who had chosen the site, planned the structure, provided the money, and promoted the erection of the State House with tireless energy and determination, should never look upon the completed Capitol. While riding over his plantation near Coosada in Autauga County, Governor Bibb, who was already in very delicate health, was thrown from the saddle and suffered a contusion of the head. This injury accelerated his decline. On July 10, 1820, realizing that death was near, he said: "My dear friends, I bid you all farewell," and died in the fortieth year of his age. The hand of death which cut down the Governor in his prime was also a mighty blow against Cahawba. Her most powerful champion and defender was lost. The new capital with its unfinished State House would miss this firm and guiding hand. No one realized this more than the citizens of Cahawba. Six days after the death of the Governor, on August 16, 1820, the Honorable Henry Hitchcock,[1] Attorney General of the State, at the request of the citizens of Cahawba, delivered a eulogium[2] honoring the deceased Governor. Among other things, Hitchcock said of Bibb's political philosophy:

> To say that his political principles were bottomed on the principles of the revolution, is asserting nothing that is not common to the great mass of the American population. The sover-

[1] Henry Hitchcock was from Vermont, kin of Ethan Allen, and was appointed by Bibb as his secretary on May 14, 1818, after Bibb was appointed Governor of the Alabama Territory by the President of the United States.

[2] *Eulogium in Commemoration of His Excellency, William W. Bibb, late Governor of the State of Alabama*, pp. 9, 10.

eignty of the people, the accountability and responsibility of officers, and the supremacy of the laws, expressions common and much discussed, have been with him themes of deep and solemn reflection. He did not, however, consider that the important secret of political science consists so much in inventing new systems of government, as in the application of known and tried principles to the habits, feelings, and dispositions of the community for which they are intended. And in his inquiry, even their prejudices were not to be disregarded, when widely variant from the principles he would introduce, however salutary might be their tendency. That the people should always control innovations upon their customs, and be consulted in everything that relates to their interest, are principles he ever admitted; yet he believed that their happiness depended not so much upon the immediate share which they have in declaring the innovations, as in the expediency and utility of the innovations themselves. Upon the intelligence of a people, and the existence of good morals, depends the existence of a capacity to exercise political liberty with benefit and permanency. He did not waste his time in speculative ideas, on the practicability of establishing a government perfect in itself, and to be perfectly administered; the improvements he hoped to see were to be effected by gradual approaches and slow operation. He would have them incorporated with the feelings of the people, and adopted in such a manner as to consolidate the whole system, by the harmony which it united with all its parts.

Hitchcock also wrote an obituary notice in which he lauded Bibb's personal and public life. In this notice there appears the following paragraph:

In the discharge of his domestic duties he was zealous, constant, and parental; he did not praise virtue without practicing it, and he was incapable of professing an excellence which he did not possess. Amidst all the vicissitudes of party, and the violence of faction, incident to a republic, and in which he held for many years a conspicuous station, his enemies never contradicted the character given him by his friends.

While Henry Hitchcock's praise of the departed Governor was fulsome, it was not exaggerated. William Wyatt Bibb was truly a gifted and superior man. To take his place successfully was the considerable task which fell to his brother, Thomas Bibb, of Limestone County. Under the Constitution, as President of the Senate, Thomas Bibb was automatically elevated to the highest state office as Acting Governor.

The new Governor was fully aware of the problems and difficulties which awaited him, but he did not flinch nor delay. He at once assumed the authority and duties of the Chief Executive and proceeded to function with dignity and courage. That he had not the talent and did not achieve the success of his deceased brother is no discredit to him. Genius is not measured unto all men in like amount.

The Year 1820

and the General Assembly—Annual Session of 1820

When the Assembly met in Cahawba for the first time on November 6, 1820, the new Acting Governor, Thomas Bibb, was prepared with a report and a program which he presented. In his message to the Assembly he had this to say about the State House:

> . . . the contract made by the late Governor for the erection of a State House at Cahawba has not been complied with on the part of the contractor within the time specified in the contract, owing to difficulties unforeseen at the time the contract was made; but the building is nearly completed and the necessity for its occupation by the Legislature so great, I have thought it would best promote the public interest to receive it, subject to be completed hereafter, and you will permit me to congratulate you on being enabled to carry on your deliberations with so much ease as the State House affords. Of the sum of $9,000 for which the house was to be built, $7,500 has been paid to the contractor, the remaining sum of $1,500 to be paid as soon as the building is completed.
>
> Of the sum of $1,000, the sum of the residue of the sum appropriated, $616 have been expended in providing the necessary furniture for your accommodation and the balance, being $384, has been deposited in the Treasury, together with the receipts for the expenditures.
>
> I submit the propriety of your making a further appropria-

tion for the purpose of providing window shutters and for enclosing the lot for the preservation of the building.[1]

Among other things, the Acting Governor also reported that he had caused to be surveyed in Cahawba an additional two hundred lots which were to be sold on the second Monday in November, 1820. The friends of Cahawba expected great things of this new city carved out of the primeval forests on the banks of the swift and muddy Alabama. Among these pioneers were some confirmed optimists, for even as these new lots were being surveyed, buyers of Cahawba lots at the first sale were petitioning the Assembly for relief on their installments because of the "pecuniary embarrassment" which had "afflicted the country for the last two years."

The members of this first General Assembly at Cahawba remembered William Wyatt Bibb as a patriotic citizen and an able public man. They did him the honor they considered his due and took what steps they could, within their limited means, to perpetuate his name and memory for posterity. In honor of the departed chief and in order to identify him with the State in a lasting manner, the Assembly changed the name of Cahawba County to Bibb County.[2] Today the county bears that name.

A committee composed of members from both houses was appointed to prepare resolutions expressive of the regret felt by the General Assembly at the death of His Excellency, William W. Bibb, late Governor of the State. Senator Nicholas Davis, of Limestone County, was chairman of the joint committee and reported the following resolutions:

The General Assembly of the State of Alabama sensibly feeling and sincerely lamenting the irreparable loss sustained in

[1] Message of Thomas Bibb, Senate Journal 1820, pp. 11 *et seq*. This recommendation was carried out by the Assembly, which authorized the Secretary of State "*to enclose the building in a cheap and substantial manner, and to have shutters made and hung*." Acts 1820, p. 90.

[2] Senate Journal 1820, pp. 18–19.

Thomas Bibb

the death of our late Governor, William W. Bibb, deem it a duty we owe to ourselves, our fellow citizens, and his revered memory, to express to the world the feelings of our hearts. We are aware that the pen of panegyric can but faintly paint his virtues . . . and should the tongue of eulogy attempt to express them it would fail in the effort.

To say he was a man without equal would be saying too much; but to say he was a man of transcendent virtue and patriotism, is nothing more than is due to his memory.

He was the friend of liberty and of man; and his increasing efforts were to perpetuate the one and promote the happiness of the other.

The archives of the nation will show to the latest posterity that he was a pure republican; the greater part of his short life was devoted to the service of his country, and his fame is impervious to the shafts of calumny.

He was an admirer of the immortal Father of his country, and it may well be said, that Washington chalked out the paths of virtue and Bibb delighted to follow them.

But Heaven has decreed that all earthly good shall pass away—and He "who maketh darkness his pavilion" has been pleased in his incomprehensible wisdom to take from us this excellent and beloved man, and we can only pray in the sincerity of our hearts, that the smile of that being who resides in the celestial mansions may be upon him; and against his name, in the books of life, may happiness be written: Therefore as a public testimony of sincere regret for the loss and in profound respect for our late Governor,

Resolved, that the members of the General Assembly wear crape on the left arm during the present session.

Be it further resolved that the Reverend Mr. Kennedy be requested to preach a funeral sermon in the State House on the day of the present instant, suited to the occasion.

And be it further resolved, that the Acting Governor be requested to cause a copy of this resolution to be transmitted to Mrs. Bibb expressive of our condolence on the late afflicting dispensation of providence.[1]

[1] Senate Journal 1820, pp. 18–19. Thomas A. Rogers, Esq., Secretary of State, informed the Senate that on November 18, 1820, the Acting Governor approved and signed the Resolutions "expressive of the feeling of the General Assembly on the loss of our late Chief Magistrate, W. W. Bibb." Senate Journal 1820, p. 35.

Even these laudatory resolutions were not enough to satisfy the Assembly. An official funeral procession and sermon was arranged by the joint committee. John D. Terrell was in charge of this tribute of respect. He planned the rites with great care and presented them with dignity. The order of this ceremony was as follows:

1st. The members of both branches of the legislature shall assemble at Mr. White's long room at 11 o'clock on the 26th instant.

2nd. The front of the Speaker's seat shall be clothed in mourning under the direction of the President of the Senate and the Speaker of the House of Representatives.

3rd. His Excellency, the Acting Governor, and the Rev. Mr. Kennedy shall head the procession. The Senate shall proceed the next in order, in pairs arranged by the President who, associated with the Secretary of the Senate, shall head that body.

4th. The Representative Branch shall move in like order.

5th. The heads of the Departments of State, and the Judges of the Supreme Court shall move next in order, to be arranged by the Secretary of State.

6th. Four chairs shall be placed on the Speaker's seat for the reception of the Governor, the President of the Senate, the Speaker and the Divine.

7th. The Senate shall takė seats on the right. The Representatives on the left. The heads of departments and the judges in the center. Seats shall be prepared by the respective doorkeepers.[1]

The sermon by the Rev. Mr. Kennedy concluded the official honors paid to the deceased Governor by his adopted state, but the influence of the man has lingered long in the law and tradition of Alabama. That this influence was strong enough to endure many years in the State's law, but not powerful enough to hold the capital at Cahawba is but further proof that politics attend men while the law follows principles.

The law of Alabama was the common law of England, brought into the State by people born into and accustomed

[1] Senate Journal 1820, p. 39.

to it and its traditions for generations. The form of government erected upon this basic law followed the Federal pattern by establishing in the Constitution a division of powers between legislative, executive, and judicial branches. The Constitution of Alabama made the legislative branch the strongest of the three, and the judicial the weakest.

The lack of proportionate power in the judicial branch stemmed directly from a constitutional provision which took from the people the right to elect their judicial officers and gave it to the Assembly. Since the judges held office by grace of the Assembly, it was perfectly natural that the Assembly should regard itself as superior to the judiciary.[1]

This superiority was asserted by the first elected Alabama Assembly, in the Huntsville session in 1819, when it enacted a law instructing the judges of the Circuit Courts, who also made up the Supreme Court, and the Attorney General of the State "to compile a digest in a volume of convenient size of the laws in force in the State." The law required them to provide an index and to entitle the volume *The Laws of the State of Alabama*. They were required also "to prepare such amendments as they thought the laws required and submit them to the General Assembly." Section Three of the act was indicative of the times. It provided: "That it shall be the duty of the Judges and the Attorney General aforesaid in all acts containing technical phrases or words in other than the English language to translate same."[2]

This was quite an order, and the new Judges must have mulled over the situation at length, but neither they nor the Attorney General did anything about it. In their hearts, being schooled in the common law, the Judges and the At-

[1] At this time Representatives in Congress were elected by the people and United States Senators were elected by the Assembly. Consequently in national affairs the General Assembly in communications addressed to these officers always meticulously used this language: "Instruct our senators" and "Request our representatives."

[2] Acts 1819, p. 133.

torney General realized that they were properly subordinate to the law only and not to be instructed in a matter of this kind by the Assembly. It was a delicate situation for Alabama's first court, but by common consent a course of non-action was pursued.

The aggressive Assembly was not willing to let the matter go unnoticed. The Court had met in May, 1820, and again in November, 1820. Not having heard anything about the status of the Digest, the Assembly appointed a select committee "to inquire of the Judges what progress they had made in preparing the Digest as required by the law of 1819."

The Judges replied to the Committee by a letter written at Cahawba on November 20, 1820, in which they stated that because of the arduous duties imposed upon them as Circuit Judges and Supreme Court Judges, and the fact that the Attorney General had to prosecute the State's cases in the Circuit Court, there was no time to do the work or get together for consultation. This was the practical answer to the Assembly. Since they were Judges and also men of high caliber, their own self-respect required them to go further and delicately but nevertheless firmly to inform the Assembly that the writing of such a Digest at the order of the Assembly was not a proper duty of the Judges of the Court. To convey this idea the Judges added another paragraph which read:

> With due regard to their own characters and to the welfare and interest of the public, the undersigned feel their inadequacy to a proper compliance with the provisions of the law of the last General Assembly, whilst they perform their own duties. With great respect we have the honor to be your obedient servants.
>
> C. C. Clay
> Reuben Saffold
> Abner Lipscomb
> Richard Ellis
> Henry Hitchcock[1]

[1] Senate Journal 1820, pp. 56, 57.

The Assembly accepted this gentle and masterly rebuke and looked elsewhere for an author for their Digest. For the Court this small victory was a great one, for it marked the beginning of the Court's independence of the legislative department. Before it achieved complete independence, it was to eat humble pie more than once and on two occasions its members were to be subjected to trial by the legislative branch in cases where the charge was not sufficient for the institution of impeachment proceedings.

The second sale of lots in Cahawba spoken about by Acting Governor Bibb in his message to the Assembly was held on the second Monday of November, 1820. One hundred and ninety-one lots sold for $21,727. This sale was also handled by Willis Roberts and Benjamin Clements, but at this second sale they were assisted by Matthew D. Thomason. The best lots of course were sold at the first sale, but the difference in the price realized at the first sale and that of the second was so great as to add gall to the already dissatisfied buyers at the first sale. This discontent was sufficient to produce later an organized effort by purchasers of lots bought at the first sale to obtain reimbursement from the State for losses which they contended were brought about by the removal of the capital to Tuskaloosa.

Before the adjournment at Huntsville the Assembly had considered the problems which would arise from locating the seat of government in a new and unorganized town. They, therefore, at that session provided Cahawba with a city government, which was functioning at the time the state officials moved in. An election for the purpose of choosing seven Councillors was ordered held on the first Monday in January, 1820. These seven were to elect one of their number as Intendant. Willis Roberts, Luther Blake, and Carlisle Humphreys were made managers of the first election. The Town Council was given authority to exercise police powers, including the right to license retailing of liquors and the keeping of billiard tables in the town of

Cahawba. The Council was also given powers to confine law violators to "close prison" not exceeding three days.[1]

Although the frontiersmen who composed this first Cahawba Assembly were regarded as careful spenders of the State's money, they demonstrated that they could also be fair and generous in a proper case. In 1818 the house and store of Jack F. Ross, the State Treasurer, had burned, destroying $606.35 in currency and coin. This was no inconsiderable sum for either Ross or the State. The Assembly, without a dissenting vote, fully reimbursed him.[2] This fire loss was the direct cause of the purchase of an iron chest for the use of the Treasury office, costing seventy dollars.[3] This was Alabama's first strongbox! One cannot but wonder what became of this money chest when a few years later the State managed to get into the banking business on a large scale.

The 1820 Assembly passed an act creating the Bank of the State of Alabama with a $2,000,000 capital, one-half of which was reserved to the State. The bank was by law located at Cahawba, subject, however, to be removed from that place "*whenever* the Seat of Government shall be changed." The superintendents of subscriptions at Cahawba were John Taylor (late of Pendleton), Anderson Crenshaw, Henry Hitchcock, Edmund Lane, and John Scott.[4] Leading citizens over the State were appointed subscription superintendents in their home communities, but this first plan to put the State in the banking business failed because the citizens declined to subscribe the necessary capital.

The welfare and progress of the town of Cahawba were constantly before the Assembly. A lottery for the purpose

[1] Acts 1819, p. 118. "Close prison" is to be distinguished from "prison bounds" which permitted a prisoner freedom within a certain defined area in the city.

[2] Acts 1820, p. 77.

[3] Acts 1820, p. 96.

[4] Acts 1820, p. 20.

of raising a fund, not in excess of $20,000, for the erecting and furnishing of the Masonic Hall of Halo Lodge in Cahawba was authorized.[1] John Taylor, Sr., William Taylor, John B. Norris, H. G. Perry, W. R. Peters, Jesse Beene, Jonas Brown, William B. Allen, David McCord, Dunklin Sullivan, and Edward Gantt were named to manage the lottery.[2]

The Cahawba Navigation Company, whose purpose was to improve the navigation of the Cahawba River "from the town of Cahawba to the falls of the river of the same name," was formed.[3] The Assembly granted an entire square in the town to the Intendant and Council of Cahawba for use as a public graveyard. Of the Cahawba land grant located on the east side of the Alabama River, the Governor was authorized to sell not over fifty one-half-acre lots at public sale. The town Commissioners were directed to open a ferry landing on the Alabama River "where Arch Street strikes the river."[4]

The State House itself was a matter of first importance. Even before the end of the session drew near John McKinley, of Madison, made a motion that leave be given to the citizens of Cahawba to have a *party of pleasure* in the hall of the House of Representatives. On a very close vote the motion was lost.[5] It seems that the Assemblymen either were jealous of their new State House, or else considered it as being for serious business only.

When adjournment time came near, by special act the care of the State House and public property was entrusted to Matthew W. McClellan, who was paid fifty dollars for his services. The Act provided that McClellan should not let or suffer said House to be appropriated or occupied in any other manner than provided by law *except* as a house of public worship, or for the Court of Errors and Appeals,

[1] Acts 1820, p. 20.
[2] Acts 1820, p. 83.
[3] Acts 1820, p. 13.
[4] Acts 1820, p. 83.
[5] House Journal 1820, p. 79.

the Circuit Court of Dallas, and the Federal Court of the United States.[1]

There was also the serious and delicate business of paying the Crocherons additional compensation for building the State House. A resolution authorizing the Acting Governor to adjust and settle the account of David and Nicholas Crocheron for building the State House was referred to a special committee. The committee reported that the contractors had performed extra work, and that the peculiar circumstances of expense and difficulty under which the State House had been completed entitled them to additional compensation. The committee recommended the amount of $4,992.50.[2] The Assembly, after considerable debate, granted the Crocherons an additional compensation in the amount of $4,500, which was to constitute full payment for all work done.[3] Thus Alabama's first State House[4] actually cost $13,500 not including the cost of the shutters and the picket fence which were paid for by the Secretary of State acting under special authority. The furnishings of the Capitol building cost $616, not including the seventy-dollar iron chest. The payment to the Crocherons increased the cost of the State House well beyond what was intended, but it still remains clear that the majority of the Assemblymen considered the Capitol only as a "temporary building."

There was some competition for the most desirable quarters in the Capitol. By resolution the Assembly assigned the

[1] Acts 1820, p. 97, Sec. 7. "Court of Errors and Appeals" was a name used frequently for the Supreme Court of Alabama.

[2] House Journal 1820, p. 121. [3] Acts 1820, p. 112.

[4] There is no known picture or painting of Alabama's first and vanished State House. The artist's conception of the State House was prepared by Mr. Hugh Martin from the specifications advertised in the *Halcyon and Tombeckbe Advertiser* on March 1, 1819, and from other bits of dependable information furnished to him by the author. Mr. Martin is a gifted artist as well as an experienced architect who is familiar with the early architecture of Alabama buildings. It is believed that his conception of the appearance of the State House is as accurate a reconstruction as can be achieved with the known dependable information.

The State House at Cahawba

northeast room on the second floor for the use of the Comptroller of Public Accounts, and the southwest room on the first floor for the use of the State Treasurer.[1] This information is of value in arriving at a judgment as to what was the interior arrangement of the building. The above resolution necessarily conflicts with several statements which have heretofore been given as authentic. The Governor had an office in the State House which he used during the time the General Assembly was in session.[2] This was a necessity as well as a convenience, for none of the governors during Cahawba's capital days had homes there.

All through this first Cahawba session the spectre of reapportionment of the Assembly hung over the Legislature like a pall. It followed the members from the Capitol halls into the taverns and boarding houses, where discussions were both sectional and heated. Resisting pressure brought to bear on them by the Governor and several strong leaders in the House, the Assembly adjourned without enacting an apportionment law. They did enact a census law and provided that the returns should be in by the next August 1, so that the next Assembly would have the exact population of each county prior to writing an apportionment law. It was not publicly stated, but it was undoubtedly true that the Alabama River system faction did not want to apportion the Assembly while Thomas Bibb, whom they regarded as an accidental Governor and whom they knew to be anti-Cahawba, was in the Governor's office. These politically minded men never forgot their conviction that the Senate

[1] Acts 1820, p. 114. The fixed location of these rooms serves to indicate strongly that the upstairs legislative chamber was not directly over the chamber downstairs. This arrangement would have eliminated annoying noises such as excited debate or tramping of feet. It is submitted arguendo that the hall of the House was on the first floor of the State House because of the convenience to the most numerous branch of the Assembly and also on account of the great weight when the houses met in the Representative hall in joint session. It is of course submitted that the Senate Chamber was on the second floor.

[2] Duke of Saxe-Weimar, *Travels Through North America*, Vol. II, p. 33.

which would be elected under the apportionment arrangement last made prior to the 1825 session would exercise the final power concerning the site of the seat of government. They could foretell even now that, barring a miracle, the House in 1825 would have a substantial majority in favor of removal from Cahawba. The men who wished to preserve the status quo by keeping the seat of government at Cahawba realized that with William Wyatt Bibb gone the only instrument by which this could be accomplished was the Senate. They were ready to obey the mandate of the Constitution as they construed it and to enact an apportionment law at the regular 1821–1822 session, but not before that time. Then the census returns would be in and there would also be a new Governor. But before that time neither Thomas Bibb nor any other person could induce or coerce them to pass an apportionment law. The annual session of 1820 adjourned on December 22. The apportionment law remained unchanged.

The Year 1821 and the General Assembly—Called Session of 1821

Acting Governor Bibb well understood the reasoning and motives which controlled the Assemblymen in their refusal to enact an apportionment law during the last regular annual session. But this knowledge did not ease the pains of disappointment nor lessen the desire of Bibb and his friends to use the power of the office of Chief Executive to force a new apportionment law before the end of his tenure in office.

Bibb counselled with his friends in Madison and Limestone Counties. They considered the state of the Governor's race now being warmly campaigned over the state. The news was not to their liking. The election would not be held until the first Monday in August, but it was already evident that South Alabama's Israel Pickens would defeat Madison County's Henry Chambers. Besides, if a reapportionment was to be effected, it must be accomplished before the new census was completed on August 1.

The removal partisans, led by the Huntsville group and strongly supported by other leaders in the valley of the Tennessee River and from Tuskaloosa, urged Bibb to order a called session of the Assembly. They contended that the Constitution required a new apportionment law before the annual 1821 session. The Governor agreed with them and convoked the Assembly in Cahawba on the first Monday in June, 1821.

The Governor did not deliver his message to the Assembly in person, but sent the writing by the Secretary of State, Thomas A. Rogers, Esq. It was a carefully prepared document wherein Bibb reminded the Assembly that "the unhappy difference of opinion which existed between your bodies at your last session in relation to the apportionment of representation for the next General Assembly, and which resulted in your adjournment without passing any law on the subject, involves in itself consequences, which in my estimation threaten the very existence of the legislative branch of the government." The Governor then stated that this perilous situation was the reason he had called the Assembly together. He told the Assembly that the Constitution required an apportionment law, and since they had failed to pass such a law at the annual session he urged that they do so now.[1]

The Assembly went into action at once. The Senate quickly referred the apportionment bill which it had written to a Committee of the Whole Senate. On Monday, June 18, 1821, Mr. Elliott, of Mobile, and a member of the select committee of the Senate chosen to manage the apportionment bill, reported the reasons by which the Senate was influenced on the subject of apportionment of the two branches of the General Assembly. Said Elliott, while referring to certain House amendments to the bill which had

[1] Senate Journal Called Session 1821, pp. 4 *et seq.*

originated in the Senate: "That they [the Senate] are constrained by a sense of duty imperative in its nature, and deducing its origin from the Constitution of this State, to resist the illegal pretensions (as they conceive) of the House of Representatives in endeavoring to coerce them into the apportionment of their own body."[1] After this exhibition of restrained anger, Elliott proceeded to argue the constitutional question. It was the position of the Senators that they were chosen for three years, and that the first senatorial terms under the Constitution would not expire until August, 1822. Hence they refused to apportion the Senate prior to the expiration of those terms. Elliott concluded that the Senate could not constitutionally reapportion its body until the regular session of 1821, *but that the House of Representatives could and should.* The Senate at once concurred in his report, those voting against it being President Gabriel Moore, Davis, Garth, Devereux, and Ringgold.[2]

The House disagreed with the Senate and amended the Senate's apportionment bill so as to apportion the Senate also. This amendment was the cause of Elliott's outburst of feeling. The Senate summarily refused the House amendment and the proceedings became a stalemate. The House finally, by a very close margin, yielded, voted to recede from the disagreement, and passed the Senate bill. Representative Chapman, whose vote made this possible, stated his reasons for changing his vote and passing the bill. He said, "I was of the opinion if the subject thus ended and the legislature should rise without making any apportionment whatever the government would be dissolved and society thrown into a state of anarchy and confusion, much to be deplored by every patriot. . . ."[3]

The Assembly, with the House yielding to a determined

[1] Senate Journal 1821, Called Session, p. 51.

[2] Moore was from Madison, Davis from Limestone, Garth from Morgan, Devereux from Conecuh, and Ringgold from Marengo.

[3] House Journal 1821, Called Session, p. 59.

and angry Senate, passed the bill providing for a new apportionment of the House of Representatives, but not of the Senate. On June 18, 1821, Bibb returned the bill to the Senate where it originated, refusing his signature and stating that the act was unconstitutional. Among other things, the Governor said:

> In the discharge of this painful duty of stating the reasons which compel me to refuse my assent to a bill which has undergone much deliberation and which has received the assent of both branches of the General Assembly, I console myself with the reflection, that should they be deemed insufficient they can be overruled in a constitutional manner by that body which is the immediate representation of the people, and on a subject too, which I conceive it is peculiarly the province of the people to decide.[1]

Thus did an Alabama Governor for the first time veto an act of the Assembly.

The Senate was in no wise intimidated or placated by the smooth words used by the Governor in the veto message. They at once reconsidered the bill and passed it over the Governor's veto nineteen to one, only Nicholas Davis, close friend and neighbor of the Governor, voting against passing the bill over the veto.

The Senate then sent the bill as passed over the Governor's veto, together with the veto message, to the House with information as to what they had done.

The House again considered the bill as now sent to them by the Senate and promptly took a ballot. Twenty-three voted to pass the bill over the Governor's veto, but nineteen voted with the Governor. The bill thus failed to pass. The called session adjourned the same day and the friends of Cahawba returned to their homes, no doubt feeling righteous and also more confident. They had beaten this Acting Governor from the Tennessee Valley and his anti-Cahawba friends. Others left believing that there was no constitu-

[1] Senate Journal 1821, Called Session, p. 59.

tional legislature and that our State government was dissolved.

The matter of first importance in the called session was, of course, passage of the apportionment law. While not engaged with this controversial matter the Assembly found time to pass a number of helpful and interesting laws. Master builders were given liens on buildings which they erected.[1] The Most Worshipful Grand Lodge of Free Masons of Alabama and its Masonic jurisdiction was incorporated. Major General Thomas W. Farrar was Grand Master.[2] The Town Council of Cahawba was authorized to collect toll at the Cahawba Bridge.[3] The insolvency law was amended so as to permit insolvent debtors to be discharged from *arrest or imprisonment* upon delivery up of their property for the benefit of their creditors.[4] The appropriations law discloses that the Assemblymen received $3,000. The Sheriff of Dallas County was given $200 "for attendance upon the Supreme Court." Nathan Sargent was paid $4.50 for "quills and inkstands"; Dr. Gantt received $3.75 for six dozen ink phials, and Joseph Camp received $7.50 for six dozen wood stands. For putting the phials in the stands, one Wilson was paid $2. The Secretary of the Senate was given a new table; it cost $10.[5] The called session after all was not a complete failure.

After the heat engendered by the controversy over apportionment had cooled and the participants in the battle had become composed, life in Cahawba lapsed into the usual pace for long hot summers deep in the cotton belt.

[1] Acts 1821, Called Session, p. 18.

[2] Acts 1821, Called Session, p. 22. Farrar was an attorney residing in Elyton in Jefferson County.

[3] Acts 1821, Called Session, p. 29. The rates of toll were: "For man and horse, 6¼ cents; for each led or loose horse, 3 cents; for each head of cattle, 2 cents; for each head of sheep, 2 cents; for each head of hogs, 1 cent; for each loaded wagon and team, 50 cents; for each wagon and team not loaded, 25 cents; for each four wheel pleasure carriage, 25 cents; and all other two wheel carriages, 25 cents each."

[4] Acts 1821, Called Session, p. 28.

[5] Acts 1821, Called Session, p. 32.

But this summer came something new and dangerous to hinder the residents of the new capital. The bilious and remitting fever[1] appeared in the community with unfortunate results to the people. Many citizens left the town and remained away until frost.

The interminable summer with its discomforts and sickness finally dragged to its hot and dreary end. Then, just as the leaves were beginning to turn yellow and fall from the giant poplars along the river's edge, the residents of Cahawba were thrown into a fury of excitement. A steamboat was coming up the river! Maybe William Wyatt Bibb was right! Perhaps Cahawba was to be an "inland metropolis" and, "situated on a river capable of being navigated by boates of great burthen," would, in time, be a center of great commerce. There was proof of it on the river. The long speculation was ended. A steam engine could propel a sizable boat against the strong and treacherous current of the Alabama. People lined the river banks from every vantage point watching the *Harriett*, belching wood smoke from her funnels, master the current and slowly ease alongside the river bank at the foot of Arch Street. Captain Morrill, later to become one of the most famous of the river

[1] Heustis, Jabez W., M.D., *History of the Bilious Remitting Fever of Alabama as it Appeared in Cahawba and its Vicinity in the Summers and Autumns of 1821 and 1822*, passim. The author resided in Cahawba and made a careful study and record of this terrible disease as it appeared in Cahawba in the summers and autumns of 1821 and 1822. Heustis concluded that "Heat and moisture were considered as essential causes in producing a vitiated state of the atmosphere, and in the consequent generation of endemic fever." He refers to "the heavy rains in the Spring with the rivers swollen in an unprecedented manner." The floods came again in July. In this connection it is interesting to note that the author *does not at any time state that the town of Cahawba was inundated during these unprecedented rises of the rivers.* Heustis further conceded that sickness was in proportion to rain, wetness, and heat; that the disease was much less severe upon negroes than upon whites; that hard drinkers, when attacked by the disease, suffered much, although many persons drank a pint of brandy or whiskey a day "to keep themselves above fever heat," and some of these entirely escaped the fever. Dr. Heustis reached the conclusion that "the bilious remitting fever which prevailed in Cahawba in the summer and autumn of 1821 and 1822, . . . in conformity to the modern nomenclature, with the strictest propriety might be denominated the *yellow fever*."

boatmen, was in command. This was October 20 and he was eight days out of Mobile, including a "day's detention at Claiborne." The good captain lost another day being a host to sightseers and questioners at Cahawba and still another at Selma. On the twenty-second of October the *Harriett* docked at Montgomery and thrilled the people for miles on both sides of the mighty Alabama. But the political men measured the matter with more thought than thrill. What was happening on that other river system, the Tombigbe-Warrior, said to be navigable to the falls in the Warrior at Tuskaloosa?

It was well known in Cahawba that Alabama's first steamboat, the *Alabama*, built at St. Stephens by the St. Stephens Steamboat Company, had failed to ascend the Tombigbe. Another steamer, built in Philadelphia and rigged with sails like a schooner to give added power, came to Mobile the same winter, but it too failed against the current. Finally, in May, 1819, the *Mobile*, a Boston-made boat which had very powerful engines, left Mobile for Tuskaloosa. The trip was a success as far as Demopolis, which was reached on May 18, but the word was that a very "big" river prevented the *Mobile* from reaching Tuskaloosa on that trip. The political men concluded that both rivers soon would be regularly navigated by steamboats, with neither having advantage, and that the politics of the seat-of-government issue was still a question of whether the Alabama River system group would have enough power to control the Senate in 1825.

A few days later Captain Morrill and his great boat passed Cahawba again going back to Mobile. This time the excitement was not so great because the people had now seen a steamboat in action. Another event also competed for attention. The town was preparing for the Assembly which would convene on the first Monday in November for the regular annual session of 1821.

Under the law the retiring Governor continued to hold

office until the Assembly had canvassed the election returns and declared the winning candidate for Governor officially elected. Thus Acting Governor Bibb was on hand and ready with his message to the Assembly, although he was fully aware that his influence as Governor was at an end and that his successor, Israel Pickens, would now command.

The Year 1821 and the General Assembly—Annual Session of 1821

Times were hard and money was tight as the end of the year 1821 approached. The State of Alabama did not escape the general pecuniary embarrassment. The treasury was almost bare and the strain could not be relieved by loans because the infant commonwealth had not yet an established credit. But an empty exchequer was not the only problem left by Thomas Bibb on the doorstep of his successor. The private banks of the State were not financially strong and functioned in such a manner as to merit the spirited criticism which they received. The unpopularity of the privately owned banks tended to support the general clamor for a State Bank. The leading public men all agreed that the State's only source of capital with which to put in operation a State-owned bank was to be found in the proceeds from the sale of the University's lands. This situation made it impossible to avoid the corollary question of the moral right to sell the lands of the University for the purpose of raising the money capital for a State Bank. It was not a pretty picture, but there were many more people affected by the pressure of the banking situation than were presently denied university educations. When public need generates public demand, it frequently overrides fairness as well as legal rights. Bibb considered the problem, but he had not begun to solve it. Maybe it would be too much for Israel Pickens.

Bibb's departure from the office of Acting Governor did not deter him from submitting his views in detail to the Assembly. On November 7 he told the Assembly that the two townships of land given by Congress for the endowment of a State University had been selected and patents were daily expected. Bibb recommended the sale of these lands and the conversion of the proceeds into cash capital to be vested in bank stock. He opposed renting the lands and sales on credit. What he desired was an early sale of the University's lands at a minimum cash price of not less than $15 per acre, so that "we shall be enabled to create a fund which may be, through the means of a State Bank, made both profitable to the University, and a great benefit to the community."

Bibb proposed that the Assembly incorporate a State University, giving the trustees power to sell the lands and invest the proceeds in a State Bank. Bibb said: "By adopting a plan similar in principle to the one I have here pointed out, I flatter myself that at no distant period our state may boast a literary and scientific institution possessing advantages but little, if any, inferior to any of our sister states."

The Acting Governor commented on the suspension of payment in specie by the Huntsville Bank and deplored the fact that its bills were still receivable in payment of all dues owed the State. At the time the State was taking the paper of the Huntsville Bank at par, the State's warrants were paid in notes of the Huntsville Bank at a depreciation of fifteen to twenty per cent. As a means of ending this unfair condition of affairs Bibb suggested that the several banks in operation in the State come into a plan for a general State Bank, and if they refused to come in on a fair basis, then that future reception of the Huntsville Bank's notes be contingent upon their resuming specie payments.[1] Having outlined what he considered the proper legislative course, Thomas Bibb quietly awaited the inaugural of his successor, Israel Pickens.

He had not long to wait. On November 7, 1821, the As-

[1] House Journal 1821, pp. 11 *et seq.*

sembly in joint session counted the votes which disclosed that Madison County's Dr. Henry Chambers had lost to Washington County's Israel Pickens by a vote of 9,616 to 7,129.[1] The seat-of-government question was not an issue in the campaign. The hard times had brought to the front a demand for adequate banking facilities. In general those who owed no debts or were clearly solvent opposed putting the State into the banking business. Those who had nothing to lose, or had hopes of gain, were perfectly willing to have the State go into the banking business and to do so on funds "borrowed" from the University. The electorate decided that Pickens was the man to be Alabama's Moses and lead her out of the wilderness.

This choice was a wise one. Pickens was a man of ability and high character. Furthermore he was a forthright man. This personal quality evidenced itself in his inaugural address made November 9, 1821, immediately after the Speaker of the House had administered to him the oath of office in the presence of a joint session of both Houses of the Assembly. After the customary introductory remarks, which were followed by comments on the natural advantages of Alabama, the Governor said: "The fairest portion of our territory, and even the spot where we are assembled was but yesterday unknown as the residence of civilized man." Pickens then outlined his desire to improve both the land and river communications. Said he: ". . . the geography of no state represents a country more happily united in interest, so far as this is affected by mutuality of situation and similarity of pursuits. We may indeed be divided by imaginary landmarks, formed by evil and designing counsels, but it is hoped the good sense and liberal sentiments of our citizens are sufficient to resist an influence so destructive of the public good."[2] The Governor, without equivocation,

[1] House Journal 1821, p. 25.

[2] House Journal 1821, p. 60. It is believed that Pickens was referring to the differences between the Tennessee Valley and the rest of the State.

directly expressed concern "that a serious difficulty had been presented so early in our political progress and before our government had assumed its permanent organization concerning the constitutional question of apportionment which raised doubts as to the legitimate existence of the legislative department and virtually of the whole government." Pickens was sure that the Constitution required apportionment of one or both branches of the Assembly; but in an effort to promote harmony he said: "The old questions canvassed upon it are settled and forever laid to rest. . . . It is but common charity to allow to all parties to the dispute the credit of sincerity; and to attribute the unfortunate result to that necessity arising from the varying operations of the human judgment, which may sometimes be as unavoidable as the act of God or of a public enemy."

Pickens further declared: "In every governmental difficulty the people have a redeeming control over their government. This may be exercised by acquiescence in the existing state of operation, as the most convenient course, until the more regular organization can be effected: or, if the magnitude of the occasion require it, they may rise in the majesty of their power, and resolve it into original elements, at the same instant reorganizing it under any modification not inconsistent with their federal obligation."

"No resort to this last extremity has been deemed advisable by any portion of our citizens. They have as by unanimous impulse chosen the present representative body to cooperate with the existing senate, in forming the General Assembly." Thus did the Governor express his opinion that the present assembly was a constitutional body.

The Chief Executive deplored the pecuniary difficulties which had visited the State with their enervating influence and cramping of active industry. He expressed the belief that speculation in public land sales was partly responsible for this condition. Concerning the depreciated currency which was afflicting the State, he said that he thought Alabama could overcome this because "our chief staple production will always command its current value in specie or its equivalent. The crop of a single year thus realized, which cannot be estimated at less than $2,000,000 would fill our circulation with a wholesome medium ample for all our purposes."

The Governor promised that he would initiate reform and exclude this depreciated currency from the State and: "If in addition to this, a prudent retrenchment of expenditure on foreign articles, be observed, the desired end, will at once be accomplished."

In the matter of the education of our youth, the new Governor was very careful. He did not mention that he contemplated using the University's educational grant for a State Bank. This was not material for an inaugural address —it could better be told in his message. But Pickens did indicate that there would be funds for investment when he stated: "On this score we have a valuable charge in trust for the present and future generations. The endowments in our hands for this purpose are ample, and by being prudently husbanded will prove a permanent resource for furnishing within ourselves the rudiments of useful learning. . . . It should ever be the policy of those who may administer our affairs to regard this fund as sacred to its purpose."[1]

The new Governor had spoken to an attentive and united Assembly insofar as he was concerned, but partisan feeling against the Acting Governor was still hot. The House of Representatives was still loyal to Bibb, but the Senate, with the exception of one or two members who were his personal friends, still regarded him with suspicion and bitterness. The House, and the House only, resolved in praise of the departing Governor.

The resolution read:

Resolved unanimously that the thanks of this *House* be presented to his excellency the Acting Governor, for the ability

[1] House Journal 1821, pp. 58–64, inc.

with which he has discharged the arduous duties of Chief Magistrate; and that this House duly appreciates the patriotic motives by which he has been governed in entering upon and continuing in the discharge of the executive duties up to this time.

Two members of the House were appointed to wait on the Acting Governor and present him with the Resolution conveying the thanks of the House to him. After the Resolution was presented to Bibb, the chairman of the committee reported to the House his answer, which was as follows:

Executive Office Cahawba
November 9, 1821

GENTLEMEN: You will permit me to express to you and through you to the House of Representatives my unfeigned thanks for the expression of approbation contained in the resolution of that Honorable Body, you have this morning presented to me. The countenance and support of my fellow citizens is at all times the most grateful and sufficient return for the responsibility of office; and is to me in this instance a peculiar gratification, as coming from the immediate representatives of the people.

I have the honor to be, your most ob't humble servant.

THOMAS BIBB

To Messrs. GREENING & VINING
A Committee etc.[1]

This intentional slight on the part of the Senate, which was intended to be an affront and was so received by Bibb, did not go unnoticed in the State. Public notice was taken of it in Huntsville by a dinner given in Bibb's honor. As soon as he concluded his business in Cahawba, Bibb began the long and hard trip from Cahawba to Huntsville.[2]

The dinner honoring Bibb was given in Huntsville as soon as the ex-Acting Governor was home and the details

[1] House Journal 1821, p. 26.

[2] The best route was to go northwest from Cahawba toward the town of Erie in Greene County and at a road junction where today stands the town of Greensboro turn north up the valley of the Black Warrior to Tuskaloosa, Jonesboro, Elyton (today's Birmingham), Blountsville, Ditto's Landing (today's Whitesburg), and so to Huntsville and then to his home in Limestone County. This ride on horseback was of itself sufficient reason why the Tennessee Valley people wanted the capital moved from Cahawba.

could be arranged. The toasts spoken on that occasion disclose the political philosophies and alignments of the sponsors. The following is quoted from the *Alabama Republican*, printed at Huntsville, November 30, 1821:

On Tuesday the 27th instant a public dinner was given to the late Acting Governor Thomas Bibb, Esq. by the citizens of Huntsville and the adjoining county as a manifestation of their personal regard and of their approbation of his political conduct. Among the set toasts was the following:

Thomas Bibb, Esq.—He disregards personal responsibility when it conflicts with public duty and his political conduct merits the approbation of his fellow citizens.

To which his Excellency made an appropriate reply which concluded with the toast:

The State of Alabama—may her citizens be prosperous and happy!

Volunteer Toasts

President: The memory of William W. Bibb.

Vice President: The constitution of Alabama. It cannot be dissolved by a faithless Senate.

Col. LeRoy Pope: Party spirit, may it cease to mar our political prosperity.

John H. Lewis, Esq.: Governor Andrew Jackson—in peace or war ever prompt and energetic, alike removed from the "love of praise or fear of censure."

Dr. Miles S. Watkins: The Huntsville Bank—beyond the pale of legislative acts and responsible to the judiciary only, time will rectify her errors and raise her paper to the proper level.

Dr. Thomas Fearn: The Senate of Alabama—Today overshadowed by clouds and darkness; may a refulgent sun illumine the morrow.

There is no record that the Senate or any of its members noticed or replied to the sentiments expressed at the dinner, but there is cause to believe that it provided Thomas Bibb some consolation for the slights of the Senate.

While Bibb was being lauded by his friends in the Tennessee Valley, Israel Pickens and the Assembly were still struggling with matters of state in Cahawba. On November 13, four days after taking the oath of office, Governor

Pickens delivered his message[1] to the Assembly. It was a lengthy but direct statement of his policies.

Pickens touched the tenderest spot first. He called attention to the fact that the new census returns were in and that the Constitution required a new apportionment law. With this declaration behind him, he then proceeded to matters of policy. He agreed with Bibb that the University of Alabama lands should be sold but differed on Bibb's advice to sell only for cash. Pickens suggested that sales be made on a plan to pay in four-, five-, or six-year annual installments because, in his opinion, this method would yield one hundred per cent more than sales for cash.

The new Governor also agreed with Bibb that of its funds the University of Alabama should be permitted to invest not over $100,000 in stock of an Alabama State Bank; the residue of the proceeds after buying the stock and putting the University of Alabama in operation he said was a "sacred trust for the future as well as the present generation." He suggested that it be invested in United States Government stocks at six per cent because the national fund was to be preferred over the new State Bank which would be created.

Pickens skillfully arranged to avoid having the demands for cash by the proposed Bank and the University come at the same time by recommending that the *location* of the University be a proper work for a future session and that in the meantime an act of incorporation, empowering the trustees to sell the land and invest the proceeds, would be sufficient. As long as the location of the University was not determined, of course no money would be required to build or operate it.

The Governor recommended that the State Treasury exclude all paper not the equivalent of specie.[2] This was a

[1] House Journal 1821, pp. 40 *et seq.*

[2] The Assembly enacted a law to this effect. Acts 1821, p. 23. This Act also had a provision for quo warranto proceedings to forfeit the bank's charter. See also Acts 1821, p. 41, Sec. 14.

vastly different policy from that proposed by Bibb and for which Bibb had been praised by Dr. Watkins in his toast at the Huntsville dinner. Pickens also suggested that "this may be a proper period for paying off the loan obtained from the Planters and Merchants Bank of Huntsville *in its own paper*." The paper was not worth its face value, so to discharge the State's debt in this manner meant forcing the Bank to take a considerable discount.

Yet Pickens was not oppressive in his attitude toward the private banks. He openly repudiated the plan to force the Planters and Merchants Bank to meet its engagements by the imposition of a tax. Said he, "Take care not to ruin debtors of the bank while securing the creditors."

In conclusion Pickens asked the Assembly to appoint a committee to examine the executive records of the two Bibbs, his predecessors in the office. "Owing, it is understood," said Pickens, "to the want of proper books for the department, these records have not been kept up from the commencement."

The Governor's message to the Assembly was delivered on November 13. On November 27, just fourteen days later (a little more than the time required for the mail to travel to Huntsville and back to Cahawba), Pickens informed the Assembly that the Planters and Merchants Bank had asked that the loan of $10,000 due it by the State be paid "to enable the bank to resume specie payments at no very distant day." Pickens recommended that the Assembly provide the funds to pay the Huntsville Bank[1] and also defer

[1] The Assembly authorized the Governor to pay the Huntsville Bank loan in its own paper and to borrow $15,000 from the St. Stephens Bank. Acts 1821, p. 68. In order to get the money the State had to issue and put in circulation some Treasury Notes. Acts 1821, p. 95. The State did not actually get the money from the Tombeckbe Bank until 1823. Acts 1822, p. 145. The Huntsville loan was paid by requiring the tax collectors of Madison and Limestone Counties to deposit their collections to the credit of the Governor in the Huntsville Bank, to be applied by him on the debt. Acts 1821, p. 114. On November 18, 1822, there still remained unpaid on this loan $350 (Pickens' Message, House Journal 1822, p. 9) and the tax collector of Madison was ordered to pay the balance. Acts 1822, p. 142.

"to a reasonable day the operation of any definitive proceedings against that institution. . . . In any event, the policy of excluding from the treasury the paper of all banks that do not pay specie, will not be the less obvious."[1] As the contestants in the bank struggle jockeyed for position the pressure from the people for a State Bank steadily increased. This is what Pickens wanted. If the people needed it enough, and demanded it strongly enough, he felt he would be justified in putting the State into the business of banking. If he did do it, he was determined that it should be according to a plan of his own and not that offered by Thomas Bibb. For this he could wait if necessary.

The need for a digest of the laws of the State continued to increase. Having failed to make the Justices of the Supreme Court prepare the Digest, the Assembly now elected Harry Toulmin to do this important work.[2] But this was not the end of the Assembly's assertion of supervisory powers over the judiciary. A committee was appointed to ascertain if the Judges of the Supreme Court had reduced their opinions to writing and filed them in the Clerk's Office as required by law. The report of the committee disclosed some interesting information.

> That the Judges had not filed their opinions in writing as required by law. But as apology for the non-performance of this part of their official duty your committee would state, that so many duties necessarily devolved upon the Judges arising from the new organization of the judicial system and from the unsettled state of the law in this country, that it has been an arduous task on them to perform those duties which were more immediately essential to the administration of justice. Your committee are also informed that shortly after the organization of the Supreme Court a number of decisions of the Judges, and without their approbation, were published by some person in a

[1] House Journal 1821, p. 106.

[2] House Journal 1821, p. 113. Acts 1821, p. 18. By a joint resolution the Assembly made it the duty of Toulmin and of the Judges of the Supreme Court to report to the Assembly any defects which they discovered in the statutes of Alabama. Acts 1821, p. 114.

mutilated form, which had a tendency to give the community incorrect information. Your committee are satisfied that the Judges will hereafter reduce their opinions to writing and file them with the Clerk as well in cases already decided, as in those which may be hereafter adjudicated. Your committee are therefore of the opinion, and recommend, it is inexpedient at present, to take any further measures on the subject.

W. CRENSHAW, *Chairman*[1]

The tone and the content of this report indicate that the Court promised to do better and that for the present the Assembly would take no action. But the significant fact is that both the Assembly and the Court seem to agree that the Assembly had the right and power to supervise the Court.

Throughout the session the famous Indian scout, militia-man, and, according to Woodward, fist-fighter, Sam Dale, had been working on his fellow Assemblymen to grant him a pension. Dale was now getting along in years and was without means. The Assembly finally acted by making Dale a brevet brigadier general with half-pay for life of a colonel in the United States Army.[2] Upon being notified by the committee appointed to inform him of the honor conferred upon him Dale replied:

GENTLEMEN: Permit me through you to return to the Legislature my unfeigned acknowledgment for the honor they have been pleased to confer upon me in bestowing the appointment of brevet brigadier general of the militia of the State of Alabama. It will be a source of unfailing pleasure to me, to reflect, that although I have expended the vigour of a strong constitution in discharging the arduous duties to which I have been subjected it has been my peculiar good fortune to meet the approbation of my fellow citizens and permit me to assure you, that while it shall please divine providence to enable me, gratitude for the

[1] House Journal 1821, p. 192.

[2] Acts 1821, p. 60. Dale was also relieved of a debt of $229.04¼ owed the State for taxes collected by him and not remitted. Acts 1821, p. 53, Sec. 14. Jeremiah Austill, who was also a hero in the canoe fight which brought fame to Dale, was extended the thanks of the Assembly by resolution but was not awarded any pension. Acts 1821, p. 115.

expression of public confidence which you have this day made shall stimulate me, to the exercise of my best exertions for the good of my country; and, will you, gentlemen, accept my sincere thanks for the marked and polite manner in which you have conveyed to me the sense of the legislature upon the present occasion.

SAMUEL DALE

To Messrs. WEEDON, ARMSTRONG AND BAGBY,
The Committee, etc.

So did the State of Alabama confer her first pension and thus did the recipient acknowledge the grant. For some reason not given, the succeeding Assembly withdrew the title of brevet brigadier general, but left Dale his pension.

As the 1821 session drew near to a close, Governor Pickens was presented with a most important bill which had originated in the House and which had been finally maneuvered through the Senate in the closing days of the session. This bill purported to be an amendment of the law of 1820 which incorporated the Bank of the State of Alabama. The effort actually to organize the Bank under the 1820 Act had been a notorious failure, because no one would subscribe and pay in the money for the stock.

Under the new law now presented to Pickens, in which it was cleverly asserted that the act was an amendment of the 1820 law, the State would contribute two-fifths of the capital of a State Bank and be entitled to two-fifths control. After the establishment of the general State Bank the bill stated that the "*banks of the State now existing* might be admitted as branches thereof upon such terms as the legislature and the banks may agree." The act was so ingeniously devised, however, that during the formative period of the Bank the State was not given control in the Bank in proportion to its contribution and risk. In this critical time the bill gave the decisive power to the existing banks. The alert Pickens saw at once that if this bank bill became law, the State of Alabama would be risking the University's money to rescue the three banks[1] now existing in the State from what was certainly an unhealthy, if not precarious, financial situation. His study of the bank bill also convinced Pickens that the proposed State Bank would, by the process of taking in the three banks currently chartered by the State, commence its operations with an immense debt. This was not the kind of bank Pickens had in mind or the kind in which he would be willing to risk the University's dowry. The bank bill before him followed the Thomas Bibb plan and took care of the existing banks. Pickens quickly decided that he would veto the bill, but he was wise enough to use extreme care. Actually the State was at war with the Huntsville Bank and had differences with the other two, but for the Governor openly to acknowledge the fact at this time might well cause the banks, or some of them, to close, thus damaging the owners and depositors alike and leaving the people of Alabama without any banking facilities whatever. That these banks were bringing crafty political pressure to bear on the Assembly was a fact well known to Pickens. The banks were using the Thomas Bibb bloc in the House to advantage and at the same time as a business procedure the Huntsville Bank pressed the State for payment of the $10,000 owed it by the State, while the Tombeckbe Bank at St. Stephens declined the Governor's request for a loan of $10,000 to the State.[2] These various pressures were exerted from several directions at once with the purpose of inducing the State to enact a law which would lend the State's cash and credit to save and aid the existing banks, while preserving to the banks the actual control of the new State Bank. But Pickens had no intention of accepting such a bank law. In a message as remarkable for its diplomacy as for its understanding, the Governor vetoed

[1] They were: a. The President, Directors, and Company of the Planters and Merchants Bank of Huntsville (Toulmin, p. 40); b. The President, Directors, and Company of the Tombecke Bank (Toulmin, p. 40); and c. The President, Directors, and Company of the Bank of Mobile (Toulmin, p. 46).

[2] House Journal 1821, p. 195.

the bill.[1] The House failed to pass it over his veto by a vote of 26 to 20. A few days later the Assembly adjourned. Pickens realized now that the bank problem was a difficult one and that he might have to wait some time before he would get a bank law to his liking.

While the bank bill caused the Governor much concern, the question which only a few months before had split asunder Bibb's called Assembly was now disposed of without controversy. The very quietness with which the Assembly presented the new apportionment bill to the Governor for his signature indicated that its creators were sensitive to the fact that the coming battle for removal was drawing nearer; and that this new apportionment law[2] "at a ratio of 1735 for the representatives" and a regrouping of counties in the senatorial districts was one of the important preliminary skirmishes.

The Alabama River system faction, realizing that they had no chance to gain control of the House, concentrated their efforts on presently procuring a composition of senatorial districts which eventually, at the critical election, would give them the best chance to win control over the Senate. These men well knew that there must be still another apportionment law in 1824, and that the Assemblymen elected under that law would settle the "Seat of Government" question. Therefore, it was incumbent upon both factions to prepare now, insofar as possible, for the coming contest. Watching each other carefully, the Assemblymen created the following senatorial districts, each being entitled to one Senator and no more:

1. Washington, Baldwin, and Mobile
2. Conecuh, Covington, Pike, & [Henry
3. Monroe
4. Dallas
5. Wilcox and Clarke
6. Marengo and Greene
7. Perry and Autauga
8. Montgomery and Butler
9. Bibb and Shelby
10. St. Clair and Blount
11. Jefferson

[1] House Journal 1821, p. 233. [2] Acts 1821, p. 57.

12. Tuskaloosa and Pickens
13. Marion and Franklin
14. Lawrence
15. Morgan
16. Jackson and Decatur
17. Limestone
18. Madison
19. Lauderdale

When the composition of the senatorial districts was finally agreed upon it appeared to the politically wise of the day that the location of the seat of government would most probably be determined by the votes of senators representing districts composed of counties which were served equally well by both big river systems, such as Baldwin and Mobile Counties, and by those counties where there was little or no service or influence by either river system, such as Franklin, and probably Blount and Jefferson, both of which were only vaguely tied to the Warrior-Tombigbe system. Jefferson's western boundary was the Warrior, but there the river was filled with shoals and rocks and was frequently a tumultuous and dangerous stream. Only very small boats of shallow draft could navigate above the falls at Tuskaloosa, the head of navigation on that stream. The smaller but less dangerous Cahawba flowed through the entire eastern section of Jefferson County and probably was as serviceable to Jefferson County at that time as the Warrior. The Tennessee River Valley had a large vote and this would weigh heavily and perhaps decisively in the final result, but the public men did not consider that the Valley had any chance to get the seat of government for itself.

While Pickens had failed to get the State Bank which he wanted, his Assembly had dutifully passed at his request an extensive act[1] supplementing the act which created the Seminary of Learning, denominated "The University of Alabama."[2] This new law provided that the destiny and control of the University of Alabama be in twelve trustees, to be elected by the General Assembly. Two trustees were

[1] Acts 1821, p. 3. Pickens was a great believer in higher education for women and at his request the trustees were empowered to select a site for a "female institution" to be a branch of the University.

[2] Acts 1820, p. 4.

to be elected from each of the six judicial circuits and were to continue in office for three years. The trustees were empowered to sell the lands of the University and to invest the proceeds. These trustees had at this time no educational institution to operate or direct, but in their hands lay the fate of Pickens' plan for a State Bank, as well as the future of the University. Not only the Governor, but the whole State, watched the election of the twelve trustees with interest. The trustees elected were:

From the 1st Judicial Circuit: George W. Owen and John Murphy
From the 2nd Judicial Circuit: Dr. George Phillips and Henry Hitchcock
From the 3rd Judicial Circuit: Jack Shackelford and Hume Field
From the 4th Judicial Circuit: John McKinley and Nicholas Davis
From the 5th Judicial Circuit: Henry Minor and Thomas Fearn
From the 6th Judicial Circuit:[1] Clement C. Billingslea and R. W. Carter

It was an excellent board. All the members were men of the highest character and integrity. Among them were scholars and business men—a good division in a case where a bank must be provided with capital and a University cared for from one and the same money source.

The 1821 Assembly was not spectacular in any way. Governor Pickens controlled it with a fair and firm hand. Most of its work was practical and useful. The successful trip of the *Harriett* up the Alabama River in October, 1821, no doubt influenced John B. Hogan, Stephen Chandler, Lewis Judson, Henry Gunnison, William Roser, and Benjamin Vincent, of Mobile, to incorporate the Mobile Steam

[1] The several judicial circuits at this time were composed as follows: *First*—Monroe, Clarke, Washington, Baldwin, and Marengo; *Second*—Dallas, Wilcox, Perry, Bibb, and Autauga; *Third*—St. Clair, Shelby, Jefferson, Tuskaloosa, Greene, and Blount; *Fourth*—Pickens, Limestone, Lauderdale, Lawrence, Franklin, and Marion; *Fifth*—Jackson, Decatur, Madison, and Morgan; and *Sixth*—Covington, Henry, Pike, Montgomery, Conecuh, and Butler.

Boat Company.[1] Another law relative to Mobile was for the benefit of the Church. The Catholics of Mobile, so lately subjects of His Catholic Majesty, the King of Spain, thought it necessary to have an act of the Assembly in order to sell their lot of ground on the west side of Royal Street on which the Chapel of the Congregation was long since erected and which is now in a state of complete dilapidation. The Assembly appointed John B. Hogan, Terry McCusker, Diego McVoy, Daniel Duval, and Dominique Salles commissioners for the Roman Catholic Congregation of Christians in the City of Mobile to make the sale.[2]

The appropriations made at the 1821 session were carefully considered. The cost of the Assembly was $20,000. The Governor received $2,000 for a year's salary. William T. Gamble, doorkeeper of the House, was paid $269.25 for stationery furnished both houses. Mathew McClellan got $113.87 for stationery and wood furnished the Senate. The Comptroller was allowed $63.25 for postage and $75 was appropriated to buy a desk for the State Treasurer. On December 21, 1821, the Assembly adjourned. There was no affluence in the Capitol at Cahawba, but the ship of state was on an even keel and Israel Pickens knew the course which he was steering.

The Year 1822

and the General Assembly—Annual Session of 1822

The Assembly of 1822 was purposely more concerned with political matters than with legislation. Its accomplishments were more those of a convention than of a lawmaking body. In this session two United States Senators were elected. In each instance the "Georgia Men," that group of political men who acknowledged William Wyatt Bibb as leader during his lifetime, were defeated.[3] Governor Pickens himself

[1] Acts 1821, p. 87. [2] Acts 1821, p. 103.

[3] The stronghold of the "Georgia Men," or "Royal Party," as they were sometimes called, was around Montgomery, but the headquarters of this frontier

had once been aligned with the Georgia men but he had left them and defeated their man Chambers for the governorship. Pickens' supporters or the People's Party now consolidated their gains and confidently followed the leadership of this tall, thin, dyspeptic lawyer who had learned the ways of politics in North Carolina before moving to Alabama.

The growing season of 1822 had produced good crops in Alabama and the spirits of the people were rising. After a long absence steamboats were again on the rivers. On August 5, 1822, Captain Roman brought the *Tensas* on her first trip to Montgomery. Just a few days behind the *Tensas* was the *Cotton Plant*, commanded by Captain Chandler, who arrived in Montgomery on August 17 towing a large barge.[1] The landings of these boats at Cahawba cheered the depressed citizens and lot-owners in the stagnating capital. Visions of a metropolis here were renewed. But a similar scene was also being enacted on the Tombigbe. The steamboat *Tombeckbe* was operating on that river system.[2] The improvement in commerce and agriculture were encouraging signs to Israel Pickens as he journeyed to Cahawba for the annual session of the Assembly.

On November 18 the Governor delivered his message[3] to the Assembly in writing. Pickens reminded that body that "you compose the First General Assembly chosen under the permanent system of representation provided by the constitution," and that the diversity in regard to that vital point which once prevailed no longer existed. With this salutation as an introduction the Governor proceeded to business.

Tammany was in Huntsville. Leaders in the Montgomery section were W. W. Bibb, at Coosada; Bolling Hall, who lived across the river from Montgomery; and Dr. Clement C. Billingslea. Huntsville had LeRoy Pope, John W. Walker, C. C. Clay, John McKinley, Dr. Henry Chambers, and Thomas Bibb, of Limestone County.

[1] Blue's *History of Montgomery*, p. 69.

[2] *Mobile Register*, June 10, 1822.

[3] House Journal 1822, p. 9.

An improved financial condition was reported. The Treasury's depreciated warrants were all paid and its paper was circulating at par. The Huntsville Bank loan had been repaid, excepting $350. The Assembly was informed that of the $15,000 which they had authorized him to borrow at the last session, he had arranged to take only $4,500 from the Tombeckbe Bank,[1] as this was sufficient for the needs of the State.

Pickens cautioned the Assembly that upon them rested the duty of devising a judicious plan for a State Bank. Said he: "So essential do I consider the plan of a charter of such an institution that on this mainly will depend the question of its expediency. This is to determine whether it may be an evil or a blessing." These were strong words for a Governor who was nurturing a plan of his own to say to a group of legislators which contained plenty of opposition.

The Governor said he wanted a State Bank established conformable to the Constitution—on correct principles—wisely and honestly conducted. He did not want an experiment. He reminded the Assembly that the Constitution, in authorizing the State Bank, restricted the Assembly to one distinct institution which was expected to afford reasonable security for public purposes, and not become a dangerous monopoly. To achieve that security Pickens listed several "almost indispensable" requisites:

First—The State should at all times have a material influence in the government of the corporation—and *that* whatever may be its interest in the capital.

Second—The State should have an interest in the capital in some degree proportionate to its control. Here Pickens listed the difficulties the State would have in providing the cash. He stated that one way would be a mutual agreement between the State and the Trustees of the University who, having determined to sell its lands, might find it expedient

[1] Pickens was one of the original organizers and had been a Director and President of this bank.

to invest a portion of the proceeds in the bank. "This idea," he said, "is suggested without knowing the disposition of the Trustees, whose concurrence would be indispensable. The approaching session of that body will afford, however, all necessary facilities for ascertaining their views on the subject."

Third—"A most critical and delicate point will be, the connexion to be formed between the State Bank and the local ones, in the adoption of the latter as branches." Here Pickens was treading on controversial ground. This was the real crux of the bank battle. But the Governor was determined *not* to let the existing banks come in as a part of the State Bank at the *time of its creation.* "The most ordinary prudence," said Pickens, "dictates that the former should not only be organized, previously to the arrangement of the terms of the connexion, but that each should have a thorough knowledge of the concerns of each other." The experienced Pickens was determined not to have a "wedding in the dark" between the private banks and the State's money.

Fourth—"Late experience is felt to show the necessity of power in the State to correct with ease the violation of the charter, as well as to punish the officers and agents for the abuses of their trusts." Pickens was here referring to the continual and arrogant misconduct of the Planters and Merchants Bank of Huntsville.

Fifth—"Whether a restriction on the issue of paper to a proportion less than thrice the capital would not be expedient, at least for about the first six years of its business."

Pickens concluded with the statement that for a successful bank it was necessary to have the actual existence of competent disposable banking capital. "This," said he, "cannot be created by fiction—but in all events a correct system will prove safe."

The Governor then informed the Assembly that the Huntsville Bank had not resumed the payment of specie within the time required by an act passed at the last session of the Assembly and that he had instructed the solicitor of the Fifth Circuit to proceed against the corporation by writ of quo warranto. Further he advised that he had employed William Kelly, Esq., as assisting counsel in the prosecution.

The Governor laid before the Assembly the ordinances and minutes of the first meeting of the Board of Trustees of the University of Alabama held at Tuskaloosa on the first Monday in April, 1822, and advised that a second session would be held in Cahawba in December when the Board would make its annual report. The Governor continued: "It may become necessary to make some legislative regulations in regard to the lands of the institution and the investment of its funds. As, however, most of these acts will require the concurrence of the Board, I defer making recommendations of any specific measures, until that body shall have convened."

The Governor then proceeded to discuss the probable recommendations of the Board to the Assembly as to the location of the University. He counseled the Assembly to keep in mind only the prosperity of the University and to allow no other distinct subject to become entangled with it.

He also reported that: "The twenty lots advertised to be sold on the east side of the Alabama, within the limits of Cahawba, have been laid off and sold accordingly."

Two things above all others stood out in the Governor's message: first, that he was determined that if a State Bank was created it would be free of entanglements with the private banks at the time it came into being and, second, that the University's endowment would not be used without the accord and concurrence of its trustees.

The Assembly was barely organized and just getting under way when the Governor received an important letter. He at once transmitted it to the Assembly for the contents were strictly political. John W. Walker, United States Senator from Alabama, had resigned his high office. The Assembly would choose a successor. The political pot in Cahawba began to boil at once. Here was another test of strength between the Georgia Men and the People's Party. The letters of both Pickens and Walker are of interest.

Executive Department
December 2, 1822

Gentlemen of the Senate and
the House of Representatives:

I have this day received the resignation of the Hon. John W. Walker, a Senator from this State in the Congress of the United States, and I have to add with much concern and regret, that extreme ill health has been the cause of denying to the State a longer continuance of his services in that important station.

I take this early occasion to communicate this information, to allow you the full time for deliberation in the selection of a successor, which is required by the importance of the grade of service, and by its length of continuance. The period of vacancy left by this resignation will expire on the 3rd of March, 1825.

Israel Pickens

Huntsville
21st November, 1822

Sir: The state of my health has been so precarious, and so much worse than usual during the past summer, as to render it for some time doubtful whether I should be able to attend the approaching session of Congress. As a citizen recognizing the paramount claim of the State upon his services I felt it my duty to remain in the station to which it had called me, so long as I enjoyed sufficient strength to discharge its functions. Some improvement for the last two months flattered me with the hope, that I might yet complete my term but the time for decision has arrived, and I still feel myself too feeble to attempt it. A journey to Washington, would not, even now, in the opinion of my friends be prudent, if it were practicable, nor a winter of residence there safe. Though improving, I improve but slowly; and though I may eventually be so fortunate as to regain my wonted strength, the period is uncertain and may be distant. Meantime the State ought not to suffer, nor lose a portion of its representation on account of my infirmities. I must therefore beg leave to retire from its service; requesting your Excellency to consider and accept this as a resignation of my seat in the Senate of the United States. In doing so I shall ever cherish a deep sense of gratitude for the unmerited distinctions which have been conferred upon me; and I cannot forbear the expression of an ardent wish, that in the choice of a successor, the General Assembly may fix on an individual, who, to equal zeal and devotion for the interests of Alabama, may unite happier talents and more vigorous health. This communication would have been made by the last mail but for a mistake in the day of its departure.

I have the honor to be with great respect and consideration your most obedient servant,

J. W. WALKER

HIS EXCELLENCY, ISRAEL PICKENS

The choice of a successor lined up in opposition the same forces which had contested for the governorship in the last election. True, the People's Party candidate, William Kelly, was not as popular as Israel Pickens, but he was a North Alabama man and it was generally accepted that the Senator to fill the unexpired part of Walker's term must be of that section. John McKinley was put up by the Georgia Men. The election was close, but Kelly won by a vote of 39 to 38. It was another blow for the Georgia party.

Immediately after Kelly's victory another election was conducted for the full term of the senatorship held by William R. King. One of the leading candidates was William Crawford, President of the Tombeckbe Bank and dealer of federal patronage in the State under the grace of the Secretary of War who bore the same name. He resided in Washington County but he was a strong Royal Party man. William R. King, from Dallas County, the other leading candidate, stood for re-election. Almost the same division which prevailed in the Kelly-McKinley election was present, but two new elements were introduced by the appearance of two unexpected candidates.

One William King was a candidate. It was the old device of using a candidate bearing a name almost identical with that of another man in the same race. Some of the Assemblymen in these early days were unlettered and others given to drinking stout potions. A slight mistake might cost William R. King re-election. There is little doubt that the Crawford crowd put William King in the race. The William R. King group probably retaliated by offering John McKee as a counterbalance. McKee was from Crawford's home section and a member of one of the oldest, largest, and most influential families in the lower Tombigbe region.

Seven ballots were taken before an election was achieved. William R. King was re-elected, 38 votes to 35.[1] The Georgia Men in Alabama were out of the United States Senate.

On Wednesday, December 11, a memorial was presented to the General Assembly by the trustees of the University of Alabama wherein they stated that they had studied the charter of the University of Alabama and found defects therein arising in some instances out of a lack of certain necessary powers, in others from the fact that their powers were too unlimited and undefined, and in still others from injudicious and impolitic direction for the disposition of the endowment. They also noted the entire omission of certain privileges which they considered necessary for the "safety, security, and prosperity of the institution." By the memorial they submitted fourteen changes which they desired the General Assembly to make in the charter of the University. Briefly, these were:

I. Provisions to continue the present Board in office for three years, and for filling vacancies.

II. Giving the President and two Trustees, or three Trustees without the President, power to call special meetings.

III. Providing that only at annual meetings of the Board could permanent officers of the University be elected and salaries fixed.

IV. That the President of the University shall not hold the office of Trustee so long as he shall hold the office of President.

[1] House Journal 1822, p. 83.

v. That a majority of the whole number of trustees shall always be present when any business is transacted and that a majority of the members present at an annual meeting shall have the power to expel a student or students.

vi. Providing in detail for the sale of lands of the University at public auction and the terms of sales.

vii. That the title to said lands shall vest in the present trustees and their successors in office forever.

viii. Requiring three members of the Board to attend each sale.

ix. Authorizing the trustees to invest $100,000 in a State Bank, if one be created.

x. Students of the University exempted from taxation and working on public roads.

xi. Trustees given power to establish three institutions for female education, one to be located in the northern, one in the middle, and one in the southern part of the State.

xii. Six additional trustees, living not over fifty miles from the University to be elected after site of University selected.

xiii. Providing for a sinking fund.

xiv. Trustees given power to lease University's lands.

The following names were signed to the memorial:

Israel Pickens, *President*	Henry Hitchcock
Thomas Fearn	J. McKinley
G. W. Owen	Hume R. Field
R. W. Carter	J. Murphy
Nicholas Davis	Jack Shackelford[1]

Having made their recommendations for changes in the charter of the University, the trustees' next move was to submit to the Assembly recommendations for the location of the "Seminary of Learning." The skill and deference with which the report is written suggest that it was not only signed by Israel Pickens but conceived by him.

If the General Assembly deem it expedient to locate the University in the northern part of the State, the Board considered Athens, or some place near it, most desirable.

[1] House Journal 1822, p. 75. The trustees who did not sign the memorial are: Dr. George Phillips, Henry Minor, and Clement C. Billingslea. Most of the recommendations were carried out by the Assembly. Acts 1822, p. 26, *et seq.* The Assembly provided for three branches of the University for female educa-

If located in the middle section of the State, then some point within Township 17, Range 13, in Autauga County—Wilson's Hill in Shelby County, the place called Gages in Perry County, and some place near the town of Tuskaloosa.

(*Signed*) ISRAEL PICKENS

The Board carefully refrained from going into details or committing itself to specific reasons for its recommendations. The plans of Israel Pickens required that the location of the University should not be decided until after the State Bank was put into operation. By dealing in generalities the Board raised the desire and hope for the University in many sections. Contests for this rich prize would insure further delay. Meanwhile, Pickens continued to work for his State Bank. The time for adjournment was near at hand, and he knew that the Assembly would not charter such a bank at this session. Before another convention of the Assembly an election would be held for the governorship. Pickens intended to be a candidate to succeed himself and to make the proposed bank an issue.

Meantime Pickens approved an act by which the quo warranto proceedings begun by the State to forfeit the charter of the Huntsville Bank were suspended. The directors of the bank made a solemn pledge to resume specie payments within the year 1823, and to meet all its engagements. It was provided that failure to meet their pledge would operate to forfeit the bank's charter on January 1, 1824.[1] Thus Pickens kept the Huntsville Bank alive for at least another year.

Two other matters of lively interest required the Assembly's attention and action before adjournment. The most personal was the attack on Sam Dale's pension granted him at the last annual session. A special committee had been appointed to consider the matter and reported high

tion (see XI) but said that not over $100,000 should be spent on buildings for them. Acts 1822, p. 31, Sec. 17.

[1] Acts 1822, p. 32.

praise for Dale and his claim to the gratitude of the country, and the committee, in recommending repeal of the law allowing a pension to Colonel Sam Dale, stated they were sensible of the difficulty which they would have to escape the censure of ingratitude which had been too often a stigma of republics; "but they have to remark that it appears to your committee that no precedent is more dangerous in government than the establishment of a pension list from the great number of indigent individuals who have distinguished themselves in this and many other states encouraged by the example, which it is believed throw themselves upon the bounty of their respective states, and while it is acknowledged none could be found whose services were more useful than Col. Sam Dale's, yet it is believed that many could be found whose pecuniary situation is more desperate, who are highly deserving, and to whom it would not be good policy to extend the favors. The public treasury is a fund drawn alike from the poor and the rich and never was designed for charitable purposes, and as this donation was given without the request or solicitation of Col. Samuel Dale it is believed by your committee that it cannot be considered a reflection on the merits or worth of that distinguished individual to withdraw it. . . ." While the Senate voted to amend the act by withdrawing the pension, Dale's friends in the House managed to save for him a portion of his grant. The Assembly finally acted by repealing that part of the act which gave Dale the rank of Brigadier General while in service. They also provided that Dale was not to receive any allowance for forage or rations. The bare pension was not disturbed.[1]

The Toulmin Digest was before the Assembly for approval, and if it was to be accepted, compensation for it had to be authorized. The joint committee which examined the manuscript reported that the statute law of state was digested with accuracy, correctness, and much ability, and

[1] Acts 1822, p. 138.

that the arrangement was good; that the plan was far superior to that of the late Mississippi Digest.[1] The committee said that Toulmin's work was very good, and that there was great need for such a digest in the state. A bill was reported by the committee whereby the State accepted the Digest and paid Toulmin for his services. Here came the rub. The Digest was a magnificent work and the State wanted it, but Alabama's treasury was low. The Assemblymen haggled about the price. Poor old Harry Toulmin, meantime, waited in Cahawba for action. He was sick and old and knew he must soon die, but he stood up manfully for his rights. Knowing of the debate, the old judge dispatched a letter to the Assembly saying:

To the General Assembly:

The undersigned having some reason to believe that a difficulty exists as to the compensation he ought to have for digesting the laws of the State of Alabama, begs leave to make the following observations:

1. In the year 1806 he was employed to digest the statutes then existing—which were those of six or seven sessions only.

For that work he received twelve hundred dollars—the digest contained four hundred and twenty-six pages. The digest now prepared and laid before the Assembly would if printed on a similar page and with the same type occupy sixteen hundred pages—and were the compensation allowed for it in proportion to the compensation in 1807 it would amount to upwards of four thousand five hundred dollars.

But in addition to this, it is but merely just to remark that the digest of 1807 was composed of entire acts while the digest now submitted is arranged under distinct heads, or titles, and care has been taken not only to arrange the acts themselves under the title to which they belong, but to divide those very acts, where they relate as they often do, to several subjects and to place the several sections under their proper titles.

2. The undersigned has known from long experience, what are the labor and the expenses of attending seven circuit courts twice a year and discharging the duties not only of a Territorial but of a Federal Judge; he can say with confidence that neither

[1] Prepared by Edward Turner and printed in Natchez, 1816.

the mental exertion nor the personal expense (even including clerk hire) has been equal to that of preparing the digest now presented to the Legislature.

It was necessary that the compiler for the purpose of making a contract with the General Assembly, should attend here two weeks, at the last session. He has been obliged to attend at the present session about four weeks, in order to facilitate an examination of the digest. He conceives therefore that his traveling expenses (having been obliged to bring a wagon for the purpose of conveying the digest and original acts of the Legislature on which the digest is formed) together with six weeks' attendance cannot be estimated at less than two hundred and sixty-four dollars.

His clerk hire and paper have cost him about two hundred fifty dollars. His labour for one year, taking that of a circuit judge as a criterion is worth seventeen hundred and fifty dollars (total twenty-two hundred and sixty four dollars).

3. The compiler of the digest now in use[1] had before him the digest of 1807 and of nine subsequent sessions some of which were very short. An appropriation was made to him of $1,000 in 1816 before the work was completed. The State of Alabama was severed from the Mississippi at the same time. What appropriations were made afterwards is not known. The present digest will contain the acts of sixteen sessions besides those of the digest of 1807.

If it be supposed therefore that Mr. Turner received no more than $1,000 for the chaos he created, it will surely be a subject of very rational investigation what sum, when a man has been paid $1,000 for mangling and murdering the laws, ought to be paid to anyone who has brought them to life again.

The acts of seven sessions are also incorporated with those exhibited in Turner's Digest. The undersigned has endeavored not only to gratify but to be useful to the public. He cannot receive for his services a less sum than about $2,000. If the General Assembly do not deem his services worthy of that compensation he prays permission to withdraw his manuscript.

He has labored incessantly and what he solicits is not from the generosity, but the justice of the General Assembly.

(*Signed*) HARRY TOULMIN

Dec. 23, 1822.[2]

[1] Turner's *Digest*. [2] Senate Journal 1822, pp. 143–144.

This was a gallant stand by an old and loyal friend of Alabama. Harry Toulmin had served her people when the State was a part of the Mississippi Territory and continued his loyal and learned services until the last. The Assembly finally authorized a payment of $1,500[1] to Toulmin with the proviso that he prepare an index and superintend the printing of the book.[2] It was a hard bargain but Toulmin accepted less than his manuscript was worth because he had need of the money now, knowing that the hand of death was already upon him.

The laws passed by the Assembly have already been commented upon. Perhaps the most novel was the grant to John Fowler of the right to operate a steam ferryboat between Mobile and Blakely capable of carrying six horses and to be ready at all times for such services except in July, August, and September, when Fowler was permitted to use either a steamboat, rowboat, or sailboat.[3] Athens got a female academy;[4] Jefferson Academy was organized in Elyton;[5] Huntsville incorporated a Fire Engine Company;[6] and Big Spring changed its name to Tuscumbia.[7] The cost of the Assembly was $25,000. W. T. Gamble was paid $114 for hire of a servant and wood and articles furnished both houses. Forty dollars was appropriated for postage. Stationery and candles cost $184.78. The sum of $86.25 was allowed for repairs to the Senate chamber and the President's chair and for locks for the tables and doors.[8]

Appropriations were made to discharge many claims against the State. Of interest among these are: John B.

[1] Acts 1822, p. 15.

[2] Before his death Toulmin prepared the Table of Contents of this most famous of Alabama lawbooks and greatest depository of historical facts, but died before making the index. The versatile Henry Hitchcock took over, wrote the index, and went to New York, where he superintended the printing.

[3] Acts 1822, p. 132. Fowler named his steam ferryboat *The Emeline.*

[4] Acts 1822, p. 122.

[5] Acts 1822, p. 122.

[6] Acts 1822, p. 123.

[7] Acts 1822, p. 131.

[8] Acts 1822, pp. 65 *et seq.*

Patrick, Deputy Sheriff of Dallas County, got $15 for serving ten days as constable to the Supreme Court. The late Sheriff of Dallas County was paid $19 for his service to the Supreme Court at the last June term. The new Sheriff, John B. Norris, received $74.50 "for room rents and services furnished the Supreme Court during the December, 1822, term."[1]

The Assembly adjourned January 1, 1823. Israel Pickens had completed the first year of his two-year term which would expire in December, 1823. Meantime, he would stand for re-election and, if successful, he would have two years more in which to carry out his program for Alabama.

The Year 1823
and the General Assembly—Annual Session of 1823

When the Assembly of 1822 completed its work and departed from Cahawba the pattern for action by Israel Pickens was complete. He would stand for re-election and ask the people to give him another term so that he could put into operation his plan for a State Bank. The remnant of the Royal Party would no doubt put forward a candidate. Pickens hoped they would, because a clear victory on this issue settled by the ballot box would assure success of his program in the legislature. Other important matters collateral to the Bank question would of necessity follow the trail broken by the Bank.

The Governor remained in Cahawba attending to the many details of state which a thorough and conscientious man like Pickens would neither delegate nor postpone. The prospective monotony of his extended residence in the city was immediately relieved by the advent of a full river which brought new steamers to the Cahawba landing. On January 1, 1823, the *Osage* with Captain Bond in charge docked at the foot of Arch Street. Two weeks later the *Elizabeth* arrived, being commanded by Captain Duncan. These, the

[1] Acts 1822, pp. 67 *et seq.*

fourth and fifth steamboats to ascend the strong Alabama current, brought an end to most of the speculation concerning the certainty of river transportation. But the overwhelming answer to all doubters was the appearance at Cahawba of the steamboat *Columbus* under the command of Captain Ashbridge on February 16, 1823. She was just six days out of Mobile and a marvel of size and splendor. Her length was 154 feet and she was 53 feet wide, costing, it was reported, $80,000. Later in April, with more knowledge of the river, her captain brought her from Mobile to Montgomery in three and one-half days.[1] Henceforth the cotton planter in this section could count on a steamboat to carry his crop to Mobile, where it would be transferred to ocean-going steamers for New England or Europe. The destiny of the river valley seemed assured. There was plenty of rich land, slaves to work it, and now sure and cheap transportation to market. This was an ideal situation, needing only a sound local circulating medium to convert it into abundant wealth. It was on this issue—the providing of such a circulating medium—that Pickens asked the people for another two-year term as Governor.

The Georgia Men, although now without their leaders, W. W. Bibb and John W. Walker, refused to let the election go by default. Dr. Henry Chambers again carried their banner to defeat, Pickens winning and again becoming "Governor and Commander-in-Chief of the State of Alabama" by a vote of 6,942 to 4,604.[2]

After the election, which was by no means exciting, a quietness settled over the State. When her citizens did gather together, the talk was mostly of cotton, acres, mules, and plowhands. Around the post offices, taverns, and business houses when politics was mentioned the name of Andrew Jackson was foremost. The people of Alabama wanted the hero of the Horseshoe and of New Orleans for President.

[1] Blue's *History of Montgomery*, p. 48.

[2] House Journal 1823, p. 25.

The country west of the Appalachians had grown in numbers and strength. This yeomanry was now striving to make its power extend to Washington. They were demanding that one of their own, a man from west of the mountains, be President of the country.

Such was the political pulse when Alabama's 1823 Assembly met in Cahawba.

The Governor sent his written message to the Assembly by J. J. Pleasants, Secretary of State. He wasted few words on formalities, but at once went straight to the question of founding the State's public institutions. The first discussed was the University. In commenting on the law already passed providing for three female institutions Pickens proposed to postpone their founding until after the site of the principal university was decided upon. Said he: "Although female education has ever been one of my favorite objects," still he was of the opinion that the establishment of these branches should be postponed. The Governor went further and declared a doubt "whether the health of any place has been sufficiently tested to warrant a preference in its favor as a site for the main institution." It is apparent that Pickens planned to delay further the establishment of the University.

The Governor made an analysis of the conditions of the circulating medium in the state, and demonstrated the unfavorable results which came to Alabama from having a large debit against it in the annual balance of trade. This situation could, in his opinion, be remedied by the Assembly's providing a sufficient and sound currency. To do this it was necessary to create a State Bank, which he believed would not only be useful to the people, but also profitable to the State.

Pickens deplored the current state of affairs in the judiciary department where litigation was disposed of on technical legal points and not on the merits. He said it rendered "the law itself a subject of reproach," and suggested as a remedy a law to exclude all questions not affecting the merits from further investigation after the rendition of judgment. Pickens also called to the Assembly's attention the fact that the decisions of the Supreme Court, while having the force of law, had never been reported. The Governor recommended that they be regularly reported and published after each term. Thus did Israel Pickens become the Father of Alabama Reports.

Pickens also recommended a general incorporation law which would relieve the Assembly of the tedium of so many incorporations and amendments thereto. The progressive-minded Governor favored improving navigation on the Tennessee and the Black Warrior, and co-operation with citizens of Tennessee in a scheme to connect the waters of the Tennessee and the Coosa, but carefully stated that the State would give encouragement and direction only to a "well adjusted individual association."

Pickens said he opposed the introduction of slaves into the State for the purpose of traffic. He declared such practice to be a public evil. He wanted to prevent such traffic if possible, but wisely warned the Assembly that "penal or restrictive laws habitually evaded or openly violated have ever proved to be demoralizing and worse than useless."

The Governor reported that he had contracted for the printing of Toulmin's Digest in New York for the sum of $4,200, and that upon Mr. Toulmin's declining the task of superintending the printing he had designated the Attorney General, Henry Hitchcock, to write the index and supervise the printing.

One of the Supreme Court Judges, Henry Y. Webb, died during the adjournment and Pickens gave notice that he had temporarily appointed Henry Minor to fill the vacancy. There were two vacancies in the Board of Trustees of the University of Alabama. R. W. Carter had died, and George W. Owen had resigned.

On Monday, November 25, the Speaker administered

the oath of office to Israel Pickens in the presence of both houses, after which his Excellency delivered an address elevated in tone and excellent in composition. He reiterated a theme ever present in his public declarations in saying: "Whatever errors our public administration may present, under whatever changes it may pass, there will remain one consolatory reflection, that a preserving principle will ever be found in an enlightened public sentiment."[1]

Very soon after this statement of policy by the Governor, Senator Hugh McVay proposed a salutary amendment to the Bank bill. The purpose of the bill was to prevent Assemblymen from doing business with the Bank by way of loan, discount, indorsement or guaranty. It also made the Assemblymen ineligible for office in the Bank until the expiration of five years, beginning January 1, 1824.[2] The Senate declined McVay's proposal except that portion dealing with eligibility for office in the Bank. In doing so it rejected a wise safeguard—one which if it had been written into law would have saved immense sums to the Bank and many unhappy experiences for Alabama's citizens.

On December 10 the bill to repeal the charter of the Planters and Merchants Bank of Huntsville was brought up in the Senate, and on motion indefinitely to postpone further consideration of the bill John Wood, Senator from Jefferson County, voted against postponement. He wanted to annul the bank's charter, but he was with the minority and the motion carried. This was the first of two historic votes cast by John Wood, of Jefferson County, in the Alabama State Senate. The full import and resulting effect of these votes could not now be foreseen or estimated, but John Wood was quite aware that his votes had considerable political sting for he obtained leave to spread his reasons for his position in the Senate Journal in order that the constituents might read them and that a true record might be

[1] Senate Journal 1823, pp. 26–27.

[2] Senate Journal 1823, p. 54.

established. He offered the following reasons to constituents for voting for the bill to annul the charter of the Planters and Merchants Bank of Huntsville:

I believe that the power that creates is competent to dissolve. If it were not the case, the safety of the people would be endangered beyond their control, providing any legislature should prove so corrupt, or so ignorant as to grant privileges to any individual or individuals, corporation or corporations that would be calculated to prejudice the interest of the great mass of the people of this State. The only alternative being to apply to a judicial tribunal, the progress of which is slow, and in some cases would amount to a denial of justice; where it would become the interest of those holding bank charters, to comply on their part so as to prevent a judicial tribunal from giving the necessary relief,[1] although calculated to destroy the best interests of the people through time.

Such a doctrine is preposterous, and fraught with all the ill consequences calculated to destroy the rights of a free people. I conceive the constitutional scruples urged against the competency of the legislature to annul or dissolve bank charters, to have no just weight; such charters not standing on the same footing of contracts contemplated in the constitution, there being no consideration paid to the State by the opposite party. The only inducement on the part of the State to grant such charters being to promote the public good; therefore it seems that whenever any institution or bank charter fails to answer the purposes for which they were intended and instead of proving a blessing, proves a curse, as the Huntsville has not[2] done, it becomes imperiously the duty of the legislature to interpose their authority in repealing such charters; any failures on their part, in my opinion amounts to a neglect of duty, as well as a flagrant violation of the constitution and a full denial of the sovereignty of the people.

(*Signed*) JOHN WOOD[3]

[1] Here Wood was referring to the fact that although quo warranto proceedings to annul the charter of the bank had already been filed in court for eighteen months, no trial had been had because the Judge of that circuit, C. C. Clay, was a stockholder and director in the bank, and being interested had disqualified himself to hear the case on its merits; yet he entered orders of continuance or postponenment.

[2] Wood later amended this "not," stating that it was a misprint.

[3] Senate Journal 1823, pp. 63–64. After John Wood published his reasons for

The mere fact that Wood thought it wise to state his reasons to his constituents and record them in the journal shows that he was aware of his political danger in casting his vote. The only bank serving the people of Jefferson County was the Huntsville Bank, and the paper of the bank was held in considerable amount by citizens of the county. It was almost the only circulating medium in use in the neighborhood. True, the paper passed at discount, but if the charter was annulled the holders feared they would lose almost all instead of about twenty per cent, and at the same time they would be deprived of their only circulating medium. Only those people who had or depended upon "hard money" were so void of self-interest as actually to support Wood even though many cordially agreed with him. Furthermore, among these Jefferson County citizens the Huntsville Bank had supporters, because many of them had come from Tennessee by way of Tennessee Valley and had friends and relatives in Madison County and Huntsville. While Wood's constituents did not love the Planters and Merchants Bank nor approve its conduct, they did not want their friends to suffer and hence did not look with favor upon the Senator's attempt to annul the bank's charter.

Three days after his vote on the Huntsville Bank matter—on December 10—John Wood cast his second historic vote. Disregarding the political consequences he again voted his conviction—he was that kind of man. Time would determine whether John Wood was strong enough with his people to vote his convictions and still be re-elected. A resolution was before the Senate proposing General Andrew Jackson as a suitable candidate for President of the United States. It passed on the third reading, 12 for and 7 against.[1] John Wood voted against the resolution—and Jackson.

voting to annul the bank's charter David Moore, Senator from Madison County, set forth the reasons for his vote, stating therein why the Huntsville Bank's charter should *not* be annulled. Senate Journal 1823, p. 68.

[1] Senate Journal 1823, p. 83.

This vote, when taken together with his vote on annulling the charter of the Huntsville Bank, was by a twist of fate to have a far-reaching influence in Alabama. Time would bring his action to fruit. Meantime, the same resolution was before the House, where it passed by a vote of 39 to 18.[1]

Most of the negative votes on the Jackson resolution in the House were from Representatives from the planter counties of South Alabama. These men were fond of the General as a military man and a patriot, but they feared him as a President. They were not so much anti-Jackson as they were pro-conservative. Regardless of the good faith of those in Alabama who opposed Jackson, the mere fact of opposition to the hero of New Orleans, and of Pensacola too for that matter, raised a storm of indignation from Jackson partisans all over the state. So strong and fervid was the reaction that the men who voted against the General in the House felt constrained to set forth in the House Journal their reasons for voting against the Jackson resolution. The anti-Jackson men stated:

> We neither condemn nor censure the opinion of those who voted in the affirmative; nor do we intend any detraction from the well earned character and splendid reputation of General Andrew Jackson. We view him as a sound politician, a true republican, and a firm friend of the rights of man. But . . . [and here they offer three reasons why they voted against the Jackson resolution]:
>
> *1st.* Suffrage was given to the people by the constitution and nowhere in that instrument is power given to the legislature to determine by law, resolution or otherwise, whom the people should vote for for President of the United States. We believe the resolutions go beyond the constitutional power of the General Assembly.
>
> *2nd.* Legislative capacity to give assistance to a candidate for office is deprecated and dreaded.
>
> *3rd.* We have no general expression from our constituents authorizing the declarations contained in the resolutions.

[1] House Journal 1823, p. 77.

This statement was signed by the following men:

JOHN BECK	Z. MERRIWETHER
JOHN G. CREAGH	JOHN M. MCLAUGHLIN
CHARLES A. DENNIS	SAMUEL W. OLIVER
JAMES H. FITTS	GEORGE PHILLIPS
WILLIAM FLUKER	GEORGE WEISSINGER
ISHAM HARRISON	HARDIN PERKINS
SAMUEL HAINES	JULIUS H. SIMS
J. D. LISTER	JOHN W. SMITH
W. W. M'CONNICO	JOHN L. TINDALL[1]

These may or may not have been sound and fair reasons for voting against the General, but they certainly did not convince or satisfy his friends. He who held elective office and was *not for* the General need must be a strong man in his own bailiwick to hold that opinion and still remain in popular favor.

Almost in that very position was Governor Pickens. He was not against Jackson, and still he was not an advocate of the General's policies. When the resolution was presented for his signature he declined to sign it, but uttered a veto message which was perhaps more pleasing to the Jackson men than the resolution itself. Among other things, the veto message stated that "no language would be too strong for the Governor's official and cordial assent. . . . Indeed, our language is wanting in richness to furnish adequate terms of commendation of the military service of our hero." Pickens refers to Jackson as one of the saviours of the country, and added, "and to none is the recollection of his services more dear than to the people of Alabama."

The Governor then set forth the reason for his veto to be "because the resolution was not fairly within the legitimate sphere of legislation," and concluded with the flattering statement, "I can also add with the most perfect sincerity, that there is no individual among the distinguished sages whose names have been in contemplation for the high office

[1] House Journal 1823, pp. 120–121.

in question in whose favor I would more reluctantly withhold my signature."[1]

No effort was made to override the Governor's veto because Pickens was a powerful and popular man in Alabama and had the respect of all the Assemblymen. They knew it was a conscientious decision and, besides, the veto message itself pleased them. What the House did was to order the public printer to print immediately two hundred copies of the message. Next year, 1824, was a Presidential election year in which its political usefulness would be greatest. General Jackson was definitely on his long and tumultuous upward course to the Presidency of the United States.

On December 20, Governor Pickens finally got his long-wanted State Bank. The preamble to the act declares its purpose:

> Whereas it is deemed highly important to provide for the safe and profitable investment of such public funds as may now or hereafter be in possession of the State, and to secure to the community the benefits as far as may be, of an extended and undepreciating currency:[2]

The law provided that the capital of the Bank be composed of $100,000 subscribed by the Trustees of the University, the proceeds of the three-per-cent grant to the State, other State funds as from the seat-of-government land grant, and a loan to be effected by the Governor aided by five commissioners appointed by the Assembly.

As soon as the Governor signed the Bank law the Assembly met in session in the evening of the same day for the purpose of locating the Bank. The seat of government was chosen with 42 votes over Florence, which received 19, Tuskaloosa 9, and Mobile 6. It is perhaps significant that the ballot was taken on "Seat of Government" and *not* on Cahawba, the suggestion being that wherever the seat of

[1] House Journal 1823, p. 138 (December 22, 1823).

[2] Acts 1823, p. 3.

government might be, there also would be the headquarters of the Bank of the State of Alabama.

In joint session the Assembly chose Andrew Pickens as President of the Bank. He had no opposition for the post, but when the directors were chosen there were twenty-six nominees for the twelve places. The following were elected:

Alexander Pope	David White	Horatio G. Perry
William Aylett	Gilbert Shearer	Joseph Pickens
William Taylor	William Chisolm	Thomas B. Rutherford
Thomas H. Wiley	Jesse Beene	Henry Hitchcock[1]

The Commissioners elected to serve with the Governor in effecting a loan to the Bank were:

George Phillips	Thomas Casey	Thomas H. Wiley[2]
Alexander Pope	Walter Crenshaw	

Governor Pickens had reason to be satisfied with the performance of the 1823 Assembly. Most of the program presented by him had been carried out as he had presented it. He now had the sort of State Bank he wanted, with good men chosen as officers and directors. He had met the "Jackson for President" group in collision without suffering any loss of favor. Even the unexpected shifts and changes in the state's official offices had been taken in stride. George W. Owen resigned as a Trustee of the University because he had been elected a Representative in Congress. George Buchanan, a friend of Pickens, was chosen as his successor.[3] Bolling Hall was elected as a Trustee in place of Henry Hitchcock, resigned, and Arthur F. Hopkins took the place of John McKinley, resigned. R. W. Carter died, and Samuel Oliver was chosen in his place as Trustee. Henry Minor resigned, and David Moore was elected Trustee in his stead.

William I. Adair, from Madison County, suddenly resigned as Speaker of the House without stating any reason.[4] It appeared that he did so in order to become a candidate

[1] Senate Journal 1823, p. 122.

[2] Senate Journal 1823, p. 125.

[3] Senate Journal 1823, p. 60.

[4] House Journal 1823, p. 124.

for the circuit judgeship which C. C. Clay, of Madison, resigned. However, Henry Minor defeated Adair for the place, 40 votes to 35.[1] None of these changes damaged the young commonwealth of Alabama. It is a compliment to her citizens that those who were qualified were ready to serve the State although frequently they did so at a sacrifice.

Pickens not only guided the ship of state, but he personally attended to many small matters which required patience and skill. He commissioned one Ferdinand Sannoner to make a map of the state. Sannoner completed the map from the available information, and promised a more perfect map later. The Governor informed the Assembly that the map was in the Executive Office for use and inspection by the General Assembly.[2] Pickens, in his double capacity as Governor of the State and President of the Board of Trustees of the University, also procured (and probably designed) the seal of the University of Alabama. He purchased it from George S. Gaines at a cost of $50.[3]

The Assembly enacted Alabama's first law controlling the practice of "physic and surgery" in the state. Five medical boards were created, one in each of the towns of Huntsville, Mobile, Tuskaloosa, Cahawba, and Claiborne.[4] This was a necessary and progressive law. The fundamental principle of the law, that of letting the medical profession regulate itself, is still in full and successful operation in Alabama one hundred and twenty-four years later.

The appropriations made by the Assembly in 1823 were the usual and ordinary sort except in a few instances. Henry Hitchcock was paid $1,200 for preparing the index to

[1] House Journal 1823, p. 124.

[2] House Journal 1823, p. 114. Sannoner was paid $120 for making the map. Acts 1823, p. 106. Today it would be priceless.

[3] Senate Journal 1823, p. 101.

[4] Acts 1823, p. 45. See "Alabama Doctor," *The Alabama Lawyer,* July 1945; and *The Journal of the Medical Association of the State of Alabama,* October and November 1945.

Toulmin's Digest and for his expenses to New York.[1] Jesse Beene, Clerk of the Supreme Court, was awarded $268.13 for services rendered in State causes, and for *recording in a well-bound book the decisions of the Supreme Court from its commencement to this time.*[2] This book was certainly the first volume of Alabama Reports, even if it was not printed. Henry Minor, however, does not mention Beene's book in his "Introductory Notice" in his Volume I of Alabama Reports.

The Assembly provided $800 for the purpose of carrying the State Bank into operation. The money was to be drawn on the certificate of the Governor.[3] The cost of starting the Bank was modest indeed, compared to the influence it was expected to, and did, exert.

Another amendment to the charter of the Planters and Merchants Bank was put through the Assembly by its friends and enemies acting together. The amendment kept the bank in operation but required it to resume specie payments on or before August 1, 1824, and not to suspend them thereafter without permission of the General Assembly.[4]

Several towns were incorporated. Among them were Greensborough[5] and Greenville.[6] The town of Claiborne started an Academy.[7] The Assembly chartered a company[8] to improve the Coosa and unite its waters with those of the Tennessee. The law contemplated the financial support of the citizens of the Alabama River basin. It was definitely

[1] Acts 1823, p. 107.

[2] Acts 1823, p. 101 (Sec. 48). [3] Acts 1823, p. 103 (Sec. 63).

[4] Acts 1823, p. 28. A resolution was also adopted by the Assembly to prevent any judge from riding the Fifth Circuit (which included Madison County) who was interested, however remotely, in the Huntsville Bank until quo warranto depending in said court was finally decided. Acts 1823, p. 119. Another resolution provided that the State Treasurer should present the Planters and Merchants Bank notes to it for payment and if not paid that he might sue the Bank, and in case of an appeal, the appellate court was to add a penalty of 15 per cent to the judgment and costs. Acts 1823, p. 118.

[5] Acts 1823, p. 58 (December 24, 1823).

[6] Acts 1823, p. 60 (December 30, 1823).

[7] Acts 1823, p. 59 (December 31, 1823).

[8] Acts 1823, p. 62.

a bid for progressive business enterprise, coupled with the intent to influence political forces to continue the seat of government in the valley of the Alabama. The plan contemplated boats up to fifty tons burthen to Wetumpka, and twenty tons above the shoals.[1] The Huntsville Library was chartered.[2]

Sam Dale finally completely lost his pension. The Assembly repealed the grant in toto,[3] but Dale liked the flavor of the State's money. Having had a taste of it he was determined to hang on if he could, so he went to Court only to have the Supreme Court declare that the Assembly had the right to take his pension away.[4] State pensions were not favorably regarded in Alabama, even for heroes.

The Year 1824

and the General Assembly—Annual Session of 1824

The people of Alabama received their first fervid partisan interest in national politics from the inspiring personality of General Andrew Jackson. This frontiersman had become a popular hero to them by marching his troops all over North Alabama and finally destroying the Creek war party in the dramatic battle at Horseshoe Bend. After the victory the General had erected Fort Jackson in the center of the state and thence gone down the Alabama River to Mobile. His campaign against the British in Louisiana, resulting in his most celebrated victory at New Orleans and his subsequent strong-arm invasion of Spanish Pensacola, had endeared the gallant soldier to the residents of the state living in that border region. The man had established himself step by step with the people in all sections of the state. In the

[1] Two weeks before this law was signed, on December 16, the steamboat *Henderson* arrived at Cahawba from Mobile in less than three days, the quickest trip yet made. The Assemblymen envisioned a mighty inland system of waterways as they enacted this legislation to join the Coosa with the Tennessee.

[2] Acts 1823, p. 71. [3] Acts 1823, p. 115.

[4] Dale vs. The Governor, 3 Stewart, p. 387.

General was a fine combination: a man of the people, from west of the Appalachians, and a national hero with apparently enough strength to crack the tradition and sequence of eastern Presidents. Jackson, in spite of his almost universal popularity, did have some opposition in Alabama from the John Quincy Adams supporters. One of the first evidences of the efforts of this group was disclosed when in November, 1823, Israel Pickens advocated that Alabama's Presidential electors be chosen by districts.[1] Pickens knew that if the electors were chosen on a state-wide basis General Jackson would receive all five of Alabama's votes. If a district basis was used, perhaps two electors from Southern Alabama, where Carolina and Virginia planters were influential, might be snared for Adams. This plan failed. Later in this same session of the Assembly the resolution approving Jackson as a candidate for the Presidency was adopted by a substantial majority only to die by Governor Pickens' veto. These maneuvers had definitely stirred in the state an interest in national politics and a passion for Andrew Jackson.

When 1824, the Presidential election year, came around local issues were put aside for the bigger event—the nationwide contest for the Presidency. This attitude of quietness in local public affairs was intensified by reason of the fact that most of Alabama's necessities had already been achieved. Her general and local governments were established and functioning satisfactorily. Moreover, under the Constitution adopted in Huntsville in 1819, if major changes in the state's government were desired they must be made by the General Assembly in the annual 1825 session. The contribution of the 1824 Assembly to any developments which might then come to pass was to write the apportionment law under which the momentous Assembly of 1825 would be selected.

Cahawba, lethargic, and in a sort of nervous repose like

[1] Senate Journal 1823, p. 12.

a man waiting to stand trial for his life, nevertheless was still the seat of the state's government and as such commanded a certain respect and authority in spite of her vulnerable position. The town had stagnated. People were afraid to make plans and even those established in the city were apprehensive. Nevertheless, then as now, what political activity did arise over the commonwealth finally funneled on the capital. Because of the absence of any general party organization in the state and perhaps also because of the Pickens effort in 1823 to devise a plan to make possible the capture of some electors for Adams, a sort of informal campaign by groups came into existence to make sure that Alabama's electors would be Jackson men.

This movement finally developed so that a planned meeting was held in the courthouse in Perry County in May, 1824, in which it was decided that the Jackson supporters should choose representatives from all over the state to meet at Cahawba during the June term of the Supreme Court.[1] The Adams supporters quickly copied the plan and so did the Crawford partisans. The Georgian was vigorously trying to win Southern and Western support.

The purpose of the several conventions was to frame a sort of organization which would aid in the choosing of electors favorable to the group's candidate. The Jackson men did the best job, and they also had the best candidate. When the ballots were counted in November the General had a majority in every Alabama county excepting Montgomery, Greene, and Butler. The state's five electoral votes were Jackson's and her people were his loyal supporters. Woe to the political security of him who opposed the General in the state of Alabama.

The Assembly of 1824 convened in Cahawba on November 15, 1824. One week later the election returns were published in the local paper.[2] The overwhelming victory of

[1] *Cahawba Press*, May 8, 1824; June 18, 1824; June 28, 1824; and July 7, 1824.

[2] *Cahawba Press*, November 22, 1824.

General Jackson was the main topic of conversation among the Assemblymen. His supporters were jubilant, the Crawford men were openly disappointed and those for Adams reserved.

Governor Pickens, being wise in politics, no doubt foresaw Jackson's victory, but this same wisdom guided him to avoid the subject in his message to the Assembly. The message,[1] delivered November 16, six days before the details of the vote were known in Cahawba, was confined to what Pickens considered the internal affairs of Alabama, deserving the attention of the Assembly. National politics were not mentioned even by indirection.

The Governor referred to General Lafayette, now a visitor in this country, in glowing terms. He expressed the opinion that our remote situation might deny us the honor and gratification of a particular visit from this generous benefactor of our country. Pickens just did not know his man, as his later experiences were to prove.

Pickens mentioned that the site of the University had not yet been selected and recommended that this be settled *before* or *after* the 1825 session because of the weighty subjects to be considered at that session. His real object was to defer further the establishment of the University of Alabama, because the Bank had not yet received the $100,000 which the University was to contribute to the Bank's capital. At the time $39,667.31¼ of the University's funds had gone into the Bank fund. For this money Pickens said that the faith and credit of the State and the whole of its productive resources and the conscience of every succeeding legislature acting under oath of the Constitution was a guaranty of security. "To question these securities," said the Governor, "would be a reflection on the honour and good faith of our own Government and people."

The "three per cent fund" provided the Bank with $31,-711.01, and the Cahawba grant $37,835.49½. The three

[1] Senate Journal 1824, pp. 5 *et seq.*

funds together totaled $109,213.81¾, so Pickens called the President and Directors together in Cahawba on July 2, 1824, and completed the organization of the Bank. An additional $100,000 was borrowed for ten years from the Phoenix Bank in New York at six-per-cent interest payable semi-annually.[1] The Governor further stated that the necessary materials had been procured and the Bank was expected to commence its operation in a few days.

The Assembly was informed that the Huntsville Bank situation was still unsettled. The quo warranto proceedings had been dismissed, but only partial resumption of specie payments had been effected and annulment of the Bank's charter appeared imminent.

The old Pickens theme of protesting against the technicalities of the law appeared again—this time more in detail because the Governor had little else to submit to the Assembly. In apparent wrath, Pickens said: "The mere formality of pleading requires a distinct class of legal professors." He repeated his suggestion of a way to remedy the evil.

The Governor told the Assembly that the census returns would shortly be available for their use in writing the apportionment law required by the Constitution. He laid before the Assembly a communication from the State of Ohio proposing a plan for gradual emancipation and colonization of the slaves, and then awaited the action of his legislature.

The first business was a motion for a committee to consider the expediency of establishing a branch of the State Bank at Huntsville or some other place in the Tennessee Valley. A committee was appointed for this purpose. When the same action was tried for Montgomery, the motion was rejected.[2] Under the Constitution only one branch of the

[1] The five loan Commissioners appointed Senator William R. King as their agent, and he procured the loan. Senate Journal 1824, p. 66.

[2] Senate Journal 1824, p. 15.

Bank could be established at any one session of the Assembly. Huntsville had beaten Montgomery to the punch—at least for the year 1824.

The Assembly fixed a time for a joint session in which to elect a United States Senator. Dr. Chambers, after observing the political barometer, had swung toward the Jackson line. He was opposed by the fading but still dangerous William Kelly. Representative Beck notified the Assembly that he was confined to his room and too ill to come to the State House and cast his vote. The Assembly appointed a committee to receive Beck's vote in his room. This action was strongly opposed.[1] Mr. Beck voted for Kelly, but Chambers won the senatorship 41 to 36.[2]

A report on the Bank was made by the Committee. It contained about the same information given the Assembly by the Governor, but added that "Everything seems favorable to the successful progress of the institution."[3]

The Assembly unanimously re-elected Andrew Pickens President of the Bank and chose for Directors for the next year

Thomas M. Wiley	Uriah G. Mitchell
John J. Crocheron	Edwin Curtis
Alexander Pope	David White
Dr. George Phillips	Jesse Beene
Gilbert Shearer	James Saffold
Horatio G. Perry	Thomas D. King[4]

The next day after the election Alexander Pope resigned and Thomas M. Wiley and David White declined to serve.[5] In the places of these three, Fielding Vaughan, Robert G. Gordon, and Jason Gardner were elected.[6]

The Trustees of the University of Alabama were elected by districts as follows:

1st Judicial District: William Crawford and James Dellett

[1] Senate Journal 1824, pp. 69, 70.
[2] Senate Journal 1824, p. 73.
[3] Senate Journal 1824, p. 73.
[4] Senate Journal 1824, p. 99.
[5] Senate Journal 1824, p. 116, p. 123.
[6] Senate Journal 1824, p. 143.

2nd Judicial District: Dr. George Phillips and Bolling Hall

3rd Judicial District: Dr. Jack Shackelford and Hume R. Field

4th Judicial District: Nicholas Davis and Thomas Wooldridge

5th Judicial District: Thomas Fearn and David Moore

6th Judicial District: Samuel W. Oliver and Clement C. Billingslea

The most important law enacted during the session was the apportionment law.[1] The distribution of power according to population under the democratic process would determine the fate of Cahawba as the seat of government. The Representatives were apportioned as follows:

County		County	
Jackson	4	Greene	3
Madison	5	Marengo	1
Limestone	4	Perry	2
Lauderdale	3	Dallas	3
Morgan	2	Wilcox	1
Lawrence	3	Autauga	2
Franklin	2	Montgomery and that part of Pike taken from Montgomery	3
Marion and that part of Fayette and Walker taken from Marion	1	Butler	1
St. Clair	2	Henry, Covington and that part of Pike taken from Henry	2
Shelby	1	Washington	1
Blount	1	Monroe	2
Jefferson and that part of Walker taken from Jefferson	3	Conecuh	2
Tuscaloosa and that part of Walker and Fayette taken from Tuscaloosa	4	Clarke	1
Pickens and that part of Fayette taken from Pickens	1	Baldwin	1
		Mobile	1
		Bibb	1

The senatorial districts were made up as follows, each district being entitled to one Senator:

Mobile, Washington, and Baldwin

Jefferson

Tuscaloosa

[1] Acts 1824, p. 3.

Pike, Covington, and Henry
Butler and Conecuh
Monroe and Wilcox
Clarke and Marengo
Greene
Montgomery
Dallas
Bibb and Perry
Shelby and Autauga
Blount and St. Clair
Pickens, Fayette, Walker, and Marion
Morgan
Franklin
Lawrence
Lauderdale
Limestone
Madison
Jackson

Considering the great preponderance of population of the Warrior-Tombigbe and Tennessee Valley sections over the Alabama River system section, the latter did not fare too badly in composition of the senatorial districts. Considered from the geographical point of view, it appeared possible that the Alabama River system group might gain control of the Senate. In event of circumstances resulting in a tie vote in the Senate, the seat of government under the law would remain at Cahawba. For this to happen a Senator would have to be absent or fail to vote because there were twenty-one Senators. Such a situation might develop in event of a close vote. Of course geographical appraisals of the expected vote could be based only on the interest of a district. The final vote of any Senator on the question of removal of the seat of government would be determined by who that Senator was, as well as by the pressure exerted on him by his constituents.

The Assembly marked time with legislation at the 1824 session, taking care of routine matters only. One exception was the repeal of the June term of the Supreme Court.[1] The appropriations were about as usual. William Kelly was paid $100 for assisting in the quo warranto proceeding against the Huntsville Bank.[2] The heirs of Harry Toulmin received $100 as a final payment for his services in digesting the laws of the state.[3] There were several payments

[1] Acts 1824, p. 7.
[2] Acts 1824, p. 48 (61).
[3] Acts 1824, p. 48 (63).

for repairs to the State House. These appear to have been small jobs because Phillip Flanagan got only $10 "for his repairs to the State House" and Mathew D. Thomason received $54.75 "for repairs to the furniture and the State House."[1] He received another $35 for "keeping the State House, and superintending the putting in a new gutter, and repairing the roof, and repairing the Representative Hall and the furniture belonging to the State House."[2]

The Mobile Republican Greens were incorporated with Jeremiah Austill as Captain.[3] A similar company styled The Montgomery Light Infantry, with J. Goldthwaite as Captain, was chartered for Montgomery.[4] The Mobile Society of Literature was chartered.[5] Many of the charter members were former residents of St. Stephens. During the two terms of Governor Pickens laws emancipating slaves were numerous and followed a set form, but the 1824 Assembly enacted a manumission law which differed from its predecessors in that a large number of persons were freed at the same time with the recital that they were "sundry persons of colour, descendants of the ancient creole population" of the city of Mobile.[6]

In one of the most ornate and extravagant resolutions ever adopted by an Alabama Assembly, the Governor was directed to invite Major General Lafayette "to honor the State of Alabama with a visit, and in event of his acceptance of such invitation, he be received in such manner as shall best comport with the important services he has rendered the American people." The Governor was authorized to draw on the treasury for the funds necessary to carry the resolution into effect.[7] After the French General had completed his tour through the state and the Assemblymen

[1] Acts 1824, p. 48 (64).
[2] Acts 1824, p. 48 (66).
[3] Acts 1824, p. 89.
[4] Acts 1824, p. 91.
[5] Acts 1824, p. 103.
[6] Acts 1824, p. 122.
[7] Acts 1824, pp. 131, 132.

were informed of the cost they were amazed at their own extravagance.

Another resolution was passed praising Sam Dale for gallant service in the Creek and Seminole wars and asking the Federal Government to pay him for his expenses and losses, and for furnishing supplies to troops. The resolution included a vivid account of many of Dale's most dramatic experiences.[1]

On Christmas Day, 1824, the Assembly adjourned, having first by resolution delivered the care of the State House and furniture to the doorkeeper of the Senate, excepting the "room occupied by the Secretary, Comptroller and Treasurer," and having directed him to cause all the furniture belonging to the State House to be deposited in the Senate Chamber, and to lock the door and retain the keys thereof until the next session of the General Assembly.

To make doubly sure that no one would induce the doorkeeper to permit use of the furniture during the adjournment, the Assembly *resolved further*, "That it shall not be lawful for any use to be made of the furniture deposited as aforesaid under any pretense whatever previous to the meeting of the next legislature."

It would seem that someone had been poaching on the State House equipment, probably under pretense of authority to use it. The Assembly meant to stop the practice.

The Year 1825

Seventh Annual Session Begun on the Third Monday in November, 1825

For sheer excitement and enduring interest, the year 1825 exceeds all others in the history of Alabama. Perhaps waiting for the dramatic events which were known to be coming added tension and suspense to the interest of the times. In the sober records of the state's annals the year 1825

[1] Acts 1824, pp. 137, 138.

stands apart, aflame with feeling and action which lasted far longer than the lives of the men who created it.

In this memorable twelvemonth came the shocking news that the adored Andrew Jackson, after receiving 99 electoral votes to the 84 received by John Quincy Adams, was still short of a majority and, the election of a President being thus thrown into the House of Representatives, the mighty warrior had lost to the little man from Massachusetts.

The Alabama partisans just couldn't accept an Adams victory; they had convinced themselves that Jackson couldn't lose. It was known that the General had many more popular votes and about 15 more electoral votes than any other candidate in the race. With Henry Clay, a Kentuckian, polling 37 electoral votes and controlling the votes of three states, and the fourth candidate, William H. Crawford, of Georgia, polling 41 electoral votes and sure of controlling three states, it seemed utterly impossible that the little Easterner from the Bay State could win the Presidency from the hero of New Orleans.

But Adams did it! When the result of the count of the electoral vote disclosed that no candidate had a majority, the Senate withdrew and the House proceeded to elect a President, voting by states. Henry Clay, having received the fewest number of electoral votes, was eliminated and the contest was between Jackson, Adams, and Crawford. There were twenty-four states and 24 votes. A tense gallery awaited the announcement of the result by the tellers, Daniel Webster and John Randolph.

Adams received the votes of thirteen states—a majority of one—and thus was chosen President. General Jackson received the votes of seven states and Crawford that of four states. "There was some clapping and exultation in the galleries and some slight hissing followed. The House suspended its proceedings until the galleries were cleared."[1]

The news of the defeat of General Jackson at first stunned

[1] Gales & Seaton, *Debates in Congress*, Volume 1, pp. 526–527.

and then embittered the Alabamians. They regarded the choice of Adams as a cheat and a steal which circumvented the will of the people of the nation. Jackson's defeat was looked upon as a calamity to the nation and an affront to the suffrage of the citizens. There was some loose talk of not accepting the result and more to the effect that they wanted to fight the campaign over again and hold the election over again. When it was learned that Henry Clay, the Kentuckian, a man from west of the mountains, had delivered to Adams the votes which made him President and at the same time vanquished Jackson, the Alabama partisans were astonished and angry. It was like being deserted by one of your own for a stranger. Later, after Adams had become President, he made Clay his Secretary of State, and many were the Alabamians who openly charged that Clay had traded the winning votes to Adams for the high post. Many, too, there were who now were determined that Henry Clay should never realize his ambition to be President. Among these was Andrew Jackson.

The circumstances of the defeat of Jackson served to cause men to make of their hero a martyr too. Jackson men who had been mere followers or mild in their loyalty now loved him with a fury which would not countenance even a difference of opinion. One had to be a Jackson man or be against him. This surge of spontaneous feeling was general over the state. It entered into every fabric of life. Its effect was mainly in matters public and political, but friendships were born or severed because of Jackson, business connections were altered on his account, and duels were fought in blind efforts to appease the feelings of men.

So intense was the Jackson devotion that there was scarcely any abatement of feeling between February 8, the day of his defeat, and the August elections, although in the interval between the State officially received the American friend, the celebrated Marie Joseph Paul Roch Yves Gilbert du Motier, Marquis de Lafayette.

Governor Pickens had told the Assembly in November, 1824, that our "remote situation" would deprive us of seeing the Marquis. However, before Christmas Senator King sent the word from Washington that the "Nation's Benefactor" would accept an invitation to visit Alabama, and the Assembly outdid itself with its resolution inviting the distinguished guest. Senator King advised Governor Pickens that the Marquis's itinerary was by ship to Charleston, South Carolina, then a short stay in Savannah, a stop in Milledgeville, the capital of Georgia, and thence through the Creek country to Montgomery. From Montgomery to Mobile the French nobleman would travel by river boat and from Mobile to New Orleans by lake steamer.

With this communication Senator King retired from the scene and the glory and the burden of entertaining the famous guest fell to Israel Pickens.

The Governor, in order to be ready for his coming guest, needed to move fast. It was almost time for the Assembly to adjourn, but Pickens immediately apprised them of the situation as disclosed to him by Senator King, and the resolution of invitation, which also included authority to pay the expenses of entertainment out of the public funds, was quickly adopted.[1] Immediately thereafter the Assembly adjourned, the members leaving for their homes by steamboat and horseback. Within a week they had spread the news so that the entire population of Alabama knew that this almost legendary hero of the Revolutionary War would visit Alabama in the coming March or the first days of April. Everyone was excited.

The business of preparing to receive the great man required planning and execution under the most trying circumstances. The mails were slow, irregular, and undependable. Still mail by "express," that is, by mounted courier, was a help but it was not available between all stations. There was no other method of public communication. From

[1] Acts 1824, p. 131 (December 24, 1824).

William R. King

his plantation home near Greensborough Israel Pickens considered the intricate problems which would be presented in sequence once the French nobleman arrived in the frontier state of Alabama, and decided that Alabama would spare no effort or expense in honoring her renowned guest. Pickens had been informed by Senator King of the travel route of the expected visitor and the approximate schedule. Basing his plans on this information, the Governor carefully selected committees in Montgomery, Cahawba, and Mobile, through which local organizations the hospitality of the State was to be made personal and effective.

In Montgomery, the first town Lafayette would reach after leaving the Creek Indian Nation, it was proposed to have a public reception to be followed by a formal ball in the evening. But Alabama had no orchestra or band measuring up to the demands of this gala occasion. The Governor immediately met this need by writing to New Orleans and making arrangements for a band to make the long trip across Lake Pontchartrain and up the Alabama River to Montgomery.[1] Arrangement of details at such great distances required so much time that it was well that Pickens had nearly three months in which to perfect his arrangements.

Because Lafayette's route from the Ocmulgee River in Georgia to Line Creek in Alabama, not far east of Montgomery, was through the Creek Nation, some place had to be selected at which the Alabama emissaries could first see and welcome their guest, and also agreement had to be made with the State of Georgia as to the place where it would surrender the Marquis and Alabama would receive him.

Pickens solved this perplexing social problem by naming General Thomas W. Farrar, a lawyer residing in Elyton,

[1] The band arrived and performed, but one of the members, Joseph Toussint, never got back to New Orleans. One Reuben Green Bates murdered him in the night time. Blue's *History of Montgomery*, pp. 54–55.

Jefferson County, as ambassador to meet General Lafayette in Georgia and to present to him Alabama's official invitation. Farrar requested two gentlemen from Mobile, Anthony Labuzan and Major Willoughby Barton, to accompany him on his mission. The Governor also designated two military men to accompany his emissary. They were Colonel Dickson and Major Coles. These five men journeyed to Georgia, passed through the capital, Milledgeville, and rested in Augusta.

Here Farrar formally delivered Alabama's invitation and the General made a warm-hearted reply, acknowledging his friendship for his hosts and his pleasure in accepting the hospitality tendered him. He also insisted that the Alabama Committee travel with his entourage through the Indian country. Recognizing his responsibility, General Farrar accepted for himself and Anthony Labuzan and they remained with the French General until he was safely delivered to Governor Pickens in Montgomery.

Meanwhile, the Governor had not been idle. He was in constant correspondence with his committees at Mobile, Cahawba, and Montgomery, arranging the exact details for the entertainment of the General as he toured through the state. A special welcoming group to receive General Lafayette from the Georgia escort at the Chattahoochee was named. Here the military men were pre-eminent. Major General William Taylor, highest ranking officer in the state, was in command. General Thomas S. Woodward was charged with the duty of seeing the guest safely through the Creek country. Woodward was part Creek Indian, spoke the language, was acquainted with the country, and had the respect of every chief and warrior in the Creek Nation. Colonel John Murphy, of Monroe County, later to be Governor, was there. General Sam Dale, the old Indian fighter, in full uniform, could not miss the show although he had to ride two hundred and fifty miles on horseback in order to be present. Two cavalry troops in full force and in dress uniform were present to honor the General when he should set foot on the soil of Alabama. Captain Moore's troop from Claiborne had ridden over two hundred miles, and Captain Abercrombie's troop from Montgomery had ridden a hundred miles under adverse conditions and at their own expense to provide a mounted guard of honor when the Georgia escort should surrender the famous visitor.

Perhaps the best account of Lafayette's reception is given by General Woodward.[1] He says it was the "most imposing show he ever witnessed." When the Georgia escort approached the east bank of the Chattahoochee River they were met by Chilly McIntosh, son of William McIntosh, Creek Chief of Coweta, and fifty Indian warriors "stripped naked and finely painted." The Indians had a sulky to which was attached drag ropes. The General entered the sulky and was drawn on the ferry by the warriors. When the ferry reached the Alabama side of the river the Indians seized the drag ropes and rapidly hauled the sulky with the Marquis aboard, some eighty yards to the top of the river bank where stood the Alabama delegation.

Chilly McIntosh now stepped in front of his warriors and introduced Lafayette to Governor Pickens' representative, Bolling Hall, with these words: "General Lafayette, the American friend. Mr. Hall, of Alabama." Mr. Hall then presented the other members of the delegation to General Lafayette.

After the ceremonies at the river the throng proceeded to Fort Mitchell hill near by, where a large group of Creek Indians with the Little Prince at its head was gathered. The Little Prince made a speech of welcome to the French Chief in the Indian tongue. This was followed by a ball game in which two hundred Indians participated, each trying to outdo the other in the presence of the honored visitor.

Woodward also recounts how Whiskey John, a Creek warrior notorious as a whiskey-drinker, met the Marquis.

[1] Woodward's *Reminiscences*, p. 66, *et seq.*

One Captain Anthony, a practical joker, told John that since everyone else had addressed the French Chief it was his duty to say something to him on behalf of those who loved whiskey. John watched for his chance and when it came he bowed low to the General as he had seen the others do. The General immediately removed his hat, thinking he had met another Chief. John straightened himself to his full height: "You French Chief. Me Whiskey Chief. You give me one bottle full. I drink him good." The General, quickly comprehending the situation, told John that while he didn't drink whiskey he would see to it that John's bottle was filled.

After the ceremonies attendant upon the reception of the General were over the hard business of getting everybody to Montgomery began. It was indeed a picturesque and colorful cavalcade—the aging but robust General wearing a resplendent uniform, accompanied always by his dog, "Quiz," and attended by his faithful but harassed manservant, Bastien. Also accompanying the Marquis was his son-in-law, Lavasseur, who acted as his secretary. The great man rode in state in a four-wheeled barouche, while his uniformed escort preceded him, flanked him, and followed him on this long journey through the primeval forests of Alabama. It was in the early spring and the rains had swollen every creek and made the road a quagmire. The bright blue broadcloth and gold-trimmed uniforms of the cavalry troopers were soon covered with mud. Many a spirited thoroughbred wallowed on his belly in the bog up to the ornamented saddlecloth as the cavalry divided the job of testing the road and bridges and patrolling the guests, both as a mark of respect and to insure protection.

General J. B. Chambers was stationed at Line Creek, westerly boundary of the Creek Nation. From this post he received messages by riders informing him as to the progress of the Lafayette party toward Montgomery. From time to time he dispatched couriers with this information for the Governor, who had come from the capital at Cahawba to receive his guest in Montgomery.

At long last, on Sunday, April 3, 1825, the great man arrived in Montgomery. He and his escort were greeted by the cheers of a great crowd. Leading citizens were busy everywhere seeing that no detail of the welcome was overlooked. Captain J. Goldthwaite with his handsomely uniformed Montgomery Light Infantry made a dazzling show, even when compared to the dashing cavalry escorts who had now been riding together every day for almost a month. Atop Capitol Hill Lafayette was received by the Governor and other distinguished citizens of the state amid the cheers of the multitude. The General responded warmly to the addresses of welcome made by Governor Pickens, John D. Bibb, and Bolling Hall, Sr. After the curiosity of the people had been somewhat satisfied, the Lafayette party was escorted to the residence of Mr. John Edmondson on Commerce Street. This was perhaps the finest home in the city and had been procured and fitted out especially for the occasion. The pantry was stocked with the finest French food and wines for entertainment of the General and his party. Israel Pickens was a magnificent host.

The following night a grand ball, with Lafayette as guest of honor, was given in the second story of Colonel Freeny's brick building at the southwest corner of Commerce and Tallapoosa Streets. Invitations to this ball were at a premium. Only those of recognized position and influence in the State's official family and the ranking officers of the militia were present, with their ladies. The New Orleans band charmed the assembled guests with both martial and ballroom music. It was a glamorous occasion, flavored with excitement, as it joined together in this frontier village the show and polish of French nobility with the strength and directness of pioneer democracy. The memory of this event will never perish in Montgomery.[1]

[1] The Montgomery Committee was composed of Colonel William Peacock,

At eleven o'clock General Lafayette retired from the ball and shortly thereafter boarded the steamboat, *The Charles Carroll of Carrolton,*[1] which was to carry him to Cahawba, the capital of the state, where the populace patiently waited, eager to see him and pay him homage.

John J. Crocheron was in charge of the general arrangements at Cahawba. He wrote the Governor that he was erecting an additional arch and flag upon the bluff where Mr. Henry Hitchcock would deliver his address of welcome at the foot of Second Street, North. He informed the Governor that the escort from the landing would be footmen instead of cavalry. Crocheron also suggested to the Governor that a public barbecue be given as well as a dinner—this to please the multitude. He suggested that after a few toasts had been drunk at the dinner, the General could leave and appear at the barbecue and give a toast. He wrote:

This arrangement will give general and public satisfaction; for all of course cannot dine with the General; few can pay $5.00 for a dinner and not a great many can be accommodated at the public houses; but with this plan all can be accommodated with fare and drink, and that, too, in a manner with the national guest, and in a manner, too, that will suit them best; *id est* the multitude, I mean.

Very respectfully, your obt. ser't,
JOHN J. CROCHERON

But Mr. Thomas Casey, the Senator from Dallas County, was not of the same mind as Crocheron. He wrote Governor Pickens, who was then at Greensborough: "Would it not be well to have a ball as well as a dinner? This would give the ladies an opportunity to pay their respects to him. . . .

Colonel James W. Johnson, Benjamin Fitzpatrick, Esq., John Bailey, Esq., William Cook, Esq., Major Thomas Scott, J. D. Bibb, Esq., Dr. Billingslea. This committee selected a subcommittee composed of John D. Bibb, William Sayre, and Henry Goldthwaite to represent Montgomery in the ceremony at the state boundary. At one time the committee despaired of getting the proper carriages in Montgomery to transport the Lafayette party, and considered borrowing several from affluent Lowndes County planters, but did not do so. Benjamin Fitzpatrick, Henry Goldthwaite, and William Cook served as Chairmen of the Montgomery Committee.

[1] Lavasseur states that it was the steamboat *Anderson.*

Mrs. Casey will attend to fixing up the rooms at the State House. I feel some pride not to be outdone by the capital of Georgia."

Mr. Crocheron requested the Governor to have the signal guns of all steamboats fired to announce Lafayette's approach to Selma and Cahawba, and asked that the Captain of the steamer bearing the distinguished visitor be instructed exactly where to tie up his boat at the landing. While crewmen were carrying out Crocheron's suggestion about firing signal guns, one Roberts was injured by the firing on the steamboat *Elizabeth.* General Lafayette sensed the human interest created by the unfortunate accident. He visited the wounded man, and his last words to General Woodward were, "Take care of the wounded man."[1]

General Lafayette did not spend much time at the seat of government. The citizens had done their utmost in cordial reception and entertainment, but the guest was running behind schedule. He remained only long enough to attend the dinner and express his thanks and appreciation of the honor accorded him. He then boarded his steamer for Mobile.[2]

Mr. Greening, of Claiborne, was invited by the Governor

[1] Woodward's *Reminiscences*, pp. 72, 73. The wounded man, however, took care of himself by suing Mr. Rhodes, the owner and master of the *Elizabeth*, and recovering a verdict of $1,500, which was affirmed by the Supreme Court of Alabama in the case of Rhodes v. Roberts, Stewart, Vol. 1, p. 145. This is really the first personal injury negligence damage suit decided by the Supreme Court of Alabama. Of course, there were cases before this of slander and libel, assault and trespass.

[2] The Mobile Committee had been selected by J. B. Hogan at Governor Pickens' request. Hogan named General Judge Hale, Captain Root, Captain Easter, General Everett, T. T. Holt, Phillip McCloskey, Dr. Carthy, H. Gunnison, S. A. Garrow, S. J. Swift, Major Armstrong, Captain Ross, B. Ames, Joseph W. Moore, H. Stickney, H. V. Chamberlain, Dr. Chernse, Dr. Lane, Colonel Smoot, W. Barton, W. H. Robertson, Col. William King, Major Montgomery, and Dr. Webb. In writing to the Governor concerning the members of the Mobile Committee, Hogan said that he "had an eye on to such as are known for their public spirit as well as knowledge in such matters." The Governor added his old friend, Silas Dinsmoor, to the committee, and still later appointed Mr. Batre. The chairman was S. H. Garrow, and Thomas L. Carthy signed as secretary.

to serve on the general committee. He accepted and in turn requested the Governor to arrange for Lafayette to stop at Claiborne on his way down the river to Mobile. The Governor so arranged it, but since the General's party was late in arriving at Cahawba, there was little time left for Claiborne. He did, however, make a brief appearance there, during which time he attended the ceremony in which the cornerstone of the Masonic Lodge building was laid.

When the General reached Mobile he was lavishly entertained by the committee for the one day during which he was there. The committee attended him as far as Mobile Point, where he was delivered to the Louisiana escort. It was over. Alabama had done her best, and considering her meager resources for entertaining French nobility, it was a performance of which she could afford to be proud. The Governor was pleased. Now he could relax from the long strain—and count up the cost.

Governor Pickens had not expected the visit. He just did not know this man Lafayette. The Marquis was hale and hearty, full of the zest of living and having a gay time visiting the States. The Congress of the United States had recently made him another fine present—this time $200,000 in cash. This sense of wealth, added to the vigor of a robust man, who was accustomed to the luxuries of Europe, made Lafayette a difficult and expensive guest. He loved rich food and fine wines and consumed them in abundance. Alabama did not disappoint his appetites. These and many other things for the comfort and pleasure of the guest could be provided by Governor Pickens only by great effort and at a high cost, but they were provided. When the noble guest departed and Governor Pickens checked his accounts, he found that the visitor had cost the State $15,715.18, to which would have to be added $1,350, a pro rata part of the additional expense of transporting the General from Alabama to Louisiana. This hospitality strained the slender resources of the six-year-old commonwealth in spite of the fact that the escorts, including two whole troops of cavalry, had individually paid their own expenses. When the sum of $12,713 had been paid out, the State's contingent fund was completely consumed. The unpaid balance of $3,002.18 was on the cuff, but the State's first big party was distinctly a success.[1]

Lafayette's departure from the state terminated Alabama's responsibility for the famous man and at the same time ended that anxiety which ever goes with being host to a celebrity. The multitude enjoyed the holiday atmosphere which prevailed generally during the time the General was the State's guest, and many of them also had the satisfaction of seeing for themselves this man who had become almost a legendary hero in the annals of the nation. His curiosity satisfied, the Alabama pioneer went back to his work. He was a republican, and royalty—even friendly French royalty—smacked too much of Toryism to set well with new-found independence.

The public men of the state had good cause to be proud of the way they had received and entertained their distinguished guest. Neither before nor since has Alabama done better. Yet, from Governor Israel Pickens on down to the youngest militia captain whose duty it was to see that no harm came to the Marquis from the time he crossed the Chattahoochee until he was bidden "bon voyage" at Mobile Point, there were mixed feelings of relief and pride when the guest was gone.

After the excitement of the Lafayette visit died away the spring and summer of 1825 in Alabama seemed about as usual. The same crops were planted and cultivated. Most people were busy with their personal affairs and stayed close to their homes. Whenever they gathered in groups, whether at churches or in school buildings, for business in

[1] Before this could be paid, other claims and charges increased the unpaid balance so that when the Assembly met in November, 1825, it required an appropriation of $4,000 to clear the cost of entertaining the French nobleman. Acts 1825, p. 88.

the towns and at the steamboat landings, the talk was usually first of weather and the crops, but it inevitably drifted to praise of Andrew Jackson, abuse of Henry Clay, and disapproval of John Quincy Adams. There were also quiet and thoughtful discussions concerning a new dueling law and about the reorganization of the Supreme Court, but the subject which interested the citizens all over the state, created controversy, and aroused speculation, was the location of the seat of government.

Since this was not a Presidential year, even the still resentful Jackson partisans were lethargic. The political situation was so quiet that Israel Pickens was able to handpick, as his successor for the office of Governor, John Murphy, from Monroe County, and no one came forward to oppose him. This fact is all the more remarkable when it is remembered that John Murphy was one of the seven Senators who voted *against* the Jackson-for-President resolution—the same resolution which Pickens had vetoed. Truly, here was a high tribute to the political integrity and prestige of Israel Pickens, accompanied by a conviction on the part of the Jackson partisans that Murphy, like his sponsor, Governor Pickens, was not an anti-Jackson man.

The election was held on the first Monday in August. When the votes were counted and the winners became known, it was established that the Senate would have six old Senators and fifteen new members. This was the body with which was to rest the fate of the seat of government. In the House there were also many members serving for the first time, but the percentage was not nearly so high as in the Senate. New men, however, did not eliminate or solve the old questions. These men, both old and new, had been carefully chosen with the controversial issues of the day in mind as the votes were cast. As far as the seat-of-government issue was concerned, the electorate had purposely chosen an Assembly divided into two well-defined camps. There were very few uncertain votes in either House.

That master leader and easily the most popular public man in the state, Israel Pickens, was at the helm to organize this most important Assembly. In a few days he would surrender the reins of Governorship to his protégé, John Murphy, but before doing so it was his duty and privilege to deliver a message to the Assembly.

The Assembly convened on the third Monday of November, 1825, which was the twenty-first day of the month. The Senate, as had been its custom for several years, quickly chose Nicholas Davis President of the Senate. There was no opposition to the popular Senator from Limestone County. In the House, William Kelly, from Madison County, was elected Speaker without opposition. He was not a newcomer in the Assembly but this was his first time to be elected presiding officer of the House. The Cahawba partisans knew that they could not defeat either of these men. For not offering any opposition at all they hoped for some return by way of gratitude, but their chief purpose was to avoid at this time any test of strength.

The Assembly completed its organization on the first day of the session, and early on the second day informed Governor Pickens that they were ready to receive from him "any communication it might please him to make." Pickens lost not one hour. He informed the committees that he would deliver his message in writing at twelve o'clock noon of the same day.

Pickens was aware of the melancholy fact that if the Assembly voted to remove the seat of government from Cahawba, the Governor's signature to the removal bill would not be necessary.[1] He had been a delegate in the Constitu-

[1] Art. III, Section 29, Constitution of the State of Alabama.

"The first session of the General Assembly shall commence on the fourth Monday in October next, and be held at the town of Huntsville, and all subsequent sessions at the town of Cahawba, until the end of the first session of the General Assembly, to be held in the year one thousand eight hundred and twenty-five; during that session the General Assembly shall have power to designate by law (to which the Executive concurrence shall not be required) the permanent Seat of Government, which shall not thereafter be changed;

tional Convention in 1819 when this provision had been included in the Constitution at the insistence of C. C. Clay and J. W. Walker, of Madison, and Marmaduke Williams and John L. Tindall, of Tuskaloosa. Now the foresight of these men was being vindicated. The push to remove the seat of government to Tuskaloosa was now on in full force. He, Pickens, the retiring governor, was opposed to Tuskaloosa but possessed no official power to prevent this result. John Murphy, being from Monroe, was of like mind and desire, but both men knew that Murphy could not veto any bill removing the capital from Cahawba. The vote of the Assembly would be decisive and final! Within that body the contest must be won or lost.

Pickens was not the kind to take a whipping lying down. This message would be his last word to the Alabama Assembly. He proposed to let them know what their retiring Governor thought about the "Seat of Government" problem even though the Constitution politely excluded the Governor from participating in this most important business. To do so required political courage, for Pickens wanted to be a United States Senator, and the fate of this ambition would probably be in the hands of the very men who composed the Assembly. It would be an easy thing to leave the whole hot controversy to John Murphy. But Israel Pickens never faltered where courage was required. He gave his views to the Assembly and they were against Tuskaloosa.

The Governor first observed that: "It is our good fortune to commence a session which has been viewed as one *of more than ordinary importance*, under circumstances which evince the prevalence of a disinterested good feeling."[1] It is believed that Pickens was expressing a hope rather than a

Provided, however, that, unless such designation be then made by law, the government shall continue permanently at the town of Cahawba; and provided, also, that the General Assembly shall make no appropriations previous to the year one thousand eight hundred and twenty-five, for the building of any other State House than that now provided for by law."

[1] Senate Journal 1825, p. 5.

fact. He knew that the factions were organized and alert, ready for the coming contest. He hoped that there would be no bitterness.

The reorganization of the judiciary, required to be passed on by the Assembly at this session, concerned the Governor, for improvement in this field had been one of his constant objects during his four years in office. He now proposed that the Assembly consider creating a distinct Supreme Court. Pickens' own view was that this would drain the best men away from the *primary* courts where they were most needed. The Governor indicated that he was inclined to favor increasing the compensation of the Circuit Judges, and postponing to a later time the creation of a separate Supreme Court.

Pickens now warily approached the seat-of-government matter,[1] acknowledging that since the Governor's concurrence to any law passed by the Assembly on this subject was not required, he regarded the matter as one of "peculiar delicacy, and shall leave it where the Constitution has intended, to your own uncontrolled judgment." The Governor then proceeded to submit his own views under the guise of a "collateral consideration" warranted by the strongest reasons of public interest. "Should it be the will of the legislature to remove the Government from its present site," said the Governor, "it would be necessary to enact measures to select an eligible position and have the State acquire the title. In this it will be considered by every one as desirable, and if reasonably practicable it may also be regarded as a duty, to procure a tract, conditionally or otherwise, of sufficient extent wherein *to lay out and found an entire metropolis.*"

If the Assembly followed the course recommended by Pickens Tuskaloosa would have been eliminated as a prospect for the seat of government, for it was already a surveyed and thriving little town. Here one could not "lay out and found an entire metropolis." The Pickens plan also

[1] Senate Journal 1825, p. 7.

made it feasible for the legislature to abandon Cahawba as a capital and yet give the Alabama River system region an open chance to retain the seat of government at some new place not subject to the objections which could be made against Cahawba. Under the circumstances this was the best Pickens could do. That it was not enough was no fault of his.

The Governor thought it wise under the circumstances to postpone the location of the University to a future session. He did not want this important decision to become entangled with the seat-of-government contest. He seized the opportunity presented by discussing the University to refer again to the establishment of a department of female instruction, for the "education of our daughters in the higher branches of literature and science." He recommended that there be one female seminary instead of the three heretofore authorized. Had Pickens not been faced with the necessity of creating the State Bank, the University of Alabama would have been in operation certainly not later than 1825 and would have consisted of two institutions, one for men and the other for women.

The Governor further proposed "the introduction of rural economy, embracing agriculture in its most comprehensive understanding as an academic study." He referred to agriculture as the "nursing mother of every human pursuit" and as being so connected with philosophy and chemistry as to deserve a place among the departments of science. Surely this Israel Pickens was a practical, intelligent, and progressive man!

Next came the Bank, an institution dear to the Governor's heart. He reported that it had commenced business on March 9, 1825, with a capital of $253,646.46. This was composed of $56,612.94¼ from the University fund, $31,597.01 from the 3% fund, $37,860.49 from the Cahawba grant, $100,000 borrowed in New York, and $27,576 of ordinary State revenues left in the State Treasury beyond current public demands.[1] In the few months of its operation the Bank had paid all expenses and interest charges and earned a net profit of $2,244.46. The University funds invested in the Bank were expected to be increased to $80,000 almost any day and in the coming year to exceed $100,000. Said the Governor: "And I retain the fullest confidence that under a faithful guardianship it may answer all the purposes of its institution."

A summary report was made of the Lafayette visit to the state. Pickens pointed out that his route through Alabama was of unusual length, one hundred miles in the Indian country, through which he was conducted with civil and military escort, to Montgomery by land, and thence by steam transportation to Cahawba, Claiborne, and Mobile, and Mobile Point, a total distance of over 500 miles. The cost of entertaining the celebrated visitor, reported the Governor, was $15,715.13. To this would have to be added $1,-350 more, which was Alabama's share of the cost in transporting the visitor from the limits to this state of Louisiana. The Governor called attention to the fact that these expenses did not include the cost of two gallant troops of cavalry who escorted Lafayette from the Chattahoochee, as these gentlemen declined to accept indemnity from the State for their expenses.

The Governor submitted to the Assembly the Ohio Resolutions proposing a plan of emancipation and colonization of slaves. Pickens disliked and deplored African slavery, yet he resented affronts from other states who attempted to violate our sovereignty. He observed that "the interests affected by the propositions under consideration are older than the government and confirmed by all its sanctions."[2]

The message concluded with a short but appropriate ref-

[1] Senate Journal 1825, pp. 9–10.

[2] Pickens' discussion of the slavery problem in this message to the Alabama Assembly is the ablest exposition of this difficult problem to be found in the books. Senate Journal 1825, pp. 13–14.

erence to his years of service as Governor. The next day the Assembly in joint session opened and published the returns for Governor. John Murphy received 12,511 votes and was declared elected.[1]

This necessary formality of declaring Murphy the duly elected Governor having been disposed of by the Assembly, it now settled down to earnest endeavor in true bicameral fashion. It was conceded by everyone that the main business of this session was to fix the location of the seat of government in accordance with the mandate of the Constitution. The contest between two sections of the state, arising out of this duty, resolved itself into two separate battles, one in the Senate and the other in the House.

In the Senate conflict the issue was quickly joined when John Wood filed a memorial contesting the Senate seat of John "Red" Brown,[2] of Jefferson County, who had already been appointed a member of the Select Committee of the Senate on "the Seat of Government" by Nicholas Davis, President of the Senate. This Select Committee was composed of Levin Powell, Senator from Tuskaloosa County, William Crawford, who represented the district composed of Mobile, Washington, and Baldwin Counties, John "Red" Brown, from Jefferson County (all of whom were known to favor removal of the seat of government to Tuskaloosa); Thomas Casey, Senator from Dallas County, and Dunklin Sullivan, who was Senator from the district composed of Bibb and Perry Counties, both of whom were strongly opposed to Tuskaloosa. John Wood had been ready with his memorial contesting the right of John "Red" Brown to represent Jefferson County in the Senate since the election in August, but it appears that he purposely waited until after the appointment of the Select Committee before presenting

[1] Senate Journal 1825, p. 16.

[2] John "Red" Brown was called "Red" because of his red hair and to distinguish him from that other John Brown (Black), also from Jefferson County (Teeple and Smith's *History of Jefferson County*, 1887, p. 55), who was serving in the House at this time as one of the three Representatives from Jefferson.

it to the Senate. Nick Davis appointed Brown on the Seat of Government Committee late in the afternoon of November 24. When the Senate met on the morning of November 25 the first business transacted was the reception of Wood's memorial.[1] Upon the outcome of this contest hung the destiny of Cahawba.

The contestant was, of course, no newcomer in state and county politics. John Wood was Jefferson County's first Senator. He had served with satisfaction to his constituents in the sessions of 1822, 1823, and 1824. But the count of the 1825 ballots showed that John "Red" Brown had defeated the veteran Senator. The Browns were politically very powerful in Jefferson but so was Wood,[2] who had the allegiance of all the old Justices of the Quorum and Justices of the Peace, and, furthermore, he was esteemed as an intelligent, patriotic citizen who with entire candor voted his convictions on all occasions. Why then had this good and popular man failed of re-election? What forces and what combination of circumstances produced the defeat of the one man whose vote would probably have kept the capital at Cahawba, or if not there, certainly in the Alabama River system basin? John Wood had a good record in the Assembly and he was certainly not through in politics, for as soon as John "Red" Brown's term expired the citizens of Jefferson again returned their old friend, John Wood, to the State Senate.

Political necessity and expediency seem to offer the only explanation of Wood's defeat. He was known to be a very

[1] Senate Journal 1825, p. 19.

[2] John Wood was an early settler, having located near Jonesborough, where he was living when the Assembly created Blount County (which at that time included most of the territory which later became Jefferson County). Wood was selected to organize Blount County. He divided the County into battalions and beats. The military officers were *elected* and then commissioned by the Governor, but the Justices of the Quorum and Justices of the Peace were selected by John Wood and upon his recommendation the Governor issued them their commissions. (*History of Blount County*, by George Powell, p. 40.)

close friend of the pro-Cahawba Senators, Casey and Sullivan, and was generally friendly to the planter group representing Montgomery, Dallas, Wilcox, and Monroe Counties. It was generally believed that he was opposed to locating the seat of government at Tuskaloosa, and if this were true, Wood's unfaltering integrity, together with his known reputation for voting his convictions, made him a dangerous foe to those who favored removal. The pro-Tuskaloosa group considered it far safer to have "Red" Brown, who was known to favor Tuskaloosa, than to risk John Wood, whose vote would have to be won on the merits of the question. The anti-Cahawba men decided that John Wood had to be defeated. This task was made easier by the overconfidence of Wood and his friends, an overconfidence born of knowledge that his record as Senator was good. Yet that record, clear and staunch as it was, had two vulnerable points. Wood had voted against the "Jackson-for-President" resolution and thus incurred the displeasure of a considerable number of citizens. Many of these Jackson partisans in Jefferson County had "soldiered" under General Jackson, and with the hardships of camp and campaign long ago forgotten they now held for the General such a fanatical loyalty that they would not tolerate any man as a candidate for public office unless he was *for* Jackson.

The other politically weak spot in Wood's record was his unrelenting fight summarily to close the Huntsville Bank. The closing of the bank early in 1825[1] had brought very considerable losses to the holders of its notes and some inconveniences to Jefferson County people. Those voters and citizens of Jefferson County who suffered losses by the decline in value of the Huntsville Bank notes blamed John Wood. A voter has no tenderer spot than his pocketbook, so Wood suffered politically regardless of whether his stand on the Huntsville Bank had been right or wrong or had in fact contributed to the depreciation of its notes.

[1] Senate Journal 1825, p. 10.

One other unavoidable situation contributed to Brown's election. This was the Tuskaloosa County influence upon the residents of the southern and western portions of Jefferson County. Capture of the capital meant more than a political achievement to the citizens of Tuskaloosa; it meant a vindication of their protests made when Governor William Wyatt Bibb in the year 1818 had ignored the Commissioners and by his own fiat had located the seat of government at Cahawba. Realizing their desperate need of the vote of the Senator from Jefferson, loyal Tuskaloosa men worked on their friends across the county line and won them over for Brown. They were helped no little by the common interest of both communities in the Warrior River and by the fact that some residents of southern Jefferson did their trading in Tuskaloosa.

After accepting Wood's contest the Assembly received its first petition asking for the seat of government. It came from Centreville, in Bibb County,[1] and was presented by a woman, probably Alabama's first business woman, Sarah F. Chotard. This enterprising lady of French descent had for a number of years conducted a successful business near the falls of the Cahawba. By this effort to procure the capital for Centreville, Sarah Chotard probably became Alabama's first woman actively and openly participating in the politics of the state. She did not succeed but she certainly selected for participation the best fight yet to be conducted in the state under the rules of republican representative government. Sarah must have been a sophisticated woman. The rest of that day was given over to the inauguration of Governor Murphy, who delivered an appropriate address to the Assembly.[2]

John Wood had presented his contest against John "Red" Brown on Friday, November 25. On Monday, November 28, Mr. Jackson, of Autauga County, for the Committee on

[1] Senate Journal 1825, p. 20.

[2] Senate Journal 1825, p. 20. The address appears on pages 24 and 25.

Privileges and Elections, reported to the Senate adversely to the claims of Mr. Wood in favor of the right to the seat of the said John Brown.[1] The report was read and ordered to lie on the table. The lines of the opposing forces were almost formed, but uncertainty was unavoidable until this contest was decided. Without the vote of the Senator from Jefferson each side could claim ten votes. The next day the Senate Committee on Privileges and Elections reported the following members as being duly elected to represent the senatorial districts designated:

From the senatorial district composed of:	
Mobile, Baldwin, and Washington	William Crawford
Pike, Covington and Henry	William Irwin
Butler and Conecuh	William Jones
Monroe and Wilcox	Arthur P. Bagby
Clarke and Marengo	George S. Gaines
Greene	Zachariah Merriwether
Montgomery	James Abercrombie
Dallas	Thomas Casey
Bibb and Perry	Dunklin Sullivan
Shelby and Autauga	James Jackson
Blount and St. Clair	John Ash
Tuskaloosa	Levin Powell
Pickens, Fayette, Walker and Marion	Jesse Vanhoose
Morgan	Thomas D. Crabb
Franklin	Theophilus Skinner
Lawrence	Matthew Clay
Lauderdale	James Jackson
Limestone	Nicholas Davis
Madison	Thomas Miller
Jackson	Robert M'Camy

The report does not mention Jefferson County, nor John "Red" Brown, nor John Wood. By the omission of any mention of the election contest its importance was emphasized. But the report laid to rest any question about the

[1] Senate Journal 1825, p. 23.

election of any of the Senators named in the report. It had been necessary for the Committee on Privileges and Elections to receive parol evidence concerning the election of Matthew Clay, Senator from Lawrence, and this had caused some talk around the State House, for Clay was known to favor removal. This Committee, like the Seat of Government Committee, had a majority of members opposed to Cahawba. From the present indications it appeared that if the anti-Cahawba men hung together they would succeed in removing the seat of government from that place.

The Senate was now ready to hear the report of the Seat of Government Committee. Needless to say, the Committee was ready to be heard. The Chairman, Levin Powell, of Tuskaloosa, submitted the report in writing.[1]

After setting forth the constitutional provisions the report said:

It was undoubtedly the intention of the framers of the constitution that the Seat of Government should not be permanently fixed at Cahawba, unless it should be found, after an experiment of six years, to be the most eligible site. Taking this to be their intention, as expressed in that instrument, your committee have endeavored to ascertain, whether Cahawba combined more advantages for the permanent Seat of Government than any other place which might probably be selected.

They have ascertained that Cahawba is on a low situation, and liable to be inundated by the waters of both the Cahawba and Alabama rivers. The inundation of a part of the town occurs almost annually; and at times it has been impracticable to reach the State House without a conveyance by water. It has been ascertained that during the last session of the legislature every street leading from the country into the town was overflowed to the depth of several feet; and that it was impossible to reach the town even on horseback, without deviating from the public highways. One part of the town was inaccessible to persons residing in another part, without the medium of water communication. Your committee further learn, that when the Supreme Court was directed by law to be holden at Cahawba

[1] Senate Journal 1825, p. 27.

in the month of June in each year, that many of the members of the bar did not attend the court at that session, from an apprehension of sickness; and that the Judges themselves were reluctant to perform the hazardous duty of holding the Supreme Court at that season of the year. By the constitution the Supreme Court can be holden only at the Seat of Government: it is therefore important to the due and regular administration of justice, that the Seat of Government should be fixed in some healthful situation. Your committee are informed that most of the inhabitants of Cahawba are unwilling to risk their health in that place during the summer; and that they are in the habit of removing, during that season, to some situation which promises better health.

From these facts, your committee have been constrained to come to the conclusion that Cahawba is not an eligible situation for the permanent Seat of Government. Your committee have given due weight to the considerations which oppose the removal of the Seat of Government.

These are the loss of public property and the expenses incident to a removal. The State House is a temporary building, and not calculated to accommodate the representatives of the people, even if the Seat of Government were to be permanently fixed at Cahawba. The arsenal is almost worthless, and is certainly entirely useless, as the public arms would be better preserved in the hands of the militia. A temporary building has been used for the bank, which is insufficient either for security or convenience.

It therefore appears to your committee that the sacrifice of property, by the removal of the Seat of Government, would be inconsiderable, and would weigh as the dust in the balance, when opposed to the weighty considerations which urge to a removal.

Your committee have also had under consideration that part of the message of his excellency the Governor, which suggests the propriety of procuring a tract of land "whereon to lay out and found an entire metropolis." It occurs to them that the Seat of Government alone cannot impart much value to real property in any town. In this town, where the Seat of Government has remained for six years, and which has been a favourite object of legislation, real property appears to be of little value. It gives no impulse to trade. If the Seat of Government be of any advantage to a town, why does commerce in this village languish? why is business thus dull? The town of Washington, the metropolis of the late Mississippi Territory, declined while even the Legislature held its sessions in its bosom. The history of every inland town in every state in which the Seat of Government has been placed, shows that the Seat of Government alone cannot give value to real property. The Seat of Government in Pennsylvania, and Frankfort, in Kentucky, illustrate this position. It is evident, that if "an entire metropolis" destitute of commercial advantages, should be founded by the Legislature, very little revenue would arise from the sale of lots in such a town. If a commercial town should be selected, the lots would be sold on account of the commercial advantages belonging to them, and not from the location of the Seat of Government.

Your committee are convinced, that no practical good would result from the establishment of a town in which to locate the Seat of Government; and believe that much inconvenience and expense would be avoided, if the Senate should come early to this conclusion.

They, therefore, recommend to the Senate the adoption of the following resolutions:

RESOLVED, That the Seat of Government ought not to remain at the town of Cahawba after the end of the present session of the General Assembly.

RESOLVED, That it is inexpedient to appoint commissioners to procure a tract of land "whereon to lay out and found an entire metropolis."[1]

This report was a terrific indictment of Cahawba. Indeed it is difficult to see how any arguments could be made in favor of Cahawba if all the statements contained in the report were true. Careful reading of the report, however, reveals its purpose is to picture Cahawba in the worst light possible. At no time is it stated that the State House itself was flooded, or that it was impossible to reach it while the Assembly was in session. Yet the impression created is that this was true. Other reliable records indicate that if "at times it has been impracticable [note the report does not

[1] Senate Journal 1825, pp. 27–28. Following the reading of the Report a bill establishing and permanently locating the Seat of Government of the State of Alabama was introduced by Mr. Jackson, of Lauderdale, and read the first time. P. 29.

say 'impossible'] to reach the State House without a conveyance by water," such times were in the spring when the rains were heaviest and floods greatest.

The main cause of flood in the town of Cahawba was due to the fact that the town was about one half encircled by the Cahawba River. The Alabama River made the entire eastern boundary. When the Alabama was high and the Cahawba full, the Alabama, being much the larger and stronger stream, acted as a dam holding the waters of the Cahawba and causing them to overflow all around the high bluff upon which the center of the town was located.

Regardless of the causes of the high water and after giving some discount to the cleverness of the language used in the report describing them, the fact seems to be that there was enough inconvenience caused by rivers to provide a good argument why the capital should be moved from Cahawba. But it is very doubtful if floods by themselves were sufficient to justify a removal of the seat of government. Opposed to the dismal scene pictured by the report is the non-political account of the floods at Cahawba described by Dr. Jabez W. Heustis in his book on the yellow fever in Cahawba in the years 1821 and 1822. The doctor particularly describes the floods and states that in the spring of 1822 the rainfall was unprecedented all over the state. Yet he does not at any time say that the waters reached the residential and business sections of Cahawba, or the State House. It must also be remembered that *after* the capital was removed the town floundered for a while and then rapidly advanced to become the richest and most progressive in the state, declining again just prior to 1860 for reasons other than floods. The "*low situation*" did not prevent this remarkable development in the period from about 1830 to 1860. It appears that these floods were more powerful and effective politically than they were naturally.[1]

On the issue of health the group favoring removal had a

[1] It must be remembered that in the year 1825 the great forests covering the

sounder case. Yellow fever was a curse to Cahawba and its fury not only took a heavy toll of lives but drove its citizens away during the "sickly season."

The report does not mention *Tuskaloosa* nor any other place. It simply condemned Cahawba. But when the committee repudiated the advice of Israel Pickens by resolving: "That it is inexpedient to procure a tract of land 'whereon to lay out and found an entire metropolis,' " even the least sophisticated among the Assemblymen understood this to mean that the committee favored removal to a town already organized, and everyone knew that the town in mind was Tuskaloosa.

The removal group were now almost ready to go ahead to a vote. They only needed to settle the John Wood vs. John Brown contest. Accordingly, on November 30, 1825, Mr. Jackson, of Autauga, Chairman of the Committee, reported on the contest between "said Wood and John Brown (Red)" stating that Brown had proven his certificate of election, and that Wood had charged fraud and illegality in the election offering *ex parte* affidavits of persons taken before magistrates in Jefferson County. Since it appeared that the affidavits were taken without notice to Brown and without his being present, the committee rejected them. There then being no evidence of fraud and illegality, the committee declined to examine the ballots and offered a resolution.

RESOLVED, That John Brown (Red) is the legal senator to represent Jefferson County in the Senate of the General Assembly of this State.

The resolution was adopted. John Brown (Red) was now the undisputed Senator from Jefferson.

watersheds of the Coosa, Tallapoosa, Alabama and Cahawba Rivers had barely been touched. They served to soak up the rains and prevent floods. Many years later, about 1916, and after the great forests on these watersheds had been cut and the lands put in cultivation, and before the building of the Alabama Power Company's system of dams on the Coosa and Tallapoosa, an *unprecedented rainfall*, according to Mr. Robbie Sturdivant, of Dallas County, did cause the waters to cover the bluff where once stood Alabama's first State House.

But John Wood was not done. While the Senate was attending to the routine business of electing some County Judges and a State Printer, Wood prepared a memorial praying that he be given a rehearing in his contest for a Senate seat and requesting that further time be allowed him to take testimony. The petition for rehearing was presented by Wood's friend, Dunklin Sullivan, of Bibb County. The Cahawba faction were now openly supporting Wood.

During a short lull between the filing of Wood's rehearing petition and a consideration of the Seat of Government Act, additional fuel was added to burning controversy when James Abercrombie, Senator from Montgomery County, presented the memorial of John Scott in which he offered, as a donation to the state, 240 acres of land in the town of Montgomery upon which to locate the seat of government. It was now disclosed that if the Alabama River section faction could not retain the seat of government at Cahawba they intended to make an all-out effort to hold it in the valley of the Alabama River.

Mr. Scott's memorial was read and ordered to lie on the table. Mr. Crawford moved to take up the Seat of Government Bill. The motion carried 11 to 10. The removal men were pressing for action. No time was given to considering the petition of Sarah Chotard or the offer of Mr. Scott. They had a majority of one vote and wanted a decision quickly, fearful lest some unforeseen circumstance intervene to deprive them of that advantage.

By the same 11-to-10 vote cast by the same Senators the Seat of Government Bill was amended so as to read:

> That the town of ———— be and the same is hereby designated as the permanent Seat of Government, and that from and after the end of the present session of the General Assembly, the sessions of said General Assembly shall be held in the town of ———— as established and limited by this Act.[1]

Sullivan attempted to amend the above language by a

[1] Senate Journal 1825, p. 40.

provision that Cahawba remain the temporary seat of government until suitable buildings and accommodations could be provided at————, and that the Governor be authorized to convene the Assembly at said town on proclamation. This move failed. The majority wanted no uncertain law nor did they want to involve the discretion of a Governor.

Mr. Jackson, of Lauderdale, then offered the following amendment to the Seat of Government Bill.

> 2. That the corporate limits of the town of———— be and the same are hereby extended so as to include fractional Sections 21 and 22, and Sections 23, 26, 27, and 28, in Township 21 and Range 10 West of the basis meridian of Huntsville.

This amendment was adopted by a vote of 12 to 9. Since the sections of land named were adjacent to the town of Tuskaloosa, the amendment might just as well have inserted that name. But Levin Powell, William Crawford, and James Jackson, who were leading the Senate fight for Tuskaloosa, were not yet ready for that vote. Instead they had the resolutions of the Committee on the Seat of Government brought up and passed them: first, "That the Seat of Government ought not to remain at Cahawba," and second, "That it is inexpedient to appoint commissioners to procure a tract of land upon which to found an entire metropolis." Both resolutions were adopted, 12 for and 9 against.[1]

Meanwhile the John Wood application for a rehearing was still pending before the Senate. The handsome, popular, and intelligent Arthur P. Bagby, of whom it was said, "He had every virtue save thrift," now seemed to be in charge of Wood's case and also to be taking the lead in the fight to hold the seat of government somewhere in the basin of the Alabama River. Bagby asked that the Wood petition be referred to a special committee. The motion carried, and Nicholas Davis, President of the Senate, put the anti-Tuskaloosa men in a close place by placing two of them,

[1] Senate Journal 1825, p. 41.

Bagby and Casey, on a three-man committee. Powell, from Tuskaloosa, was the third member.

Bagby's next move was to have the Seat of Government bill "lie on the table." This lost 9 to 12. Next he moved for an adjournment and lost again 9 to 12. The bill was then read the third time.[1]

After the third reading Jackson, of Lauderdale, moved to fill in the blank with "Tuscaloosa" so as to fix the seat of government at that place. Bagby desperately moved that the bill lie on the table until the Wednesday following, but lost 10 to 11. Almost at his rope's end, Bagby moved that the bill lie on the table "till tomorrow." He now won 11 to 10. George S. Gaines, of Clarke and Marengo, gave him the vote which granted Bagby another day.

Next day, which was Tuesday, December 6, 1825, after disposing of routine matters the persistent Casey hopefully moved that the Senate adjourn until the morrow. The motion lost. Jackson, of Lauderdale, then moved to take up the Seat of Government Bill and the motion carried 11 to 10. He then quickly renewed his motion to fill in the blanks with the word "Tuscaloosa," which carried by the same 11-to-10 vote. Making one last futile effort Casey moved for adjournment and lost.

The question was then put, "Shall the bill pass?", and determined in the affirmative, yeas 11, nays 10.[2]

The battle to remove the seat of government to Tuskaloosa was over in so far as the Senate was concerned. The yeas and nays were called for and those who voted *for Tuskaloosa* were:

President (Davis from Limestone)
John Brown (Red), Jefferson
Matthew Clay, of Lawrence
Thomas D. Crabb, of Morgan
William Crawford, of Mobile, Washington, and Baldwin

[1] Senate Journal 1825, p. 44.

[2] Senate Journal 1825, p. 48.

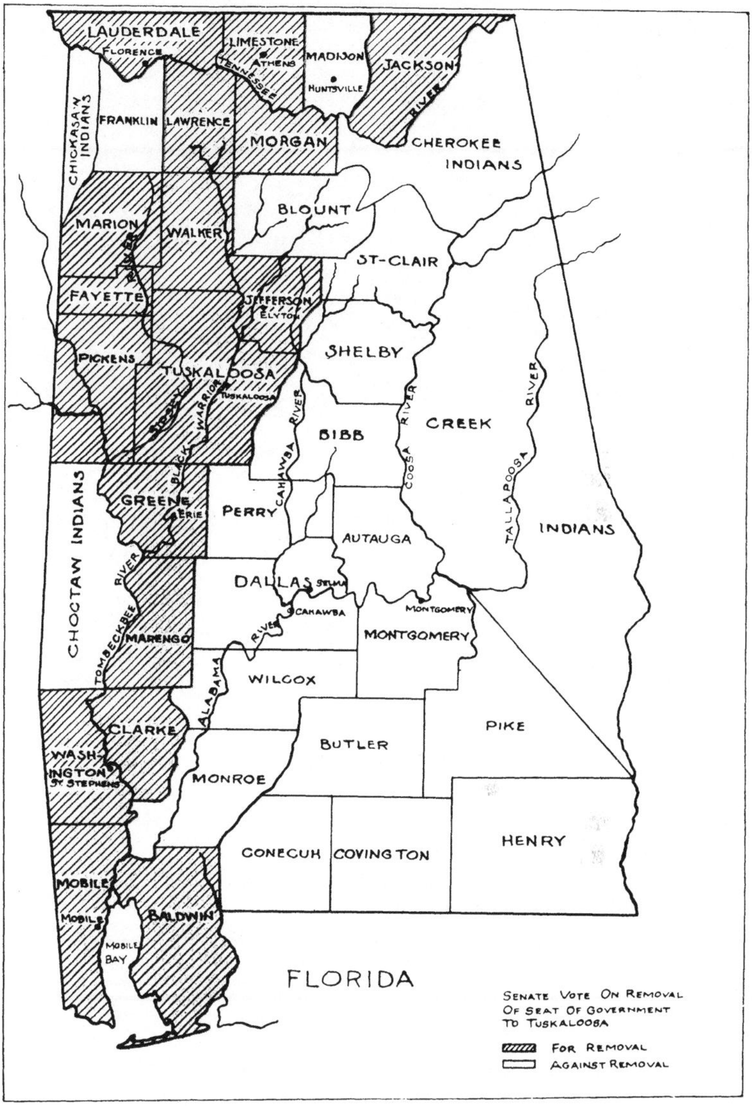

Map showing
Senate Vote on Removal of Seat of Government

George S. Gaines, of Clarke and Marengo
James Jackson, of Lauderdale
Robert M'Camy, of Jackson
Zachariah Merriwether, of Greene
Levin Powell, of Tuskaloosa
Jesse Vanhoose, of Pickens, Fayette, Marion, and Walker

Against Tuskaloosa

John Ash, of Blount and St. Clair
James Abercrombie, of Montgomery
Arthur P. Babgy, of Monroe and Wilcox
Thomas Casey, of Dallas
William Irwin, of Pike, Covington, and Henry
James Jackson, of Shelby and Autauga
William Jones, of Conecuh and Butler
Thomas Miller, of Madison[1]
Theophilus Skinner, of Franklin
Dunklin Sullivan, of Bibb and Perry

Thus, by a margin of one vote, and that cast by John (Red) Brown, of Jefferson, whose seat was contested, did Alabama's Senate decide to remove the seat of government from the basin of the Alabama River and locate it at Tuskaloosa on the Warrior. Since the Senate bill was eventually passed by the House, the whole course of political affairs in Alabama was changed for a long time to come, maybe because John Wood dared to oppose General Andrew Jackson, and spoke and voted his mind on the Huntsville Bank question.

Immediately after the roll call on the seat-of-government bill, Arthur P. Bagby reported for his special committee on John Wood's rehearing petition.[2] The committee reported against Wood, and in so doing made the astonishing statement that "the return of the sheriff of Jefferson County showed John Brown was duly elected a Senator for that county, that neither the Constitution of the State, nor

[1] This vote by the Senator from Madison is difficult to understand. Madison's five representatives in the House voted for Tuskaloosa.

[2] Senate Journal 1825, p. 48. The report was concurred in by a vote of 13 to 7, most of the opposition declining to yield even with Bagby leading.

any law made in pursuance thereof, authorized the Senate to go beyond the return of the sheriff in the investigation of a contested election." There must have been some pretty solid basis for Wood's complaint, for Bagby, before concluding his report, made this statement: "Your committee feel as deeply as it can be felt, the value of the elective franchise; and if in this case the fact really be, that the memorialist was fairly elected, they feel as deeply the regret arising out of the insuperable obstacles which prevent the memorialist from enjoying his rights."

One gets the impression that Babgy was of the opinion that Wood was the rightful Senator from Jefferson, but that since the sheriff had returned Brown as the elected Senator nothing could be done about it as the Constitution and laws of the State did not provide a remedy. Whether Brown held the office rightfully or wrongly, he *held* it, and his vote sent the capital to Tuskaloosa.

Having won in the Senate and feeling confident over achieving the same result in the House, Mr. Powell, Senator from Tuskaloosa, presented to the Senate the memorial of sundry citizens of Tuskaloosa, proposing to convey to the State one hundred and eighty acres of land, and one hundred and twenty-eight lots within the limits of the town of Tuskaloosa as defined by an Act which had passed the Senate during the present session, upon terms specified in an obligation entered into by the said memorialists, and filed in the Office of Secretary of State.[1]

There must have been some discontent among the senators, either about the Wood-Brown contest or with the gift of land made by the Tuskaloosa citizens, to have induced the experienced and sensible Bagby to offer the following resolution:[2]

Whereas, by the 29th section of the 3d article of the Constitution of the State of Alabama, it is made the duty of the Gen-

[1] Senate Journal 1825, pp. 54–55.

[2] Senate Journal 1825, p. 59.

eral Assembly, at the present session, to designate by law the permanent Seat of Government, and which shall not thereafter be changed; and whereas it is deemed inexpedient for the Seat of Government to remain at the town of Cahawba; and, whereas some point in Autauga, in Township 17 and Range 14, combines all the advantages of health, centrality, and commercial convenience; and whereas, it is considered a matter of last importance to the harmony, welfare, and prosperity of the people of the State of Alabama, that the Seat of Government should be located permanently at some point where the good people of the State will be content to see it remain, to wit—on the northeast quarter of section thirty-three: Be it therefore resolved by the Senate and House of Representatives, That it is expedient to locate the Seat of Government permanently in Township 17, and Range 14, in Autauga County;

which was read. The question was then put, "Shall the resolution be made the order of the day for a second reading tomorrow?"

Whether this try was just a last desperate effort by the Alabama Valley men or there was some undisclosed reason which gave promise of it passing, the resolution was quickly defeated on a vote to order its second reading on the morrow, yeas 12 to nays 9. Skinner, of Franklin, voted on this resolution with the Tuskaloosa group. The fight in the Senate was over. The Senators now awaited the action of the House. Indications were that the House had been delaying action to see what would happen in the Senate.

THE PROCEEDINGS IN THE HOUSE

The fight in the House of Representatives, while not so close as that in the Senate, was still so uncertain that the leaders for removal were constantly uneasy in spite of the large majority of votes which they commanded. There were 38 votes in the Tuskaloosa bloc and it was no simple matter to keep harmony among them while warding off the efforts of the opposition to break up the combination.

Almost the first matter to come before the House was a memorial presented by James G. Lyon claiming the seat in the House as the Representative from Washington County now occupied by Ptolemy Harris.[1] The committee to which the matter had been referred made a voluminous report in favor of Lyon and against Harris.[2] When the vote in the House was taken it was decided 41 to 22 that Harris was *not* entitled to the seat but the same men voted a few minutes later only 33 to 30 that Lyon was entitled to the seat.[3]

It is difficult to tell from the vote which side hoped to gain by seating Lyon. He received the vote of a considerable number of anti-Tuskaloosa men, yet Seth Barton, of Tuskaloosa, made the motion that he be seated. Perhaps both factions were wooing him. On the final vote Lyon voted for removal of the seat of government to Tuskaloosa. This was to be expected because his home county was on the Tombigbe.

Speaker William Kelly appointed on the select "location of the permanent Seat of Government" committee, Samuel W. Mardis, of Shelby, Jos. Pickens, of Dallas, Seth Barton, of Tuskaloosa, James Dellett, of Monroe, and Harry I. Thornton, of Madison. Two only favored Tuskaloosa, Barton and Thornton. The committee on November 30 reported through its chairman, Mr. Mardis:

RESOLVED: That it is expedient to remove the Seat of Government of the State of Alabama from the town of Cahawba.

RESOLVED: That it is expedient that the permanent Seat of Government be located within —— miles from the State House in the town of Cahawba.

RESOLVED: That commissioners be appointed for the purpose of examining and reporting to this House a proper place to locate the Seat of Government of the State of Alabama; and that their examination be confined within —— miles of the town of Cahawba.[4]

[1] House Journal 1825, p. 4.

[2] House Journal 1825, pp. 24–28. Although the sheriff returned Harris as the elected Representative, the House did not accord his return the same force which the Senate gave the sheriff's return in the Wood contest.

[3] House Journal 1825, p. 39.

[4] House Journal 1825, pp. 46–47.

The House received the report and ordered that it lie on the table. It appears that the Alabama River faction were conceding that the seat of government should be removed from Cahawba but that they also intended to keep it in the Alabama River valley and that they were going to prevent it going to Tuskaloosa if they could.

On December 2 the report was called up and Coalter, Lauderdale, moved that the House concur in the first resolution. It carried 37 to 25, but Mardis, Dellett and Pickens voted against it.[1] Later Coopwood, of Lawrence, moved that the second resolution be postponed to the first day of June next, which carried. This was a polite method of killing the motion. Everyone knew that the General Assembly would not be in session in June. Coalter then made the same motion with reference to the third resolution. But this time the motion failed by a vote of 30 to 34.[2]

Up to now the handsome, dynamic and reckless Seth Barton, of Tuskaloosa, had been leading the fight for removal. Another Barton, Willoughby Barton, of Mobile, picked up the challenge and for a time became the opposition champion. He was a well educated and experienced man. Israel Pickens had thought so well of his attainments that he had appointed Willoughby Barton as one of his two envoys to meet General Lafayette at Milledgeville and invite him to become the honored guest of the State of Alabama. Barton proved his talents when he discharged that delicate mission with credit to himself and his state.

When the motion to anaesthetize the third resolution failed to pass, Willoughby Barton was ready with something new. He moved to strike out the whole of the third resolution after the word "Resolved," for the purpose of inserting the following:

That three commissioners be chosen by ballot of this House to view the ground situate on both sides of the Alabama River,

[1] House Journal 1825, p. 50.

[2] House Journal 1825, p. 55.

within ten miles of said river, and between the town of Cahawba and the junction of the Coosa and Tallapoosa rivers, and report within fourteen days to the General Assembly the several sites which they may conceive eligible for the permanent Seat of Government of this State, and the country adjacent to said sites with their advantages and disadvantages, designating the particular site which they deem the most eligible for that purpose; with authority to make conditional speculations for such site or sites, and that three commissioners be appointed in like manner to examine Centreville and Tuskaloosa, and the adjacent country within ten miles of each place, and report in like manner.[1]

This resolution was so framed as to give the sites of Selma, Montgomery, and Wetumpka an even chance with Centreville, proposed by Sarah Chotard, and with Tuskaloosa, the prime contender. A division was called for and the vote on the striking of the third resolution was taken first. It was stricken unanimously. The vote to insert was then cast and it was adopted 36 to 27.[2] This vote was taken on Monday, December 5, 1825, and at a time when the House was advised that the Senate bill was certain to pass on the morrow. If the committee elected used the entire fourteen days given them by the resolution they would not report to the Assembly until December 20. There was nothing in the resolution, however, which obligated the Assembly to defer action until the examining committee reported. If, however, the commissioners chosen to view the sites were members of the House it is doubtful if the House would have proceeded with nine of its members absent. This was part of Dellett's strategy. If the decisive vote could be delayed something might happen to improve the chances of the Alabama River system group.

Next day Marston Mead, of Blount County, who had voted with the majority on the resolution to appoint commissioners, moved for a reconsideration.[3] The House by a

[1] House Journal 1825, p. 55.

[2] House Journal 1825, p. 55.

[3] House Journal 1825, p. 58.

vote of 44 to 19 granted the reconsideration. The resolution being before the House, Barton of Mobile moved to amend his own resolution:

> By striking out the word "ballot," which carried, also to strike out the words "General Assembly" and insert in lieu thereof, "this House"; also to insert after the words "in like manner," the words, "and with like powers," which were severally carried.[1]

Now it was the turn of Barton of Tuskaloosa. He moved to strike out all the resolution before the words "to view the ground, etc." and insert an amendment to the effect that the three commissioners be chosen by a joint vote of both Houses. This was ruled as being out of order because the House had "yesterday rejected a similar amendment." Mead, who had voted with the majority on that question the day before, saved Barton of Tuskaloosa, by moving for a reconsideration on that vote, and got it 33 to 29. Barton now renewed his motion to amend and won 33 to 30.

Barton of Mobile, who had voted in the affirmative on the question, now moved to reconsider the vote on his motion to strike out the words "General Assembly" and insert "this House." He lost. A vote was then taken by the House on Mobile Barton's resolution as amended by Tuskaloosa's Barton. It carried 38 to 23.[2] The House, having had enough of this parliamentary maneuvering, adjourned. The Tuskaloosans themselves didn't like this resolution, for after they succeeded in amending it, they voted against it. Their tactics this day were directed toward delay, because it was already known to them that the Senate bill, which provided for removal of the seat of government to Tuskaloosa, had been passed by the Senate. Their plan now was to get the House to pass the Senate bill. When it did so, this would end the matter, for the Governor's approval was not required.

On Monday, December 12, the bill on permanently locating the seat of government of the State of Alabama

[1] House Journal 1825, p. 59. [2] House Journal 1825, p. 60.

which had been passed by the Senate was brought before the House for consideration. The House at once resolved itself into a Committee of the Whole on the Senate bill for locating the seat of government.[1] Kelly vacated the Speaker's chair and Vining presided. The Committee of the Whole considered the bill for some time, when Mr. Speaker resumed the chair and Mr. Vining reported that "the Committee of the Whole House had directed him to report the bill without amendment."[2] The Senate bill was now before the House for action.

Mr. Dellett, from Monroe, immediately opened the attack on the Senate bill by moving to strike out all that part of the bill following the enacting clause, and to insert the following:

> *Be it enacted*, That commissioners be elected by joint vote of both houses of the General Assembly, who are hereby authorized to locate the Seat of Government of the State of Alabama within the County of Autauga upon the northeast quarter of section 33, township 17, range 14.

A division of the resolution was called for and on motion to strike out, Dellett lost 31 to 30. It was close, but some of the Representatives who voted with Dellett probably did so as an artifice.

Mr. Kelly now moved to amend the second section of the Senate bill by inserting after the word "Tuskaloosa" the words "for the purposes aforesaid." The move lost 20 to 42, the vote indicating that the House did not intend to amend the Senate bill in any manner.

Dellett tried again by moving to strike out all the second section of the Senate bill. He lost 28 to 35. Two motions to adjourn were lost. The question was then put on whether the Senate bill should be read a third time on the following day. It was decided in the affirmative, yeas 37, nays 26. The

[1] The Senate had passed this bill on December 6, 1825.

[2] House Journal 1825, p. 71.

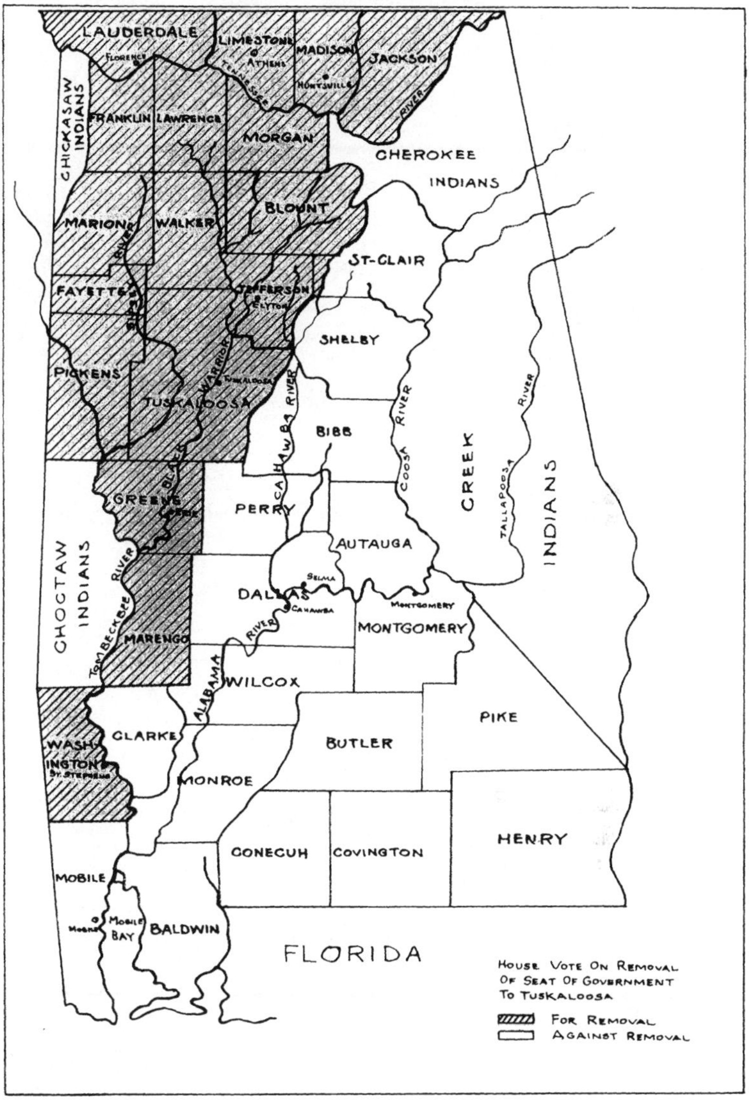

Map showing
House Vote on Removal of Seat of Government

House adjourned. Tomorrow would bring the end of the struggle!

The next day, Tuesday, December 13, 1825, after several routine matters were disposed of:

> The engrossed bill from the Senate, to be entitled an Act establishing and permanently locating the Seat of Government of the State of Alabama pursuant to the 29th section of the 3d article of the constitution, was read a third time, and the question being put, shall this bill pass? it was decided in the affirmative, yeas 38, nays 26.[1]

This is how the members of the House voted:

Aye—For Removal to Tuskaloosa

(*Mr. Speaker*) 1 William Kelly, of Madison
2 Phillips H. Armbrister, of Jackson
3 Jonathan Bailey, of Lauderdale
4 Seth Barton, of Tuskaloosa
5 W. K. Baylor, of Jefferson
6 John Baxter, of Jackson
7 Wm. Brandon, of Madison
8 John Brown, of Jefferson
9 George Coalter, of Lauderdale

[1] *Acts 1825, p. 12.*

AN ACT Establishing and permanently locating the Seat of Government for the state of Alabama, pursuant to the twenty-ninth section of the third article of the Constitution.

Section 1. Be it enacted by the Senate and House of Representatives of the state of Alabama in General Assembly convened, That the town of Tuscaloosa be, and the same is hereby designated as the permanent Seat of Government; and that from and after the end of the present session of the General Assembly, the sessions of the said General Assembly shall be held in the said town of Tuscaloosa, as established and limited by this act.

Sec. 2. And be it further enacted, That the corporate limits of the town of Tuscaloosa be, and the same are hereby extended, so as to include fractional sections twenty-one and twenty-two, and sections twenty-three, twenty-six, twenty-seven and twenty-eight, in township twenty-one and range ten west of the basis meridian of Huntsville.

WILLIAM KELLY, *Speaker of the House of Representatives*
NICHOLAS DAVIS, *President of the Senate*

NOTE: This is the only instance known to the author where an Act of the General Assembly of Alabama includes the signatures of the Speaker of the House of Representatives and the President of the Senate. Since the Constitution expressly dispensed with the signature of the Governor in case such a law was enacted, no doubt the Speaker and President signed it in their official capacities to give it authenticity.

10 Joseph Coe, of Lawrence
11 Bowley Conner, of Pickens
12 Thomas Coopwood, of Lawrence
13 James Davis, of Franklin
14 J. M. Dupuy, of Jefferson
15 Wm. Edmondson, of Limestone
16 William Fluker, of Marengo
17 Stephen Heard, of Morgan
18 John P. Hickman, of Lawrence
19 Richard Inge, of Tuskaloosa
20 Henry King, of Madison
21 Charles Lewis, of Jackson
22 James G. Lyon, of Washington
23 Joshua L. Martin, of Limestone
24 Wm. B. Martin, of Lauderdale
25 Peter Martin, of Franklin
26 Marston Mead, of Blount
27 Quin Morton of Limestone
28 Jas. C. Neill, of Greene
29 Daniel Peyton, of Jackson
30 J. H. Sims, of Greene
31 Waddy Tate, of Limestone
32 Harry I. Thornton, of Madison
33 John L. Tindall, of Tuskaloosa
34 Melcajah Vaughan, of Morgan
35 John Vining, of Madison
36 Robert H. Warren, of Greene
37 George White, of Marion
38 Marmaduke Williams, of Tuskaloosa

Nay—Against Removal to Tuskaloosa

1 John S. Bailey, of Montgomery
2 Willoughby Barton, of Mobile
3 Nimrod E. Benson, of Montgomery
4 John W. Bridges, of Wilcox
5 Robert Broadnax, of Autauga
6 Phillip Coleman, of St. Clair
7 Nathan Cook, of Butler
8 John G. Creagh, of Clarke
9 Walter Crenshaw, of Dallas
10 James Dellett, of Monroe
11 Eldridge S. Greening, of Conecuh
12 Thomas I. Hallett, of Mobile

13 Jonathon Jones, of Bibb
14 Edward J. Lambert, of Baldwin
15 Samuel W. Mardis, of Shelby
16 William McLemore, of Montgomery
17 John McNeill, of Autauga
18 John W. Moore, of Monroe
19 Sameul W. Oliver, of Conecuh
20 Jos. Pickens, of Dallas
21 Jas. Saffold, of Dallas
22 George Shotwell, of St. Clair
23 Richard B. Walthall, of Perry
24 George Weissinger, of Perry
25 William C. Watson, of Henry
26 Phillip Fitzpatrick, of Pike

The long battle was over. Not only had Cahawba lost but the whole Alabama River system section had failed in the effort to keep the seat of government. The arguments of the losers that when the Indian titles to East Alabama should be cleared and the eastern section of the State occupied by settlers, it would be necessary to move the seat of government from the western location at Tuskaloosa to a more central point[1] were ignored and pushed aside by the supporters of Tuskaloosa. These determined men had schemed to capture the capital and had assembled the votes necessary to do it. Their Act, once passed by the Assembly, was not subject to the veto power, and no argument regardless of how sound or true could deter them from the consummation of their plan.

What manner of men captained the campaign which won the seat of government for Tuskaloosa? What of the leaders who championed a losing cause?

In the Senate Levin Powell, citizen of Tuskaloosa, had charge of his home town's campaign to get the capital. Senator Powell was designated by William R. Smith as "the most level-headed man of that day in our community." He was a justice of the peace and also the postmaster. Powell in

[1] Sullivan renewed this argument after the seat of government had been placed in Tuskaloosa. Senate Journal 1826, pp. 60–61.

part made up for his lack of learning by being the close friend and constant associate of two of Tuskaloosa's most brilliant men, Judge Minor and Washington Moody.[1] Powell was also a patient and careful man in political matters. Tuskaloosa had able leadership in the Senate.

And Senator Powell had strong men to aid him. James Jackson, of Lauderdale, had come to the United States from Ireland and established himself in Nashville, only to move on to Florence, Alabama, which he helped found. He so successfully operated a large plantation that he was able to indulge in extensive philanthropies benefiting schools and churches. He participated in public affairs for years and was noted for his firmness of character and gentle disposition. He was the close personal friend of Andrew Jackson and enjoyed the respect and confidence of all who knew him.

Aiding these two stalwarts was William Crawford, of Mobile and Washington. Crawford had been the protégé of William M. Crawford, Secretary of the Treasury, and was one of the few remaining "Georgia men" still strong in Alabama politics. Crawford was president of the Tombeckbe Bank at St. Stephens, and had felt a similar blow when the seat of government moved from St. Stephens on the Tombigbe to Cahawba on the Alabama. Now he was helping to bring it back to the Warrior-Tombigbe. Crawford had been the law partner of the brilliant Henry Hitchcock, and had closely contended with William R. King for the United States senatorship. At the end of the 1825 session Crawford resigned to become United States District Judge, the second man in Alabama to hold that office. With these three men to tend her interest in the Senate Tuskaloosa was well cared for.

The opposition were men of quality, too. Arthur Pendleton Bagby was the unofficial leader. He was a member of an aristocratic family in Virginia which had provided him

[1] *Reminiscences of a Long Life*, by William R. Smith.

with a splendid education. The young man moved to Claiborne, Alabama, and in 1821 was elected to the House. In 1822 he was chosen Speaker, the youngest man ever to hold that office in Alabama. He continued to serve in the Assembly until he was elected Governor in 1837. This was followed by election to the United States Senate. President Polk appointed Bagby as Minister Plenipotentiary to the Court of the Czar at St. Petersburg, in which post he achieved great success. Bagby was a handsome, pleasant, and attractive man, and a dangerous contender for any doubtful vote.

Dr. Thomas Casey, of Cahawba, was of course the man charged by circumstances with the greatest responsibility for Cahawba. He was the Senator from Dallas. Casey was well-educated, having been graduated with honors from South Carolina College. He served his district in the Senate from 1819 to 1827, but could not stand the disappointment occasioned by the removal of the capital, so he departed for Mobile after 1827. He was known as "a skilful physician and a most worthy man." Dr. Casey was experienced in the conduct of legislative matters and extremely loyal to Cahawba. In no way did the cause of his group suffer from inattention or lack of effort.

Dunklin Sullivan, from Perry County, was Casey's co-director and constant ally through the seat-of-government battle. He too was a South Carolinian who had moved to Dallas and thence to Perry County, where he became Probate Judge. Sullivan was also a successful planter and an aggressive and defiant opponent of Tuskaloosa.

The men in the House did not suffer in a comparison with the Senators. The Tuskaloosa delegation was chosen especially for the job of bringing home the capital. Dr. John L. Tindall and Marmaduke Williams had served as delegates in the 1819 Constitutional Convention, in which the provision was written providing for an opportunity to change the seat of government in 1825. If questions were to be raised as to what had been said or understood at that time, Tuskaloosa would have in these representatives witnesses who had been present at the time, to testify in her behalf. Dr. Tindall was a practicing physician but his qualifications and habits forced him to participate in other departments of life. He was a man of marked ability and fine character, and Smith says that he "was one of the most influential of those of our citizens who secured the location of the State Capital at Tuskaloosa."

Marmaduke Williams had opposed William Wyatt Bibb in the first governor's race ever run in Alabama. He had been a protest candidate, running because Governor Bibb had appropriated the seat of government from Tuskaloosa and had placed it at Cahawba. Williams was a man born to politics. His brother was Governor of the Mississippi Territory and he held office as Assemblyman and County Judge in Tuskaloosa for a long period. He was the first secretary to the Board of Trustees of the University and continued in that job for about nineteen years. His natural political abilities, together with his constant association with many of the most influential and intelligent men in the state, made Marmaduke Williams a dangerous foe in any contest involving politics.

Dr. Richard Inge was another representative from Tuskaloosa. He belonged to a most distinguished family and was himself a man of accomplishments. Dr. Inge seems to have been the quietest and most self-effacing of the Tuskaloosa delegation, but he no doubt contributed greatly to their success.

In contrast to Dr. Inge was Seth Barton, the fourth representative from Tuskaloosa County, and the most spectacular of all the members of the 1825 Assembly. He was an arrogant fellow who was elected to the Assembly by one vote, it being cast by the sheriff to break a tie. Barton had come to Alabama from Virginia and formed a partnership at the bar with the able George N. Stewart. His legal status being thus assured, Barton participated in politics for excitement, and social life for pleasure. Says William R. Smith: "Seth Barton was a magnetic character. Of great force and intellect and commanding elegance of person, he ruled potentially in the circle of his own associates, absorbing into his own way of thinking and acting all who approached him as familiars. Though a recognized debauchee, he was nevertheless a leader in Tuskaloosa society; an especial pet with the women. He would fight a bully on the street in the morning, wash off the blood and mud and array himself like a prince for dining; and afterwards preside at the piano in the parlor at night and there sing 'Robin Adair' with a voice so melodious and an emphasis so touching as to throw the gay circle surrounding into ecstasies of delight."[1] Barton was so fascinating that the gifted Reverend A. A. Muller, D.D., pastor of the Episcopal Church at Tuskaloosa, became his boon companion, and was dismissed from his church.

This is the man who practically appointed himself to wage the "fight on the floor of the House" for Tuskaloosa. When Seth Barton set himself to be agreeable and attractive, he was a master at the business. With the flowing bowl he was both experienced and delightful. If the record of convivial persons in the taverns of Cahawba had been preserved covering the first days of December in the year 1825, one doubts not that Seth Barton's name would lead all the rest. With such a charming and audacious leader small wonder that Marmaduke Williams was quiet and Richard Inge spoke not at all.

But while Seth Barton was enjoying public acclaim, another man was doing the heavy spade work for Tuskaloosa. He was Alabama's first lobbyist and no doubt set the pattern for some master workmen who since his day have followed on the trail he blazed. This was Captain James H. Dearing, who was probably the most vigorous, energetic, and enter-

[1] *Reminiscences of a Long Life*, by William R. Smith, p. 167.

prising of the Tuskaloosa pioneers. He was not only the town's most successful merchant, but being dissatisfied with the slow barge transportation, he built the steamboat *Tom Bigbe* which was the second steamer to operate to Tuskaloosa. In connection with his mercantile business Captain Dearing operated a steam mill and carried on immense planting operations. He acquired great practical skill as a botanist and used his knowledge with advantage on his plantation, as well as to make his splendid mansion in Tuskaloosa more beautiful with a marvelous flower garden. He was for a long time a director in the State Bank. William R. Smith very conservatively records that Captain Dearing was "a close and influential lobby member of the State Legislature at Cahawba during the exciting session when the question of permanent location of the seat of government was engaging public attention, and it is believed that he exerted a material influence in favor of Tuskaloosa."[1] Dearing was accustomed to success and having the money, skill, and determination to win, when paired with the brilliant Seth Barton, the two made an unbeatable combination.

The opposition to the Barton-Dearing team was Willoughby Barton, of Mobile, and James Dellett, of Claiborne. Not much is known of Willoughby Barton. He came to Mobile as a Register in the Federal Land Office when Alabama was a territory. He was a well-educated man of some political experience. Israel Pickens chose him as one of his representatives to meet officially and invite General Lafayette to the state as its guest. Willoughby Barton's sure knowledge of parliamentary law made him a useful man in the House floor battle for the seat of government. He aided James Dellett who carried the burden of leadership. Dellett was a South Carolinian who had graduated with high honors at South Carolina College and sought his career in Claiborne. He was accepted immediately by the people of

[1] *Reminiscences of a Long Life*, by William R. Smith, p. 99.

Alabama and was elected Speaker of the first House of Representatives at Huntsville in 1819, and again in 1821. He served several terms in the Assembly before being elected to Congress. The scholarly B. F. Porter said of Dellett: "To strangers he was taciturn, and to the masses anything but dependent or conciliatory. His ideas of independence and sincerity forbade."

Although Arthur P. Bagby supplied the persuasiveness and charm needed by the Alabama River group, it appears that Tuskaloosa in addition to having the strongest geographical-political bloc also had charm and power in the Seth Barton-Captain Dearing-Levin Powell combination. These advocates were more than competent to manage her cause to a successful conclusion.

The seat-of-government struggle actually began in the year 1818 and was then promptly quieted by that master politician, William Wyatt Bibb. Thereafter, the issue smouldered until 1825 when the heat of elections again produced a glow which had flared into a hot flame by the time the Assembly convened in Cahawba in November 1825. This seasoned partisan and sectional contest served to relegate into relative obscurity other matters of great importance which developed in this the last session of the legislature at Cahawba.

The most troublesome of these other matters was the extent of the right of the Assembly to examine and inspect the affairs of the Bank of the State of Alabama. Here was a contest which exceeded the seat-of-government fight in bitterness and was almost its equal in consequences. The Bank had opened on March 9, and in its eight months of business existence, had done so much business that rumors were flying thick and fast from one end of the state to the other, some of which were intended to, and no doubt did, cause some distrust of the Bank. A disgruntled politician or a would-be borrower refused a loan would most surely not speak favorably of the Bank.

Andrew Pickens, President of the Bank, was a competent and honest man, but he was subject to the authority of twelve directors who had been elected to their posts by the Assembly. To assume that Assemblymen would not want some consideration for themselves and their friends and that the directors were not responsive in some degree is to fail to be realistic about difficulties which arise when a republican government goes into business for profit.

Pickens met the situation in the most forthright and decent manner possible. He made his report of the condition of the Bank[1] to the Assembly in a form which did not disclose any detail and entirely failed to reveal *who* had borrowed the enormous sum of over four hundred thousand dollars in eight months—at the rate of over fifty thousand dollars per mouth. To his financial report, President Andrew Pickens appended a note which read:

> As great anxiety must necessarily be felt, throughout the country, respecting the condition and operations of this institution, perhaps no statements or reports, from the Board itself, however fully or carefully drawn up, will, at all times, give entire satisfaction. The General Assembly has, very properly, reserved to itself the right of examining, by a joint committee, the general accounts and books of the Bank relating to such statement, whenever it may be deemed necessary. If such committee should now be appointed, it would be a matter of much gratification to the Directors, and they would, very respectfully, suggest the propriety and policy of making it an established custom to appoint, at each session of the General Assembly, a joint committee, to inspect the books and examine the operations of the Bank. This might be very efficacious in preventing

[1]

Capital Stock	$253,646.46		
Money Deposited	93,888.40		
Notes in Circulation	257,823.00		
		Debts due to Bank	$404,620.00
		Cash on Hand	204,019.90¼
		Due from other Banks	1,005.38½
		Banking House	1,098.37
		Books, Stationery, Bank Paper, etc.	3,394.33

(In the cash on hand is included $165.00 of counterfeit notes received from Treasurer.)

Senate Journal 1825, p. 21.

or detecting, at an early period, any mismanagement of its affairs, and would tend greatly to preserve the character of the institution, and while its funds are prudently and honestly administered, of securing to it that public confidence which is essential to make it extensively useful to the State.

Signed by order of the Board,

November 26, 1825. ANDREW PICKENS, *President*[1]

Andrew Pickens had no doubt done the best he could in lending the Bank's money, but the closing of the Huntsville Bank and the shriveling up of the Mobile and Tombeckbe banks threw the entire demand of a money-famished population on the State Bank. Andrew Pickens could not dictate to the directors, with the result that people with political influence were able to borrow from the Bank. Since the Assembly elected the directors, controlled the Bank, and had the power to examine and inspect its books, President Pickens, aware of his high duty and conscious of the danger of his position, wanted those who had the final power to also have a fair participation in the responsibility, and to know who borrowed the money, how much they got, and on what terms. The Pickens report on the Bank exploded a bomb in the Assembly. If all sections of the state had not been involved as debtors of the Bank it is likely that the Bank matter would have controlled the seat-of-government issue.

First action on Andrew Pickens' report was taken in the House when on December 2nd a resolution was offered:

> . . . to appoint three members of the House to join such committee on the part of the Senate to inspect and examine such general accounts in the books of the Bank of the State of Alabama as relate to the statement furnished by the President of the Bank to the Assembly. . . .

The House appointed Messrs. Hallett, Creagh, and Mardis as their part of the joint committee.[2]

The Senate concurred in the House resolution the next

[1] Senate Journal 1825, p. 21. [2] House Journal 1825, p. 49.

day and appointed Senators Jackson, of Lauderdale, Gaines and Crawford to the committee.[1] This was a strong committee and they were dealing with a big and sensitive matter. Many members of the Assembly had borrowed heavily from the Bank. A disclosure of the facts might well affect the political destinies of most of the members of the Assembly. The committee went to work and demanded to see the books of the Bank. The cashier of the Bank, J. B. Cook, evidently acting on orders of the directors, refused to let the committee see the crucial records, namely, the individual ledger, the discount book, the offering book, and the note book. The reason given was that these could not be shown without divulging the private accounts. The cashier refused for the same reason to exhibit to the committee the notes discounted.[2]

On December 16th the committee appointed to inspect and examine the Bank reported to the House,[3] and to the Senate.[4] The gist of the report was that the Directors and Officers claimed that the Charter of the Bank required them to refuse the Assembly access to the documents which had been denied to them. The committee was of a different opinion, and set forth in the report the reasons why the Bank law entitled the Assembly to inspect these papers, and why the Charter did not prohibit it. Along with the report the committee presented this resolution which they recommended:

> RESOLVED, That the General Assembly has the right to inspect, by joint committee, all the books of the bank, and all the evidences of debt due to that institution.[5]

The House let the report and resolution lie on the table until December 21st when Representative Vining moved that the House *not* concur in the report and resolution of the committee. On a point of order Speaker Kelly ruled that

[1] Senate Journal 1825, p. 40.
[2] Senate Journal 1825, p. 66, Ex. A.
[3] House Journal 1825, p. 83.
[4] Senate Journal 1825, p. 64.
[5] Senate Journal 1825, p. 65. House Journal 1825, pp. 83–84.

the House was competent to express its opinion on the report separately from the resolution, and might approve both, or approve one and reject the other, and the House sustained him. Greening moved that the *report* lie on the table, which carried, but when Davis moved that the *resolution* lie on the table he lost 1 to 63.[1]

Meanwhile, the Senate was struggling with the same report and resolution. They passed the resolution 18 to 3.[2] Immediately Mr. Casey offered an additional resolution:

> RESOLVED, That the committeee appointed to examine the Bank shall be under the *injunction of secrecy* . . . and that no person who is a director in any other Bank shall be appointed on said committee.

By a vote of 18 to 1 the last proviso was struck out—the Senate seeing that it was intended to eliminate William Crawford, a director of the Tombeckbe Bank, from the committee. As amended, the resolution passed and was ordered to lie on the table.[3] The Casey resolution was again amended so as to read:

> RESOLVED, With the concurrence of the House of Representatives that the examination of the affairs of the Bank of the State, by the joint committee, be conducted under the injunction of secrecy, except so far as it may be necessary to examine witnesses, and that they report their proceedings to the two Houses with *closed doors*.[4]

This resolution was presented to the House for concurrence. Barton, of Tuskaloosa, immediately opposed any accord by the House, by offering a resolution of his own:

> RESOLVED, That the joint committee of both Houses had no authority to inspect the individual ledger, discount book, the offering book, and the note book of the Bank of the State of Alabama.

Marston Mead attempted to table Barton's resolution, but failed and it was adopted 41 to 22.[5] At least there were 22

[1] House Journal 1825, p. 101.

[2] Senate Journal 1825, p. 71.

[3] Senate Journal 1825, p. 72.

[4] Senate Journal 1825, p. 76.

[5] House Journal 1825, p. 102.

members of the House who did not object to having their accounts inspected. After some parliamentary sparring the Senate resolution was adopted 52 to 10, and immediately thereafter the effect of this action was killed by adoption of Barton's amendment thereto by a vote of 41 to 20.[1]

The next day Barton, of Tuskaloosa, offered a lengthy resolution of his own. Evidently, after the adjournment the preceding afternoon, those House members who disliked the Senate action conferred together, and this resolution was the fruit of their thought. It provided for a joint committee acting under the *injunction of secrecy* to inspect the Bank's books *as far as the same may be necessary to a full development of its condition without being prejudicial to the public interest.* The resolution further provided for a specific routine in case any fraud was found to have been practiced on the Bank or its directors, and if a report of fraud be made the same be made to the General Assembly with *closed doors.* Barton went further and provided the exact words of an ironclad *oath* to be administered to the committee members so as to insure an inspection and report within the limits of his resolution, and that the facts learned by the committee members be and remain secret. With some slight amendment, the Barton resolution was adopted 43 to 20,[2] and Messrs. Creagh, Dellett, and Hallett were named members of the committee by the House.

The Senate was cold to the House resolution. After some consideration they voted to strike out that portion of it calling for the "Barton oath," and then indefinitely postponed further consideration of the measure.[3] The Senate then proceeded to try to solve the troublesome situation by amending the Charter of the Bank so that a joint committee would clearly have the right to inspect the affairs of the Bank under an *injunction of secrecy.*[4] This Senate bill did not suit the House so they struck and rewrote one of their own

[1] House Journal 1825, p. 103.
[2] House Journal 1825, p. 107.
[3] Senate Journal 1825, p. 80.
[4] Senate Journal 1825, p. 87.

along the lines of Seth Barton's resolution, but omitting the "oath" provision. The Senate, somewhat mollified by elimination of the "oath," accepted the House bill.[1] The act which was finally passed also protected the privacy of accounts in the Bank, provided for reports by the committee to the General Assembly behind closed doors, and that the injunction of secrecy not be removed except by joint resolution of both Houses.[2] The Senators in objecting to the oath evidently considered this requirement as a reflection upon the integrity of the members of the General Assembly who might serve on the Bank inspection committees.

So the measure rested until the House informed the Senate that they had chosen as their three members of the committee to inspect the Bank, Messrs. Dellett, Greening, and Hallett.[3] The Senate then elected Crabb, Jackson, of Lauderdale, and Sullivan to serve on the committee.[4] This election was held on January 3, 1826. Senators Nicholas Davis, William Crawford, Arthur P. Bagby, James Jackson, of Autauga, Matthew Clay, and James Abercrombie refused to vote when the committee members were elected. They were outraged that the amendment to the Bank Charter had failed to give the Assembly complete and absolute power to inspect the Bank and they deeply resented the Barton resolution.

These defiant Senators set forth their reasons and feelings in a long, detailed statement which constituted a complete explanation of their position, signed it and had it included in the printed journal of the Senate so that the citizens of the state might read and understand the whole controversy.[5]

When politically seasoned men like Nicholas Davis and Arthur P. Bagby were forced to resort to this method of

[1] Senate Journal 1825, p. 102. [2] Acts 1825, p. 5.

[3] Senate Journal 1825, p. 109; House Journal 1825, p. 161. (Greening replaced Creagh on the committee.)

[4] Senate Journal 1825, p. 110. [5] Senate Journal 1825, pp. 143–146.

action to be sure that all the facts were made available to the people, there must indeed have been strong feelings and deep resentment against the action of the majority in keeping secret the "inside" affairs of the Bank.

After this protest document had been spread upon the pages of the Senate Journal, Mr. Jackson, of Lauderdale, Chairman of the Committee on the State Bank, which was reporting on a bill to fix the salary of the President of the Bank, offered an additional section as an amendment to this bill.

> *And be it further enacted* that no member of the General Assembly shall during the time for which he shall have been elected become indebted to the Bank of the State of Alabama, either directly or indirectly: *Provided* that this Act shall not be so construed as to prevent any member from renewing any note which he may have previously discounted.

The above was amended by adding:

> Provided further, that this Act shall not be so construed as to prevent those members of the present General Assembly who have not already borrowed from the Bank, obtaining a loan.

But the Senate declined to include the following additional provision:

> Provided further, that no member of the General Assembly shall recommend applicants for discounts in said Bank.[1]

But this is as far as this worthy amendment ever got. It was never passed by the House. Here ended the fight for the 1825 session.

On the day before the General Assembly adjourned, the joint committee to examine into the state and condition of the State Bank reported. Thomas D. Crabb reported to the Senate,[2] and T. L. Hallett to the House.[3]

The joint committee, appointed by both branches of the

[1] Senate Journal 1825, pp. 149–150.

[2] Senate Journal 1825, p. 153.

[3] House Journal 1825, p. 228.

General Assembly, to examine into the situation and condition of the Bank of the State of Alabama, respectfully report—That the paper hereto annexed (marked A), is an exposé of the situation and condition of the Bank, up to the 9th day of January, 1826. From this statement it will be perceived that the sum of four hundred and forty-eight thousand and eight hundred and fifty-nine dollars is due to the Bank, on notes discounted to individuals. It cannot be expected from the committee, to say that this money has been loaned exclusively to solvent persons, and that the debts are entirely safe; but so far as the committee have been able to ascertain the situation of the debtors to the Bank, they have not discovered that the Institution will sustain any loss from the debts now due.

The situation of the Bank, as exhibited by the statement hereunto annexed, speaks for itself; but the interest of the Institution and of the State, may require from the committee, an expression of their opinion, as to the solvency of the Bank, and its ability to meet the demands against it. On this subject, there can be no differences of opinion.

The committee were appointed at a late period of the present session of the General Assembly; and the short space of time allowed to them has had the effect of prescribing certain limits to their examination; but they are perfectly satisfied as to the correctness of the report which they now submit, and that the Institution is entitled to the confidence of the public.

(A)

State of the Bank of the State of Alabama, on the 9th day of January, 1826

Capital Stock	$253,646.46	Notes discounted		$448,859.00
Notes in circulation	278,507.00	Banking House		1,119.17
Individual deposits	164,735.04	Due by other Banks		1,165.38
Expenses chargeable upon the Institution up to this date remaining unpaid, exclusive of the President's salary, and such amount as may be allowed to the Hon. Wm. R. King, for negotiating the loan of $100,000 in New York	3,166.80	Cash on hand, viz.:		
		Specie	$141,330.00	
		Notes of other Banks	109,210.84	
				250,540.84
Gain on the transactions of the Bank up to this date, as appears by the statement annexed, marked B	1,629.09			
	$701,684.39			$701,684.39

(B)

Statement of Expenses Incurred, and Interest Received, by the Bank of the State of Alabama

To interest on the loan of $100,000 in New York, from 1st of October, 1824, to 9th of January, 1826	$7,650.00	By discount, premium on bills, and interest received from the commencement of the operations of the Bank up to the 9th of January, 1826, as appears by the books of the Bank	$21,783.34
To interest on the University Fund, $48,063.75, from 1st Jan. 1825, & $8,-544.19 from 1st March, 1825	3,396.24		
To current and permanent expenses from the commencement of the operations of the Bank up to 9th Jan. 1826, including the sum of $3,166.08 due by the institution, and remaining unpaid	9,108.01		
To gain on the transactions of the Bank up to January 9th, 1826	1,629.09		
	$21,783.34		

Those who would keep secret the identity of the borrowers from the Bank, and the amounts which they had received, won their fight. The committee's report was a carefully worded argument to the effect that no one should have cause to doubt or lose faith in the Bank. To this farcical proceeding, after the bare report had been published, the Assembly added a face-saver in the form of a joint resolution, removing the injunction of secrecy.[1] But this was only the beginning of a long, long headache. The Bank was eventually to become a tremendous source of trouble for the State government, and before its demise did for a period challenge and overshadow the sovereign state itself.

The reformation of the judiciary was perhaps next in importance after the Bank matter. On December 27, 1825, Abner S. Lipscomb for the first judicial district, Reuben Saffold for the second, John Gayle, Jr., for the third, and Anderson Crenshaw for the sixth, were elected without opposition by the General Assembly. In the fourth district

[1] Acts 1825, p. 49.

John White was elected on the third ballot, defeating Richard Ellis and William B. Martin. The hardest fight occurred in the election of the judge for the fifth district. John Taylor finally defeated William I. Adair and Henry Minor on the seventh ballot.[1] The defeat so stung the incumbent Judge Minor that he resigned his unexpired term the next day.[2]

There had been some effort to create a separate and distinct Supreme Court, but the Assembly elected to follow the advice of Israel Pickens and retained the old plan of having the Circuit Judges serve as Justices of the Supreme Court. The Assembly did, however, restore the June term of the Supreme Court on the assumption that since the Court would hereafter meet at Tuskaloosa instead of Cahawba, the objection of jeopardy to health did not exist.[3] The Assembly also authorized the Court to appoint a Clerk of the Supreme Court to hold office for five years. The Clerk was required by the law to establish his office in Tuskaloosa before the end of March, 1826, "at which place said office shall be kept, and remain so long as the Seat of Government shall continue at said place."[4]

The Assembly elected Samuel Pickens Comptroller, and John C. Perry State Treasurer.[5] Neither man had any opposition. Daniel McGibbons was elected Harbor Master for the Port of Mobile, and Henry Gunnison, Joseph W. Moore, Samuel G. Swift, and Russell W. Lewis were designated wardens to serve with him.[6]

The Assembly by a margin of one vote in the House refused to establish a bank of discount and deposit as a branch of the Bank of the State of Alabama.[7] The Tuskaloosa bloc,

1 House Journal 1825, pp. 122–123; Senate Journal 1825, p. 89, *et seq.*

2 Senate Journal 1825, p. 94.

3 Acts 1825, p. 75. Lipscomb was appointed Chief Justice. (Minor, p. 397)

4 Acts 1825, pp. 22–23. Henry Minor accepted the appointment of Clerk of the Supreme Court, being the first man to hold that office. Acts 1825, p. 99 (Sec. 4).

5 House Journal 1825, p. 129.

6 House Journal 1825, p. 187.

7 House Journal 1825, p. 195.

having captured the seat of government, were determined also to have the University of Alabama located in their city. Israel Pickens had advised the General Assembly against making the decision at this session, and his judgment had weight with many of the Assemblymen. Nevertheless, the successful and predatory Tuskaloosans were resolved to test out their chances. They found a ready and determined opponent in Dr. Casey, Senator from Dallas, who came forward with a resolution stating the desirability of locating the University "at or near the centre of the geographical limits of the State" and the inexpediency of a site "at any extremity or on the borders of the State," and asking the Assembly to name "five fit persons" to find a suitable place for the University near the center of the State.[1]

The wording of Casey's resolution makes it plain that his main purpose was to eliminate Tuskaloosa from all consideration as a desirable site for the permanent location of the University. The House by a vote of 27 to 26 decided not to attempt to select the site for the University during the 1825–26 session,[2] but on the very same day that Casey offered his resolution the Governor approved an act reserving from sale all land owned by the University in Tuskaloosa County.[3] This was the first firm step taken by the Tuskaloosa group to capture the University. They already had the seat of government and the Bank of the State of Alabama. They could wait a little longer for the University, as this plum was not now ripe enough for plucking.

The removal of the Bank to Tuskaloosa presented no difficulty because its charter granted in 1823 provided that it be located at the "Seat of Government." Now that the seat of government was Tuskaloosa, this meant that here the Bank must be located. However, the Tuskaloosans deemed it necessary to have a specific removal law, and so one was enacted.[4] The act was significant in that it re-

[1] Senate Journal 1825, p. 135.
[2] House Journal 1825, p. 227.
[3] Acts 1825, p. 32.
[4] Acts 1825, p. 49.

quired that the Bank be moved to Tuskaloosa before June 1, 1826, and that *if the President of the Bank fail or neglect to remove* the Bank as directed by the law, the Comptroller should do so. Evidently some of the Assemblymen were still angry with Andrew Pickens for asking the Assembly to investigate the Bank, and they didn't want to run the risk of a possible fight over moving the Bank from Cahawba to Tuskaloosa.

The same Bank law provided for the election of two sets of directors of the Bank for the coming year, the first group to serve as long as the Bank remained at Cahawba, and the second group to take over when the Bank was moved to Tuskaloosa. There was some justification for this arrangement other than that of political expediency. The directors had to be reasonably accessible to the officers of the Bank. Because of the limitations of travel, this necessitated a more or less geographical selection of directors.

There was no opposition to Andrew Pickens, so he was re-elected President of the Bank, but it is a noticeable fact that a large number of the Assemblymen refrained from voting. Those elected as directors for the Cahawba Board were:

John J. Crocheron
Jesse Beene
John E. Vasser
Thomas D. King
George Phillips
R. G. Gordon
Uriah G. Mitchell
Edwin Curtis
Bernard Johnson
H. G. Perry
Fielding Vaughan
John Shields

For the Tuskaloosa Board were chosen:

James Hogan
Benjamin B. Fontaine
George Cox
James H. Dearing
Thomas Owen
William L. Adams
John B. Hogan
Garland Hardwicke
Otis Dyer
John McKee
William R. Colgin
Hardin Perkins

One of the most annoying matters before the Assembly of 1825 for consideration was the question of the Ohio Resolutions proposing a plan to emancipate the slaves. Israel Pickens had dealt with this matter in a masterly way in his message. The Senate made no formal report on the Ohio Resolutions but Seth Barton, Chairman of the House Committee, spread his report in the Journal, in which he stated that the philanthropists should direct their attention to free people of color and not to slaves. In restrained and elevated language Barton replied to the Ohioans "that at a propitious time and when there was a practicable mode of ridding ourselves of our colored population consistent with their rights and the rights of the owners, Alabama would cheerfully acquiesce in every measure calculated to effect such an object." Barton submitted a resolution providing that Alabama should not concur in the Ohio Resolutions.[1]

William Kelly, Speaker of the House, bade farewell to its members in a dramatic address in which he said: "To preside over the deliberations of this House was a proud and perilous elevation." But Kelly was always theatrical and always looking for a means of promoting himself. Three years hence he was to file charges against the Justices of the Supreme Court, and have them tried before the Senate. Now he was enjoying the applause so dear to one who loved himself.

The Tuskaloosans offered little in a material way to the State as a means of inducing the Assemblymen to locate the seat of government there. Only the site was promised, and this was a little indefinite as to size and location. Mr. Powell referred to it as an obligation entered into by sundry inhabitants of Tuskaloosa and filed in the office of the Secretary of State.[2]

The Senate, while considering the bill providing for accommodations for the Assembly for the next session, by resolution required the Secretary of State to lay before the Senate "the bonds and other papers made by the citizens of Tuskaloosa to the Governor of this State, in considera-

[1] House Journal 1825, p. 216.

[2] Senate Journal 1825, pp. 54–55.

tion of the removal of the Seat of Government."[1] The defeated but never vanquished Casey, of Dallas, offered an amendment to the bill under consideration, in which it was recited:

> WHEREAS, The memorial, presented to the General Assembly by the citizens of Tuscaloosa, among other things, agrees to furnish rooms, etc., for the accommodation of the General Assembly, for two sessions: Be it further enacted, That no money shall be drawn from the treasury for carrying this act into effect.

The amendment passed.[2] Casey wanted to be sure that the State would not have to pay rent for the rooms or quarters furnished them. The Tuskaloosans, however, got the best of the deal, for the State was forced to buy or hire all the chairs, tables, and other furniture and equipment used by them, for the Cahawba furnishings were not carried to Tuskaloosa.

The Assembly did, however, by law direct the Comptroller, Treasurer, and Secretary of State to remove their offices to Tuskaloosa by June 1, 1826. These officers were authorized

> . . . to adopt such measures for the removal of their respective offices aforesaid, as they may deem expedient or safe, either by *land* or *water* conveyance, and also for the transportation of such furniture belonging to their said offices, as may be convenient.

The Secretary of the Senate and the Principal Clerk of the House were given the duties of removing the papers and records of the Assembly, while the Quartermaster General had charge of the State Military Store and equipment.[3]

Since this Act authorizing removal was effective as of February 1, 1826, there was plenty of time within the high-water season to use river transportation down the Alabama and up the Tombigbe-Warrior to Tuskaloosa. This method was probably used instead of travel by wagon over the dif-

[1] Senate Journal 1825, p. 110.

[2] Acts 1825, p. 88.

[3] Acts 1825, p. 46.

ficult road to Tuskaloosa. The water route also had the advantage of providing the custodians of the records with a pleasant and interesting trip.

A law was enacted to take care of the leftovers. The Senate doorkeeper was given the duty of collecting all movable property of the State and storing it in the Senate Chamber; he was to lock the door and give the key to the State Treasurer. The Treasurer in turn was authorized to sell what was not removed to Tuskaloosa and to place some suitable person in charge of the State's buildings. He was also authorized to sell the "State House and the lot on which it is situated," for cash or credit, but for not less than $3,000.[1]

The 1825 Assembly was so occupied with the seat-of-government, Bank, and Court matters that little time was left for legislation for the general welfare, but non-controversial laws were readily passed.

Demands were rising all over the state for schools and academies. These were promoted by local interests, and charters were granted without argument. The Moulton Library Company was incorporated,[2] quickly followed by Moulton Academy.[3] The Coosawda Academy in the town of Coosawda was established.[4] In Montgomery, Milton Academy was chartered and given authority to raise $5,000 by a lottery.[5] The citizens of Greene County were given a charter for Concord Academy, but it was not permitted to have an annual income of over $10,000.[6] The Town of Tuscumbia incorporated two institutions—Tuscumbia Academy[7] and Tuscumbia Female Academy.[8] The trustees of the two institutions were almost identical. LaFayette Academy in the village of LaGrange was chartered and limited to an annual income of $6,500.[9] This was destined to be one of the most famous schools ever to exist within the State of Alabama.

[1] Acts 1825, p. 74.
[2] Acts 1825, p. 55.
[3] Acts 1825, p. 62.
[4] Acts 1825, p. 59.
[5] Acts 1825, p. 60.
[6] Acts 1825, p. 61.
[7] Acts 1825, p. 62.
[8] Acts 1825, p. 63.
[9] Acts 1825, p. 64.

The town of Florence was incorporated and its limits established.[1]

The Assembly provided the sum of $2,000 to pay the cost of removing the Bank to Tuskaloosa and also of "providing and fitting up a house in the town of Tuskaloosa suitable for the reception of the Bank."[2] The Governor was given $4,000 with which to finish paying the cost of the Lafayette entertainment.[3]

Although the 1825 Assembly had shown progressive characteristics by amending Alabama's dueling law so that holders of public office had to make oath they they had not engaged and would not in any way engage in the practice of dueling, almost before the ink was dry on the Governor's signature approving the law, the same Assembly relieved the popular Hiram Shortridge of its provisions. This vice of relieving men from the operation of the law was buried deep in the tradition of a people who detested the duel and yet were never quite able to enforce the laws against it when a particular person was concerned.

The years from St. Stephens to Tuskaloosa were not many, but they were tumultuous and disturbed years for the fledgling commonwealth of Alabama. Within this short span government was born, put into operation, and made to function under the merciless decrees of suffrage.

The ballot made Tuskaloosa the victor, and Alabama's diadem adorned her brow. Tuskaloosa's capital years were full of glory and excitement, but they were numbered, for even as she had lifted the seat of government from Cahawba, so did Montgomery take it from Tuskaloosa. But the annals of Tuskaloosa and Montgomery are for others to tell—this of St. Stephens, Huntsville, and Cahawba is finished.

[1] Acts 1825, p. 70, *et seq.* [2] Acts 1825, p. 87. [3] Acts 1825, p. 88.

APPENDIX

Appendix

MADISON COUNTY AND HUNTSVILLE PRIOR TO 1819

SOUTH of the Tennessee state line and within the "Great Bend" of the Tennessee River was a rich, beautiful and delightful country claimed by the Cherokee Nation, the Chickasaw Indians, and the State of Georgia. Neither tribe of Indians lived there when the white man arrived about the turn of the century. Georgia's claim was one based on sovereignty without occupation.

The United States purchased Georgia's rights in 1802, and the Indian title was extinguished by purchases and treaties made in 1805 and 1806. The land within the Big Bend became part of the Mississippi Territory which Congress had organized in 1798 and extended in 1804. Robert Williams, Governor of the Territory, by executive proclamation created Madison County on December 13, 1808. The following February 27, 1809, the Legislature of the Mississippi Territory extended the jurisdiction of the Territorial Government over the new county.

The first white settler in the county was very probably "Old Man Ditto," who lived on the Tennessee River at Ditto's landing, now Whitesburg. Ditto's name does not appear in the census of the county taken in January, 1809. He probably crossed to the south side of the river and took up residence among the Cherokees in order to avoid the activities of the census taker.

According to Judge Taylor's recollections, Joseph Criner and his brother, Isaac, together with Stephen McBroom, came into Madison County from the north and built a cabin on the Mountain Fork of Flint River. Just after the cabin was completed John Hunt and a man named Bean[1] came by searching for the "Big Spring." Later they returned to Criner's cabin and reported that Bean was going back to Tennessee but that Hunt was going to settle at the Big Spring.

John Hunt and his companion were the forerunners of a large number of unauthorized settlers who moved into the county and took possession of lands before the United States could arrange land sales. As of January 1, 1809, further settlement in the county was prohibited. At the same time President Madison ordered a census of the county in order to identify the settlers

[1] John Hunt, Isaac Criner, and a Thomas McBroom appear in the Census of 1809, but the names of Joseph Criner, Stephen McBroom, and Bean are not listed.

already there. This census[1] was completed in January, 1809, and the names listed are almost identical with those appearing on the Register of Applications to settle on the Public Lands of Madison County. These activities on the part of the United States may have retarded intruders from taking possession of Madison County lands but they by no means stopped the practice. At first the late arrivals settled just over the Madison boundary, on the Indian lands. Federal troops removed many of them, but when the intruders found that they were less severely dealt with when occupying Federal land than when occupying Indian land, the intrusion in Madison County increased.

The President moved as rapidly as possible in an effort to avoid these difficulties and disputes. About three months after the census was completed, on April 5, 1809, by proclamation he ordered land sales of the territory acquired from the Cherokees and Chickasaws in Madison County. Five days later the Secretary of the Treasury appointed John Brahan of Virginia, Receiver, and William Dickson of Tennessee, Register, for the sale of public lands in Madison County. The first sale was held in Nashville, Tennessee, beginning on the first Monday in August, 1809, and lasting three weeks. By October, in spite of threats of violence by settlers who already occupied some of the lands, the buyers at the sale had purchased 24,000 acres and paid down over $60,000 for them.

This Nashville land sale altered the course of Madison County. The gentry of Virginia, South Carolina, and Georgia were big buyers of choice lands. They soon moved in with their families and slaves, and, being numerous as well as talented, they were soon in charge of all civic offices and public affairs. This same influence quickly made itself felt in the government of the Mississippi Territory. The time was not far off when Huntsville would challenge Natchez for first place in the Territory.

The development of Madison meant public officers and patronage. Learning that the Governor would soon set up a county government in Madison, the Bar of the Mississippi Territory petitioned the President to appoint one of their members, Drury W. Breazeale, as Judge for the county. Although he had been first to apply and had the backing of his fellow lawyers, Breazeale failed to get the appointment. Stephen Neale was made Sheriff, and William Winston, Clerk of the County Court. A little later Louis Winston was appointed Attorney General of the county and was asked by Governor Williams, of the Mississippi Territory, to recommend good men to him for appointment to public office. The Governor cautioned Winston "to take special care not to enter the name of any one in the least

[1] Appendix, p. 216.

degree connected with the Yazoo Claim or whose friends or relations are interested in its establishment."

On December 23, 1809, the Legislature of the Mississippi Territory appointed William Dickson, Edward Ward, Louis Winston, Alexander Gilbreath, and Peter Perkins, residents of Madison County, Commissioners to locate the county seat. The town when laid out was directed by the Legislature to be named Twickenham.[1] The Commissioners located the town near Hunt's Spring on a portion of 1,000 acres of land which Martin Beatty had purchased at the land sale, and which included the Big Spring. The land was acquired by Beatty's exchange of his 1,000 acres for other land and by the action of LeRoy Pope, often called the "Father of Huntsville," who bought the property released by Beatty for $23 per acre, from which he set aside a plat on the bluff above the Big Spring for a Courthouse and Public Square. The town as first laid out included about 60 acres divided into blocks of two acres each, which blocks were in turn subdivided into four lots. John W. Leake was the surveyor who laid out the original plan of Twickenham. The sale of the lots brought in about $10,000, which was used for the erection of public buildings.

The day after the Mississippi Territory Legislature named the Commissioners who were to locate the seat of government for Madison County, it prepared a memorial to Congress stating that Madison County had no representative in the Mississippi Territory Legislature and that the Legislature was without power to give representation to the county. The memorial further informed Congress that Madison had at this time no court of criminal jurisdiction. Congress responded by passing a resolution which extended suffrage to the citizens of Madison County, and on January 25, 1810, authorized the President to appoint a judge with the same powers as those possessed by the judge of Washington County.

Competition for the judgeship was immediate and spirited. Governor Williams wrote the President that his brother, M. Duke Williams, had removed to Madison County, with his family, and that he was well qualified to have the office. The Governor urged the President to give him the place. Several Congressmen, including William Wyatt Bibb, asked the President to appoint Obadiah Jones to the judgeship. They also recommended

[1] Turner, p. 98. Toulmin, p. 106. Mr. Betts records in his excellent history of Huntsville that LeRoy Pope selected the name of the town, which was the name of the home of the poet, Alexander Pope. In 1811 the name was changed from Twickenham to Huntsville, in honor of John Hunt, first settler at the Big Spring or Hunt's Spring. (Toulmin, p. 774.) John Hunt evidently was unable to hold his homestead at the Big Spring after the land sales, for he abandoned his claim and moved away.

"John W. Walker, Esq., a young gentleman of talents and respectability," to be attorney general. Jones was nominated on March 5 and confirmed on March 6, 1810, thereby becoming Madison County's first judge.[1] As for Walker, he was destined to go far beyond the fine character given him by his friends.

Judge Jones' first court was held October 1, 1810. Peter Perkins served as clerk. The Court recognized as attorneys at the bar J. W. Walker, J. C. Hamilton, George Cotter, James Rogers, Gabriel Moore, Marmaduke Williams, and Louis Winston. At least three of these men achieved distinction in Alabama. Gabriel Moore also served as assessor and collector for the County of Madison during the year 1810.

The population of Madison steadily and rapidly increased. On June 29, 1811, the President ordered the land office moved "from Nashville to Huntsville, otherwise called Twickenham, in Madison County, there to be opened on or before the seventh day of August next ensuing." Governor Holmes, of the Mississippi Territory, on July 2, 1814, recommended to the President that he appoint James Titus, of Madison County, as a member of the Legislative Council of the Territory. Titus received the appointment and served continuously as Councillor until the end of the Alabama Territory. In December, 1814, Madison was awarded a second Councillor, and Robert Beatty was selected for the post.

The "Big Bend" had become such a thriving community that a newspaper was justified. The *Madison Gazette* was established in Huntsville by T. G. Bradford and Company in May or June, 1812. In August, 1816, the *Huntsville Republican*, published by Thomas B. Grantland, appeared. The name was changed to *Alabama Republican* on February 10, 1818.

On November 25, 1812, Green Academy was established in Madison County. The trustees were William Edmondson, John Brahan, William Lesley, James McCarty, Peter Perkins, Charles Buris, William Derrick, James Neely, John Grayson, Henry Cox, Bennett Woods, Samuel Allen, Andrew K. Davis, William Evans, and Nathan Power. On December 13, 1816, the Legislature of the Mississippi Territory appropriated to Green Academy and the academy at St. Stephens each the sum of $500. This was probably the first public money spent for education in what is now the State of Alabama. In 1818 Lemuel Mead,

[1] Jones was given the oath of office by William Dickson, Chief Justice of the Orphans' Court, on August 4, 1810. The losing applicant, M. Duke Williams, removed to Tuskaloosa, is known in Alabama's history as Marmaduke Williams. He opposed William Wyatt Bibb in the first election for Governor in Alabama and lost. He long served in the House of Representatives from Tuskaloosa County, was a judge there, and was for many years the Secretary to the Board of Trustees of the University of Alabama.

Henry Chambers, Henry Minor, John M. Taylor, Clement C. Clay, and John William Walker were named as additional trustees of the Academy.

A bank was needed to serve the thriving section which recognized Huntsville as its center. A charter was granted by the Legislature of the Mississippi Territory on December 11, 1816, to The President, Directors, and Company of the Planters and Mechanics Bank of Huntsville. The following leading citizens were named superintendents of subscription: LeRoy Pope, John P. Hickman, David Moore, Benjamin Cox, John M. Taylor, Thomas Fearne, Jesse Searcy, Clement C. Clay, and John W. Walker. The capital was limited to $500,000. The name of the bank was changed on February 13, 1818, to "The President Directors and Company of the Planters' and Merchants' Bank of Huntsville." This institution had a checkered career until by proclamation Governor Pickens dissolved it in 1825, using authority given him by the General Assembly.

When General Andrew Jackson marched from Tennessee in 1813 to fight the Creek War he passed through Huntsville with a large part of his army, and Mr. Betts records that four companies from Huntsville, including the "Mounted Rangers," under command of Captain Eli Hammond, together with a fifth company from Hazel Green led by Captain Jack Mosely, joined General Jackson's forces.

While the "Big Bend" community did its part in the Creek War, this creditable performance was far surpassed by peaceful achievements of the people. Many business houses were built around the public square. Thomas and William Brandon were the masons who changed Huntsville from a town of wooden buildings to one of mortar, brick, and stone. Later these same men extended their craftsmanship into the building of homes which were notable for their beauty and enduring qualities. The Courthouse was built by John P. Hickman. He was engaged in the work a number of years, and had not finished the building as late as December, 1816.

But Huntsville was ready in July, 1819, to receive the Constitutional Convention which was to bring statehood to Alabama, and more than any place in Alabama was able to care for Alabama's first General Assembly in its lone but memorable session while Huntsville was the "temporary Seat of Government" of the newly born sovereign State of Alabama.

NOTE: Carter's *Territorial Papers of the United States*, Vols. v and vi, *Early History of Huntsville, Alabama*, by Betts, Turner's *Digest of the Laws of the Mississippi Territory 1816*, and Toulmin's *Laws of Alabama 1823*, have all been consulted in preparing this brief sketch.

CENSUS OF MADISON COUNTY

[GLO: Div. E, Ohio-Miss. SG, Vol. 65, 1803–1810: ADS]

(Enumeration taken Jany 1809)

Heads of Families	*Free White Males Under 21 Years of Age*	*Free White Males Over 21 Years of Age*	*Free White Females Under 21 Years of Age*	*Free White Females Over 21 Years of Age*	*Total of Free White Inhabitants*	*Total Slaves*
Reubin Windham	1	1		2	4	
Jiles Muckleroy	2	1	2	1	6	
John Murphy	6	1	3	1	11	
John Wood	3	1	4	2	10	
Jacob Broils	2	1	1	1	5	
Levy Melvin	2	1	7	1	11	
Leban Rice	4	1		2	7	1
Aaron Rice	1			1	2	
Reubin Brock	2	1	5	1	9	
Isaac Brock	1	1	2	1	5	
Sturdy Garner	5	2	2	1	10	
William Burges	3	1	5	1	10	5
Richard Burges		2			2	2
Larkin Rogers	5	1	3	1	10	
Charles Gwinn	1	2		1	4	
Joseph Cartwright	1	1		1	3	
Littleton Felps	1	1	4		6	
Harman King	2	2	2	1	7	
James Moore	1	1	2	1	5	1
James Pybes	4	1	4	1	10	
John Murr	3	1	1	1	6	
Thomas Speaks	3	1	2	2	8	
James Fitzgerald	1	2	3	2	8	
John Helm	1	1	1	1	4	
Thomas Murphy	3	1	4	1	9	
John Jones		1		1	2	9
Jacob Clemmons	3	1	3	1	8	
Cullen Earp	2	2	2	1	7	1
Francis Shaw		1			1	5
John Shaw		1		1	2	
James Walker	5	1	2	1	9	
Mose Poore	2	1	2	1	6	
Issaiah Hamilton	3	1	1	1	6	
Alexander McCollum		1			1	
James Hamilton	1	1	1	1	4	
John Gatlin		1		1	2	
Gavin Johnston	2	1		2	5	
Francis Johnston	2	1	2	1	6	
Isaac Criner	1	1		1	3	2
Joseph Gormley	5	1	1	3	10	
Nicholas Couch	2	2	2	2	8	
George Baylis	2	1	4	1	8	
James Levingston	4	3	1	1	9	
Nathaniel Davis		1	1		2	
George Baylis	4	1	3	1	9	

Heads of Families	*Free White Males Under 21 Years of Age*	*Free White Males Over 21 Years of Age*	*Free White Females Under 21 Years of Age*	*Free White Females Over 21 Years of Age*	*Total of Free White Inhabitants*	*Total Slaves*
John Maloy	3	2	3	1	9	
Samuel Davis	3	3	1	1	8	
John R. Cook	1	1	1	1	4	
Mary Morrow	2	1	1	1	5	1
John Ridenour	3	1	5	1	10	1
Asahal Babb	2	1	3	1	7	
James Babb	1	1	4	1	7	
Aseph Wills	1	1	5	1	8	
John Harles		1	2	1	4	
John Bayzone	2	1	8	1	12	
George Bayzone	1	1		1	3	
Levi Hines	5	3	5	1	14	1
Benjamin Hines		1			1	
Absalem Colwell	1	1		1	3	
John Carter	1	1	3	1	6	5
John Bunch	1	1		1	3	4
Ebenezar Byram	1	1		1	3	4
Jacob Pence		2	3	1	6	
William Tindall	1	1	1	1	4	
James Braden	5	2	3	1	11	
Hezakiah Baylis Junr	1	1	4	2	8	4
Daniel Baylis	2	1			3	
Hezekiah Baylis Senr		1		1	2	
William Clark	5	1	6	1	13	
James McGowen	2	2	3	1	8	
Henry Maxwell	1	1	4	1	7	
John Hester	1	2	1	2	6	
John McCrimmons		1		1	2	
John Christian	3	2	6	1	12	2
Jacob McCarty	2	1	1	1	5	
James Black		3		3	6	
Mordacia Lammon		1	2	3	6	
Daniel McFall	3	1		1	5	
John Sprawl	3	2	2	1	8	
Benjamin Franks		1		1	2	
John Smith Senr	5	3	4	1	13	2
William Fields	1	1		1	3	
Daniel Morris		1			1	
George Broils	3	1	3	2	9	
John Condron		1	1	1	3	
John Lewis	3	1	1	1	6	
Henry Forgusson	3	1	4	1	9	
Robt S. Qallient	3	1	3	1	8	
John Bason	1	1	1	1	4	
William Brown	1	1		1	3	
William Brown Jun	2	1	3		6	3
Elijah Lawley	1	1	1	1	4	
Hugh Malloy	1	1	4	1	7	
Varnel Magbee	2	1	3	1	8	
Joseph Powell	1	2	2	1	5	
Willam Barlett	4	1	1	1	7	

Heads of Families	*Free White Males Under 21 Years of Age*	*Free White Males Over 21 Years of Age*	*Free White Females Under 21 Years of Age*	*Free White Females Over 21 Years of Age*	*Total of Free White Inhabitants*	*Total Slaves*
Jacob Prewitt	2	1	3	1	7	15
Joseph York	4	1	2	1	8	
William Prewit	1	1		1	3	2
James Mahan	3	2	1	1	7	
James Dayton	3	1	6	3	13	
John Grayston	4	2	2	1	9	2
Benjamin Wilson	5	1	2	1	9	2
James Wilson		1		2	3	
James Loller		1		1	2	
David Harles	4	1	1	1	7	
Thomas Jones	4	1	2	1	8	
Reece Baylis		1	2	1	4	
Robin Hampton		1	1	1	3	
John Waldrop	1	1	3	1	6	
Enoch Berry	2	1	4	1	8	
Robert Davis		3	1	1	5	
Robert Bushart	1	1	3		5	
Richard Crawson	5	1	6	1	13	2
Peter Anderson	2	1	2	1	6	
Jacob Cannimore	2	2	2	3	9	
Erikus Anderson		1		1	2	
Samuel Cannimore	6	4	1	4	15	
John Lamley	4	2	3	1	10	
Levy Byram	2	1	1	1	5	3
Reubin Stone	3	2	1	1	7	2
Jessey Cannimore	2	1	1	1	5	
David Lindsey	1	3	1	1	6	6
Benjamin Busey		2	3	1	6	8
John Gillin	2	2	2	1	7	
William Thompson	2	3	2	1	8	
Jacob Baldwin	1	1	3	1	6	1
Abraham King	2	1		2	5	
Isaac Rogers	2	1	3	2	8	
Alfred Massingale	3	1	1	1	6	
Solomon Massingale	3	1	4	1	9	3
Cason Fulch	1	1	3	1	6	
Reddin Crisp	1	1		1	3	
Isaac Lee	1	1		1	3	
William Prewit	1	1	1	1	4	
John Bowren	3	2		1	6	
William Crisp		1		1	2	
Henry Landers	4	2	1	1	8	
Amos Elliott	3	2	4	1	10	
James Walker	1	1		1	3	
George Light	3	1	2	1	7	
Jessey Sullens	4	1	3	1	9	
Levy Crow	3	1	1	1	6	
John Allbright	3	1	2	1	7	
John Hellums	1	1	1	1	4	
Alden Byram	3	1	4	1	9	3
Thos O Banian	1	1	4	1	7	3

Heads of Families	*Free White Males Under 21 Years of Age*	*Free White Males Over 21 Years of Age*	*Free White Females Under 21 Years of Age*	*Free White Females Over 21 Years of Age*	*Total of Free White Inhabitants*	*Total Slaves*
Williams Neighbours	2	1	2	1	6	
Edward Bradley	2	2	4	1	9	4
Andrew Sibley	2	3	1	1	7	
Spencer Ball		2	1	2	5	
John Hews	1	1		1	3	
Moses Seton	6	1	6	1	14	
George Poe	3	1	3	1	8	
James Criss	2	2	2	1	7	
Anthony Street	3	2	4	1	10	
John Reynolds	3	1	2	1	7	
James Shoemaker	1	1	2	1	5	
Samuel Wilson	1	2		1	4	
James Anderson	4	1	2	1	8	
James Christian		2		1	3	
Thomas Austin	2	1	1	1	5	
Allen Christian	3	1	3	1	8	
Mathew Pendall	3	1	3	1	8	
Thos Lindsey	4	1	2	1	8	
Henry Moore	1	1		1	3	
John Hatfield	1	2		1	4	1
Richard Mardis	3	1	2	2	8	3
Joseph Wafford	1	1	1	2	5	3
John Killingsworth	2	1	5	1	9	
Ebenezar Byram Junr	3	2	1	1	7	3
John Derick		1	1	1	3	1
Reynold May	2	1	2	1	6	
James Drake	1	1	1	1	4	
Edmund Clements	3	1	2	2	8	17
George Blackburn	3	1		1	5	
Benjamin Langford	1	3	1		5	11
John Couch Senr	3	2	3	2	10	
Thos Couch	4	2	1	1	8	
John Couch Junr	1	1	1	1	4	
John Allison	4	1	3	1	9	1
Waller Mathews	3	1	2	1	7	
Jospeh Mathews	4	1	4	1	0	
Archibald McDanniel		1	5	1	7	6
John Renneau	3	1	3	1	8	
John Martin	1	2	3	1	7	
John Kerksey	1	1		1	3	7
Edward Webster	3	1	2	1	7	
William Hallmark	3	1	3	1	8	
Isaac Nesmith	1	1			2	
John May	1	2		1	4	
Samuel Aklin	5	1	3	1	10	
James Cotton	2	1	3	1	7	
Charles McCartney	2	2	2	2	8	6
Joseph Hews	1	1	2	1	5	
Joseph Aklin		2	1	1	4	
Thomas McBroom	3	1	1	1	6	
Michael Montgomery	3	1	1	1	6	

Heads of Families	*Free White Males Under 21 Years of Age*	*Free White Males Over 21 Years of Age*	*Free White Females Under 21 Years of Age*	*Free White Females Over 21 Years of Age*	*Total of Free White Inhab-itants*	*Total Slaves*
George Sharp	3	1	1	1	6	6
Thomas Williams		1		1	2	
Hugh Roger	2	4		2	8	
George Dilworth	2	1	3	1	7	
Reubin Simmons	2	1	3	1	7	6
Mathew Moore		3	1	1	5	
Thomas Mimms	1	1	1	2	5	
James D. Rogers		1	1	1	3	
William W. Kavanaugh	2	2	2	1	7	
Thomas Powell		1	3	1	5	
Hugh Carothers	1	1	4		6	
John Morison	5	2	2	1	10	
William Adair	1	1	2	1	5	
Samuel Mardis	1	2	1	2	6	
Benjamin Wafford Sen[r]	1	1	2	1	5	10
Benjamin Wafford Jun[r]	4	1	2	1	8	3
William Gassaway	2	1	4	1	8	
John Nicholson	1	2	2	1	6	
John Crawford		2	3	1	6	12
Francis Johnston	2	2	2	1	7	
Daniel Harrison		1	1	1	3	
Davis Neale		1	1	1	3	
Isaac Johnston	3	1		1	5	
John Clap	2	1	1	2	6	
Robert Wright	6	1	2		9	1
Joseph Evans	1	1	1	1	4	
Francis Bell	4	1	2	1	8	
Thomas Nismith		1		2	3	
John Nismith	2	1	4	1	8	
Thomas Hewlet		1	1	1	3	2
John Kavanaugh	1	2	1	1	5	
George Hallmark Sen[r]	3	1		2	6	
George Hallmark Jun[r]	2	1	4	2	9	
John Baker	2	3	4	1	10	
James Kernes	1	1	1	1	4	
John Loy	1	1	1	1	4	
James McNutt	4	1	3	1	9	
Isreal Standefer	5	3		2	10	3
Robert Stinson	3	1	5	1	10	
Lewis Clapp	3	1	3	1	8	
Vincent Glass	3	1	3	1	8	4
William Bird	2	1	5	1	9	
Joseph Harrison	1	1	1	1	4	
Robert Liston		2	1	1	4	1
Jessey French	1	1		1	3	
James Seton	2	1	3	1	7	
John Hodges	2	1	1	1	5	
John Bayley	4	1		1	6	
William Bayles	1	1	7	1	10	
Ezekiel Clap	4	1	5	1	11	
Hugh McVay	1	2	4	1	8	11

Heads of Families	*Free White Males Under 21 Years of Age*	*Free White Males Over 21 Years of Age*	*Free White Females Under 21 Years of Age*	*Free White Females Over 21 Years of Age*	*Total of Free White Inhabitants*	*Total Slaves*
Minor Winn	3	2		1	6	
Thomas Bawlin	3	1	5	1	10	
Robert Boyd	3	2	4	2	11	3
John Keys	1	1	3	1	6	
Gamiel Findley	3	2	3	1	9	
Maynard Colly	1	1	1	1	4	
Nathaniel Austin	3	1	3	1	8	
Richard Bell	5	1	3		10	
William Lynch	1	1	1	1	4	
John Hunt	4	1	1	2	8	5
Giles McGuire	3	1	1	1	6	1
Benjamin Stegall		1	2	1	4	
William Campbell	1	2	1	1	5	1
Joseph Dougherty		2	2	1	5	
Alexander Gilbreadth		3			3	
David Gray	1	1		1	3	1
William Landram	3	1	3	1	8	1
James Smith	7	1	2	1	11	
Abel Lewis	1	1	2	1	5	1
Rodon Fulcher		1		1	2	
Alexander Campbell	2	1	2	1	6	1
Little B. Adams	1	1	4	1	7	17
Joseph Adams		1	1	1	3	1
Raleigh Hews	2	2	2	1	7	
Charles Carrell	1	2	3	1	7	9
William Carrell	2	2		1	5	
William Bloomer	1	1		1	3	
David Jones	1	1	1	1	4	
Isaac Vernon	2	2	2	2	8	1
Benjamin Stedham	2	1	7	1	11	
John Millhouse	1	1	5	1	8	5
Henry Bloodworth	1	1		1	3	
Daniel Kieth	1	1	5	1	8	1
Abraham Perkins		1		1	2	5
Robert Winn	2	1	3	1	7	
Anthony Ward		1	3	1	5	
David Henderson	2	1		1	4	
Thomas Johnson	2	2	1	2	7	
Lewis Pew	4	1	2	1	8	
George Snodgrass	2	1	2	1	6	
John Jackson	1	1	1	1	4	
James Henderson	1	1	1	1	4	
Abner Cotton	2	1	2	1	6	2
Garland Tidwell	1	1		1	3	
William Wright		1	4	1	6	
John Childers	4	3	1	2	10	
Moses Fields	1	3	4	1	9	1
William Mayson	3	1	4	1	9	
William Fowler	1	1		1	3	
William Cooper	1	1	3	1	6	
James Copeland	1	1		1	3	

Heads of Families	*Free White Males Under 21 Years of Age*	*Free White Males Over 21 Years of Age*	*Free White Females Under 21 Years of Age*	*Free White Females Over 21 Years of Age*	*Total of Free White Inhabitants*	*Total Slaves*
Benjamin Grayson	4	1	2	1	8	
Benjamin Williams	1	2	4	1	8	–2–7
Thomas Battle		1		1	2	7
Benjamin W. Battle		2	1	2	5	
Joseph Greenwood	1	2	3	1	7	
Phelix Parker	4	1	3	1	9	
John McPhail	3	2	2	1	8	
John Beason	1	1	1	1	4	
Freeman Jones	3	2	4	1	10	
William Southerland	2	1	1	1	5	
James Matier		2	1	2	5	
James Mattier	1	1	1	1	4	
Solomon Matier	4	1	1	1	7	
James McCinnis	1	1	2	1	5	
Alexander Baxter	2	1			3	
James Baxter		1		1	2	
Rowland Cornelius	1	1	4	1	7	11
Robert Harper	4	2	5	1	12	
John Conley		2	1	1	4	
David Conelly	2	1		1	4	2
Hugh Carothers	1	1	4		6	
James Hubbard		1		1	2	
John Morrison	1	1	1	1	4	
John Bird	2	1	3	1	7	
Edmund Hodges	2	1	2	1	6	
Robert Dial		1		1	2	
John Birdwell	2	1	6	1	10	
Francis Maxwell		4	2	1	7	1
John Baxter	1	1	1	1	4	
Stephen Jones	1	1	3	1	6	
Nicholas Moser	4	3	2	1	10	
Joseph Pate	1	2	1	3	7	
William Bonds		1	2	1	4	
Joshua Butcher	2	1	1	1	5	
William Reneau		1		1	2	
Richard Hallmark		1	1	1	3	
Daniel Gillis	2	1	5	1	9	1
Archibald Patterson	6	1	2	1	10	
Malcolm Patterson	4	1	4	1	10	
William Simpson	1	1		1	3	4
George Wilder	3	2	2	1	8	
John Wilder	2	1		1	4	
Horatio Aday	5	1	1	1	8	
Hugh Woollard	4	2	2	2	10	
Dillin Blevins	2	2	4	2	10	10
John Roller	2	2		1	5	
Abram Head	2	1	1	1	5	
Abner Solomon		1	1	1	3	
Michael Harrison		7	6	3	16	2
William Campbell	4	1	1	1	7	2
Patrick Burns	1	2	4	1	8	1

Heads of Families	*Free White Males Under 21 Years of Age*	*Free White Males Over 21 Years of Age*	*Free White Females Under 21 Years of Age*	*Free White Females Over 21 Years of Age*	*Total of Free White Inhab-itants*	*Total Slaves*
John Robins	2	1	1	1	5	
John Jones		1		1	2	
Total Population	677	473	685	388	2223	322

It appears from the written enumeration of the Inhabitants of Madison County Mississippi Territory—taken Jany 1809—That the population consisted of

353 Heads of Families
677 Free white Males under the age of 21 Years
473 Free white Males over the age of 21 Years
685 Free white Females under the age of 21 Years
388 Free white Females over the age of 21 Years
2223 Total white Inhabitants and 322 Slaves

THO^S FREEMAN

THE HON^BLE ALBERT GALLATIN
Sect^y of the Treasury U. S.

CAHAWBA BEFORE 1820

WHAT of Cahawba before it was selected by William Wyatt Bibb for Alabama's "Seat of Government"? The learned Peter Brannon states that there was an Indian town at the mouth of the Cahawba when De Soto passed there in the year 1540. The Spanish recorded the town as being named Casiste. Later when the French came up the Alabama River they found Indian settlements here bearing the Choctaw name Cahawba, meaning "water above"—an appropriate name for a place subject to the wrath of two great rivers. Brewer reports that the French built fortifications at Cahawba about 1750 for the protection of their trading post at this place.

Evidently there was no "town of Cahawba" in being at the junction of the Alabama and Cahawba Rivers in February, 1818, when the General Assembly created Dallas County and established its court system, for the Act provided:

> That for the time being, the said Courts, in and for said County of Dallas, shall be holden at the mouth of the Cahawba; but said Courts may, respectively, for want of necessary buildings, adjourn to some convenient place contiguous thereto. (Acts Alabama Territory, February 1818 Sessions, pp. 47–48)

The absence of buildings at the site of the old and vanished Indian village of Cahawba was due to the fact that all the land surrounding this point of union of the Rivers Alabama and Cahawba was owned by the Federal Government and had been withheld from sale and denied to settlers.

The Assembly realized that this place was a convenient and accessible location which could not be confused with any other place, and they were also informed that there were "buildings" on land "contiguous thereto." The building on land contiguous thereto was most certainly the homestead of Captain John Howard, at whose home the first court in Dallas County was subsequently held.

The first reference to the "town of Cahawba" appears in Governor Bibb's message to the Alabama Territory Assembly at its November session in 1818, and the phrasing which he used indicates that he was referring to the townsite of Cahawba instead of an actual town. A few days later, on November 16, 1818, the Assembly enacted the law which located the seat of government of the state at the confluence of the Alabama and Cahawba Rivers, and gave the Governor power to "lay off, or cause to be laid off on such plan as he may deem most suitable, a town at the place now called and known as the town of Cahawba." (Acts Alabama Territory, November Session, 1818, p. 46)

Soon after the Assembly had directed that the courts of Dallas County be held at the "mouth of the Cahawba," the Worshipful Roderick McLeod, Chief Justice of the Orphans' Court of Dallas County, held a court and his written record now in the Probate Office of Dallas County recites that he held the court at the "mouth of the Cahawba" on June 9, 1818. The business before the Court was to probate the will of Reuben White, deceased. The subscribing witnesses not being present, the Court adjourned to July 20, to meet again at the house of Captain John Howard, at the "mouth of the Cahawba." Sitting with Worshipful Chief Justice Roderick McLeod were Thomas Craig and Abner Cleveland, Justices of the Quorum. The sureties for John White, who offered Reuben White's will for probate, were John Howard and Abner Franklin. The will was proven by witness Wm. R. Pickett.

In the same Orphans' Court minutes, on page 12, it is disclosed that the Court met at the house of Captain John Howard in the *town* of Cahawba on July 19, 1819. This is the first reference in this record to the "town of Cahawba," but at this late date Cahawba had been legally created by the General Assembly, the site surveyed into lots, and most of them sold at public auction.

The records of the Commissioners' Court of Dallas County, appearing in the same book which contains the Orphans' Court proceedings, show that Abner Franklin was also a Justice of the Quorum at the April session in 1818 when the Commissioners' Court granted John Howard a license to keep a tavern in his home. They also named John Rose, Charles Rose, William Davis *et al.* to lay out a road from Cahawba to Fort Bibb on the Federal Road. This Court also served as a sort of pioneer "Office of Price Administration." At the April session of 1818 they established "Rates for Taverns."

Diet per meal 37½ cents
Taffy and whiskey 18¾ pr ½ pt cts
Medarie and cherry wines 18¾ pr ½ pt cts
Malaga and other inferior wines 18¾ pr ½ pt
Corn and fodder pr. feed 37½ cents
Corn only, 25 cts
Feed by the night pr horse One Dollar pr feed, 24
hours one dollar thirty seven and ½ cents
Lodging per night 12½ cents

In April 1818 on application of Elizabeth Campbell, it was ordered by the Commissioners' Court that the ferry on the Cahawba River near the mouth thereof be established as a public ferry and charge the following rates:

Each four wheeled carriage, $1.00
Each two wheeled carriage, 55 cents
Horse and rider, 12½ cents
Each head of horse or led horse, or cattle, 6¼ cents
Each passenger, 6¼ cents

For the ferry of Parson Davis on the Alabama River near the mouth of the Cahawba:

Four wheeled carriage, 1.50 dollars
Two wheeled carriages, 75 cents
Horse and rider, 75 cents
Each pack horse, 25 cents
Each foot person, loose or led horse, 12½ cents
Each head of cattle, hogs or sheep, 6½ cents

In April, 1819, a year later, things were booming. The Assembly in November, 1818, had named this place for the seat of government of the state of Alabama, and the surveyors had already surveyed the lots to be sold in May—next month. The Commissioners' Court reviewed the tavern and ferry situation and fixed the rates as follows:

Tavern rates for said county fixed as follows:
For breakfast, dinner, or supper, 50 cents
Feeding horse with corn and fodder, 50 cents
Feeding horses with corn only, 37½ cents
For night's lodging, 12½ cents
Rates of spirits, as formerly

The price of food for man and beast was upped while that of liquor was unchanged. One wonders if Captain John Howard, operating a tavern in his home, might not have collected a price above the ceiling for a good whiskey on a cold night.

At this time no change was made in the ferry rate, but business was so greatly increased on the ferries by developments at the seat of government that a Special Court called in August, 1819 revised the ferry rates as follows:

Cahawba River Ferry
Each four wheeled carriage, 75 cents
Each two wheeled carriage, 37½ cents
Horse and rider, 8 cents
Single horse, 4 cents
Footman, 4 cents

Alabama River Ferry
Each four wheeled carriage, $1.00
Each two wheeled carriage, 50 cents
Horse and rider, 12½ cents
Single horse, 6¼ cents

Pack horse, 12¼ cents
Foot passenger, 6¼ cents
Cattle pr head, 5 cents
Hogs, sheep and goats, 3 cents

So it was in Cahawba in 1818 and until the State of Alabama took over in December, 1819, and by law established that all the tract of land granted by Congress to Alabama for the seat of government thereof "shall be deemed and taken to be within the limits of the town of Cahawba." (Acts 1819, p. 118)

MEMBERSHIP AND ORGANIZATION OF THE SENATE AND HOUSE OF REPRESENTATIVES 1818–1825

Roster of the Legislative Council of the Alabama Territory

At the First Session of the First General Assembly

At the Town of St. Stephens

Begun January 19, 1818—Adjourned February 14, 1818

County of	
Madison	James Titus

James Titus, being the only member present, elected himself President of the Council, and appointed Curtis Hooks Secretary, and John Pearson Doorkeeper.

Roster of the House of Representatives of the Alabama Territory

At the First Session of the First General Assembly

At the Town of St. Stephens

Begun January 19, 1818—Adjourned February 14, 1818

County of	
Baldwin	Henry B. Slade
Clarke	John McGrew, Neil Smith
Madison	Gabriel Moore, Hugh McVay, John W. Walker, Clement C. Clay
Mobile	Alvan Robishow
Monroe	Sam Dale
Montgomery	Phillip Fitzpatrick
Washington	A. S. Lipscomb, John F. Everitt

Gabriel Moore was elected Speaker; Isaac Nicholson, Clerk; Samuel Smith, Sergeant at Arms; and Matthew Lasoy, Doorkeeper.

Roster of the Legislative Council of the Alabama Territory

At the Second Session of the General Assembly

At the Town of St. Stephens

Begun November 2, 1818—Adjourned November 21, 1818

County of	
Madison	James Titus, Lemuel Meade, Henry Chambers
Monroe	John Gayle, Jr.
Shelby	George Philips
———	Matthew D. Wilson

There is no known printed copy of the Journal of the Second Session of the Legislative Council. Certain references in the Journal of the House of Representatives for the Second Session disclose that the above members were present; that James Titus was again President of the Council; that Peter Martin was Secretary, and Matthew Lasoy, Doorkeeper.

Roster of the House of Representatives of the Alabama Territory

At the Second Session of the General Assembly

At the Town of St. Stephens

Begun November 2, 1818—Adjourned November 21, 1818

County of	
Baldwin	Henry B. Slade
Blount	Isaac Brown
Cahawba	Littlepage Syms
Clarke	Neil Smith, William Walton
Conecuh	Richard Warren
Cotaco	Melcajah Vaughan
Dallas	Edwin D. King
Limestone	Benjamin Murrell
Madison	Clement C. Clay, John W. Walker, Samuel Walker
Marengo	William Anderson
Marion	Charles Hudspeth
Mobile	Alvan Robishow
Monroe	Sam Dale
Montgomery	Phillip Fitzpatrick
Shelby	Jesse Wilson

Tuskaloosa	Julius H. Sims
Washington	John F. Everitt, Abner S. Lipscomb

John W. Walker was elected Speaker; John C. Goolrick, Clerk; and Littleberry Vaughan, Doorkeeper. Samuel Smith, by letter, resigned the office of Sergeant at Arms.

Roster of the Senate of the State of Alabama

At the First Annual Session of the General Assembly

At the Town of Huntsville

Begun October 25, 1819—Adjourned December 17, 1819

County of	
Autauga	Howell Rose
Baldwin	Robert A. Harwell
Blount	Gabriel Hanby
Cahawba	Littlepage Sims
Clarke	Joseph B. Chambers
Conecuh	John Herbert
Cotaco	J. W. Garth
Dallas	Thomas Casey
Franklin	William Metcalf
Lauderdale	Joseph Farmer
Lawrence	Flemming Hodges
Limestone	Thomas Bibb
Madison	Gabriel Moore
Marengo	Thomas Ringgold
Marion	John D. Terrel
Mobile	James L. Seabury
Monroe	John Watkins
Montgomery	John Gause
St. Clair	David Conner
Shelby	Bennet Ware
Tuskaloosa	Thomas Hogg
Washington	William Trotter

Thomas Bibb was unanimously elected President *viva voce*. Thomas A. Rogers was elected Secretary, and John K. Dunn, Doorkeeper.

The Senate adopted the rules of government of the Senate of New York State for their use until rules of their own could be written and adopted (Senate Journal 1819, p. 9). Later thirty-four rules of order were adopted for government of the Senate (Senate Journal 1819, pp. 31–34).

Roster of the House of Representatives of the State of Alabama

At the First Annual Session of the General Assembly

At the Town of Huntsville

Begun October 25, 1819—Adjourned December 17, 1819

County of	
Autauga	Phillip Fitzpatrick and Charles A. Dennis
Baldwin	Thomas Carson
Blount	John Brown, Isaac Brown, Benjamin Mattison
Cahawba	Jonathon Jones
Clarke	William Murrell, G. M. Creagh
Conecuh	William Lee, Thomas Watts
Cotaco	Melcajah Vaughan, John McCarley
Dallas	Edwin D. King, James Saffold
Franklin	Temple Sargent, Anthony Winston
Lauderdale	Thomas Gerrard, Jacob Byler
Lawrence	Lewis Dillahunty, Samuel Bigham
Limestone	Nicholas Davis, James W. Exum, William Whitaker
Madison	Samuel Walker, Epps Moody, J. G. Birney, Samuel Chapman, Griffin Lamkin, John L. Towns, Frederick Weedon, Isaac Wellbourn
Marion	Silas McBee
Mobile	James W. Peters
Monroe	James Dellett, William Bates, Pascal Harrison, George W. Owen, Samuel Dale
Montgomery	John Edmundson, Joseph Fitzpatrick, Larkin Cleveland
St. Clair	James Hardwick
Shelby	Jesse Wilson, Arthur Taylor
Tuskaloosa	James Hill, Hardin Perkins, Julius Sims
Washington	John F. Everitt, James Thompson

James Dellett was elected Speaker; Jonas J. Bell, Clerk; and E. M. Tate, Engrossing Clerk. Daniel Rather was elected Doorkeeper.

Roster of the Senate of the State of Alabama

At the Second Annual Session of the General Assembly

At the Town of Cahawba

Begun November 6, 1820—Adjourned December 21, 1820

County of	
Autauga	Howell Rose
Blount	Gabriel Hanby
Cahawba	Littlepage Sims
Clarke	Joseph B. Chambers
Conecuh	John Herbert
Cotaco	Jesse W. Garth
Dallas	Thomas Casey
Franklin	William Metcalf
Jackson	William D. Gaines
Lauderdale	Joseph Farmer
Lawrence	Flemming Hodges
Limestone	Nicholas Davis
Madison	Gabriel Moore
Marengo	Thomas Ringgold
Marion	John D. Terrel
Mobile	James L. Seabury
Monroe	John Watkins
Montgomery	John Gause
St. Clair	David Conner
Shelby	Bennet Ware
Tuskaloosa	Thomas Hogg
Washington	William Trotter

Gabriel Moore was elected President; Marmaduke Williams, Secretary; and Matthew W. M'Clellan, Doorkeeper.

Roster of the House of Representatives of the State of Alabama

At the Second Annual Session of the General Assembly

At the Town of Cahawba

Begun November 6, 1820—Adjourned December 21, 1820

County of	
Autauga	James Jackson, Phillip Fitzpatrick
Baldwin	Joseph Mims

Blount	Isaac Brown, John Brown, Colonel John Brown
Cahawba	Gabriel Benson
Clarke	William Murrell, George U. Creagh
Conecuh	Samuel Cook, Thomas Armstrong
Cotaco	McKinney Holderness, John T. Rather
Dallas	Isaac M'Means, Horatio G. Perry
Franklin	John Duke, Temple Sargent
Lauderdale	Hugh M'Vay, Jonathan Bailey
Lawrence	Samuel Bigham, Matthew Clay
Limestone	John S. Doxey, William Edmundson, Quin Morton
Madison	Frederick Weedon, Samuel Chapman, John McKinley, John M. Leake, John Vining, David Moore, Samuel Walker, Henry Chambers
Marengo	John Coats
Marion	James Moore
Mobile	Francis W. Armstrong
Monroe	John Murphy, George W. Owen, James H. Draughan, Samuel Dale, Thomas Evans
Montgomery	Larkin Cleveland, James Abercrombie, Joseph Fitzpatrick
St. Clair	Phillip Coleman
Shelby	Benjamin Davis, Jack Shackelford
Tuskaloosa	Hardin Perkins, Jeptha V. Isbell, James Hill
Washington	James Tagert, Benjamin S. Smoot

George W. Owen was elected Speaker *viva voce*; James J. Pleasants, Principal Clerk; and Daniel Rather, Doorkeeper.

Roster of the Senate of the State of Alabama

At the Called Session of the General Assembly

At the Town of Cahawba

Begun June 4, 1821—Adjourned June 18, 1821

County of	
Autauga	Howell Rose
Bibb	Charles A. Dennis
Blount	Gabriel Hanby
Clarke	Joseph B. Chambers
Conecuh	John W. Devereux
Cotaco	J. W. Garth
Dallas	Thomas Casey

Franklin	William Lucas
Jackson	William D. Gaines
Lauderdale	Joseph Farmer
Lawrence	Flemming Hodges
Limestone	Nicholas Davis
Madison	Gabriel Moore
Marengo	Thomas Ringgold
Marion	John D. Terrel
Mobile	John Elliot
Monroe	John Watkins
Montgomery	John Gause
St. Clair	David Conner
Shelby	Bennet Ware
Tuskaloosa	Thomas Hogg
Washington	William Trotter

Gabriel Moore was elected President, and M. Williams, Secretary.

Roster of the House of Representatives of the State of Alabama

At the Called Session of the General Assembly

At the Town of Cahawba

Begun June 4, 1821—Adjourned June 18, 1821

County of	
Autauga	James Jackson, Phillip Fitzpatrick
Bibb	Gabriel Benson
Blount	Isaac Brown, John Brown, Colonel John Brown
Clarke	William Murrell, George U. Creagh
Conecuh	Samuel Cook, Thomas Armstrong
Cotaco	McKinney Holderness, John T. Rather
Dallas	Isaac M'Means, Horatio G. Perry
Franklin	Theophilus Skinner, Temple Sargent
Lauderdale	Hugh M'Vay, Jonathan Bailey
Lawrence	Samuel Bigham, Matthew Clay
Limestone	John S. Doxey, William Edmundson, Quin Morton
Madison	Frederick Weedon, Samuel Chapman, John McKinley, John M. Leake, John Vining, David Moore, Samuel Walker, Henry Chambers

Marengo	John Coats
Marion	James Moore
Mobile	Francis W. Armstrong
Monroe	John Murphy, George W. Owen, James H. Draughan, Samuel Dale
Montgomery	Larkin Cleveland, James Abercrombie, Joseph Fitzpatrick
St. Clair	Phillip Coleman
Shelby	Benjamin Davis, Jack Shackelford
Tuskaloosa	Hardin Perkins, Jeptha V. Isbell, James Hill
Washington	James Tagert, Benjamin S. Smoot

It is probable that Mims of Baldwin County, and Evans of Monroe County, although they were elected, did not attend this session. Theophilus Skinner replaced John Duke of Franklin.

There were no new officers elected at the Called Session because it was the decision of the House that the Constitution did not require the election of officers oftener than annually. In the absence of Daniel Rather, M. D. Thomason was appointed Doorkeeper.

Roster of the Senate of the State of Alabama

At the Third Annual Session of the General Assembly

At the Town of Cahawba

Begun November 5, 1821—Adjourned December 19, 1821

County of	
Autauga	Howell Rose
Baldwin	Julius Haines
Bibb	Charles A. Dennis
Blount	Gabriel Hanby
Clarke	Joseph B. Chambers
Conecuh	John Devereux
Dallas	Thomas Casey
Franklin	William Lucas
Jackson	William D. Gaines
Lauderdale	Hugh McVay
Lawrence	Flemming Hodges
Limestone	Nicholas Davis
Madison	Isaac Lanier
Marengo	Patrick May

Marion	John D. Terrell
Mobile	John Elliott
Monroe	William Wingate
Montgomery	John Gause
Morgan	J. W. Garth
St. Clair	David Conner
Shelby	Bennet Ware
Tuskaloosa	Thomas Hogg
Washington	William Trotter

John D. Terrell was elected President; Francis S. Lyon, Secretary; George V. Dick, Assistant Clerk; and M. W. McClellan, Doorkeeper.

Roster of the House of Representatives of the State of Alabama

At the Third Annual Session of the General Assembly

At the Town of Cahawba

Begun November 5, 1821—Adjourned December 19, 1821

County of	
Autauga	William R. Pickett, John A. Elmore
Baldwin	Elijah Montgomery
Bibb	Jonathon Jones
Blount	John Brown, Moses Ayers, Washington Allen
Clarke	James Magoffin, Edward Kennedy
Conecuh	Eldridge S. Greening, John E. Graham
Dallas	Walter Crenshaw, Randall Duckworth
Franklin	William W. Parham, Theophilus Skinner
Jackson	William Barclay, George W. Hopkins, Booker Smith
Lauderdale	Gutherage Masterson, John Craig
Lawrence	Matthew Clay, Hugh A. Anderson
Limestone	William Edmundson, Benjamin Murrell, Quin Morton
Madison	David Moore, John Vining, Frederick Weedon, John Martin, Thomas Miller, William Fleming, Henry King, John M. Leake
Marengo	Nathaniel Norwood
Marion	Lemuel Beene
Mobile	Francis W. Armstrong
Monroe	James Dellett, John Carr, Samuel Dale, A. P. Babgy, Thomas Evans

Montgomery	Joseph Fitzpatrick, George Dabney, Peter Williamson
Morgan	McKinney Holderness, Horatio Philpott
St. Clair	James Hardwicke
Shelby	Benjamin Davis, Thomas McHenry
Tuskaloosa	Levin Powell, Marmaduke Williams, Sion L. Perry
Washington	James Tagert, James Thompson

James Dellett was elected Speaker; N. Dodson, Principal Clerk; Edward R. Byrd, Engrossing Clerk; Thos. W. Winn, Assistant Clerk; and William T. Gamble, Doorkeeper.

Roster of the Senate of the State of Alabama

At the Fourth Annual Session of the General Assembly

At the Town of Cahawba

Begun November 18, 1822—Adjourned January 1, 1823

Senatorial District of	
Autauga and Perry	Dunklin Sullivan
Baldwin, Mobile, Washington	Francis W. Armstrong
Bibb and Shelby	Jack Shackelford
Blount and St. Clair	David Conner
Butler and Montgomery	John D. Bibb
Clarke and Wilcox	Neil Smith
Conecuh, Covington, Henry, Pike	John W. Devereux
Dallas	Thomas Casey
Decatur and Jackson	Robert M'Camy
Franklin and Marion	William Metcalf
Greene and Marengo	John Coats
Jefferson	John Wood
Lauderdale	Hugh McVay
Lawrence	Arthur F. Hopkins
Limestone	Nicholas Davis
Madison	David Moore
Monroe	John Murphy
Morgan	Thomas D. Crabb
Pickens and Tuskaloosa	Levin Powell

Nicholas Davis was elected President; Francis S. Lyon, Secretary; George V. Dick, Assistant Clerk; and Matthew W. Thomason, Doorkeeper.

Roster of the House of Representatives of the State of Alabama

At the Fourth Annual Session of the General Assembly

At the Town of Cahawba

Begun November 18, 1822—Adjourned January 1, 1823

County of	
Autauga	Phillip Fitzpatrick
Baldwin	Lud Harris
Bibb	Jonathon Jones, John Wallace
Blount	Marston Mead
Clarke	Edward Kennedy, James Fitz
Conecuh	Samuel W. Oliver
Dallas	Thomas B. Rutherford, Walter Crenshaw
Decatur and Jackson	Alexander Dulaney, Wm. Barclay, Thos. Bailey
Franklin	Anthony Winston, Theophilus Skinner
Greene	Hiram Shortridge, Zachariah Merriwether
Henry	Benjamin Harvey
Jefferson	Isaac Brown, Thomas W. Farrar
Lauderdale	James Jackson, Francis Durrett
Lawrence	Greene K. Hubbard, Matthew Clay, Joseph Young
Limestone	Woodson Montgomery, Quin Morton, William Edmondson, Joshua L. Martin
Madison	William I. Adair, John M. Leake, John Pope, Thomas Fearn, Christopher Hunt, William Sanders, James W. McClung
Marengo	Nathaniel Norwood
Marion	John D. Terrell
Mobile	Thomas L. Hallett
Monroe	Arthur P. Bagby, John Gayle, Henry L. Riviere
Montgomery	John Browning, James Abercrombie
Morgan	John T. Rather, John Adams
Perry	George Weissinger, William Ford
St. Clair	James Hardwicke, Phillip Coleman
Shelby	Benjamin Davis

Tuskaloosa	Thomas C. Hunter, James Hill, Marmaduke Williams
Washington	James Thompson
Wilcox	Edwin L. Harris

Arthur P. Bagby was elected Speaker; Nathaniel Dodson, Principal Clerk; William B. McClellan, Engrossing Clerk; Thomas B. Tunstall, Assistant Clerk; and William T. Gamble, Doorkeeper.

Roster of the Senate of the State of Alabama

At the Fifth Annual Session of the General Assembly

At the Town of Cahawba

Begun November 17, 1823—Adjourned December 31, 1823

Senatorial District of	
Autauga and Perry	Dunklin Sullivan
Baldwin, Mobile, Washington	Francis W. Armstrong
Bibb and Shelby	Jack Shackelford
Blount and St. Clair	David Conner
Butler and Montgomery	John D. Bibb
Clarke and Wilcox	Neil Smith
Conecuh, Covington, Henry, Pike	John W. Devereux
Dallas	Thomas Casey
Decatur and Jackson	Robert M'Camy
Franklin and Marion	William Metcalf
Greene and Marengo	John Coats
Jefferson	John Wood
Lauderdale	Hugh M'Vay
Lawrence	Arthur F. Hopkins
Limestone	Nicholas Davis
Madison	David Moore
Monroe	John Murphy
Morgan	Thomas D. Crabb
Pickens and Tuskaloosa	Levin Powell

Nicholas Davis was unanimously elected President *viva voce*. Francis S. Lyon was elected Secretary; David H. Burke, Assistant Clerk; and Matthew D. Thomason, Doorkeeper.

Roster of the House of Representatives of the State of Alabama

At the Fifth Annual Session of the General Assembly

At the Town of Cahawba

Begun November 17, 1823—Adjourned December 31, 1823

County of	
Autauga	William R. Pickett
Baldwin	Samuel Haines
Bibb	Charles A. Dennis, Alexander Hill
Blount	Marston Mead
Clarke	James Fitz, John G. Creagh
Conecuh	Samuel W. Oliver, John Fields, James Salter
Dallas	Walter Crenshaw, George Phillips
Decatur and Jackson	William Barclay, Daniel Peyton
Franklin	Temple Sargent, Theophilus Skinner
Greene	Zachariah Merriwether, Julius Sims
Henry	Benjamin Harvey
Jefferson	John Brown, Isham Harrison
Lauderdale	James Jackson, Caleb S. Manly
Lawrence	Zadock M'Vay, Benjamin B. Jones, Joseph Young
Limestone	John W. Smith, Joseph Powell, William Whitaker, Joshua L. Martin
Madison	William I. Adair, William Moore, William Fleming, John Vining, Henry King, Isaac Lanier, Thomas Miller
Marengo	William Fluker
Marion	James Moore
Mobile	Thomas L. Hallett
Monroe	John Gayle, Samuel Dale, William W. M'Connico
Montgomery	William M'Lemore, John G. Ashley
Morgan	William S. Goodhue, Horatio Philpott
Perry	George Weissinger, John McLaughlin
St.Clair	James Hardwicke, George Shotwell
Shelby	Samuel W. Mardis
Tuskaloosa	James Hill, Hardin Perkins, John L. Tindall
Washington	J. D. Lister, Samuel Haines
Wilcox	John Beck

William I. Adair was elected Speaker; N. Dodson, Principal Clerk; Thomas B. Tunstall, Assistant Clerk; and R. B. Watson, Doorkeeper. William Adair resigned during the session and Samuel B. Oliver was elected to succeed him.

Roster of the Senate of the State of Alabama

At the Sixth Annual Session of the General Assembly

At the Town of Cahawba

Begun November 15, 1824—Adjourned December 25, 1824

Senatorial District of	
Autauga and Perry	Dunklin Sullivan
Baldwin, Mobile, Washington	James Tagert
Bibb and Shelby	Jack Shackelford
Blount and St. Clair	David Conner
Butler and Montgomery	John D. Bibb
Clarke and Wilcox	Neil Smith
Conecuh, Covington, Henry, Pike	John W. Devereux
Dallas	Thomas Casey
Decatur and Jackson	Robert McCamy
Franklin and Marion	William Metcalf
Greene and Marengo	John Coats
Jefferson	John Wood
Lauderdale	Hugh McVay
Lawrence	Arthur F. Hopkins
Limestone	Nicholas Davis
Madison	David Moore
Monroe	John Murphy
Morgan	Thomas D. Crabb
Pickens and Tuskaloosa	Levin Powell

Nicholas Davis was unanimously elected President *viva voce*. F. S. Lyon was elected Secretary; David H. Burke, Assistant Clerk; and Matthew D. Thomason, Doorkeeper.

Roster of the House of Representatives of the State of Alabama

At the Sixth Annual Session of the General Assembly

At the Town of Cahawba

Begun November 15, 1824—Adjourned December 25, 1824

County of	
Autauga	William R. Pickett
Baldwin	Silas Dinsmore, Jr.
Bibb	Alexander Hill, Jonathon Jones
Blount	Marston Mead
Clarke	John G. Creagh, Richard Dickerson
Conecuh	Samuel W. Oliver, Nathan Cook, John Green
Dallas	Walter Crenshaw, Joseph Pickens
Decatur and Jackson	Daniel Peyton, Wm. D. Gaines, Samuel Moore
Franklin	Theophilus Skinner, William W. Parham
Greene	Zachariah Merriwether, Ezekiel Pickens
Henry	William C. Watson
Jefferson	Thos. W. Farrar, Benjamin Worthington
Lauderdale	Jacob Byler, John P. Cunningham
Lawrence	Zadock McVay, James McCord, John White
Limestone	Quin Morton, Joshua L. Martin, James W. Exum, William Edmondson
Madison	James W. Camp, Samuel Walker, Anthony H. Metcalf, Thomas Miller, John Vining, Isaac Lanier, Wm. Fleming
Marengo	William Fluker
Marion	James Moore
Mobile	Willoughby Barton
Monroe	A. P. Bagby, Samuel Dale, John W. Moore
Montgomery	James Abercrombie, Andrew Baxter
Morgan	John T. Rather, Robert Tapscot
Perry	George Weissinger, Charles J. Shackelford

St. Clair	George Shotwell, Phillip Coleman
Shelby	Samuel W. Mardis
Tuskaloosa	Hardin Perkins, John L. Tindall, R. E. B. Baylor
Washington	——— Ruffin
Wilcox	John Beck

Samuel Walker was elected Speaker; N. Dodson, Principal Clerk; Wm. B. McClellan, Engrossing Clerk; Thomas B. Tunstall, Assistant Clerk; and Elijah Wyatt, Doorkeeper. N. Dodson resigned and was succeeded by Thomas Murray.

Roster of the Senate of the State of Alabama

At the Seventh Annual Session of the General Assembly

At the Town of Cahawba

Begun November 21, 1825—Adjourned January 14, 1826

Senatorial District of	
Autauga and Shelby	James Jackson
Baldwin, Mobile, Washington	William Crawford
Bibb and Perry	Dunklin Sullivan
Blount and St. Clair	John Ash
Butler and Conecuh	William Jones
Clarke and Marengo	George S. Gaines
Covington, Henry, Pike	William Irwin
Dallas	Thomas Casey
Fayette, Marion, Pickens, Walker	Jesse Vanhoose
Franklin	Theophilus Skinner
Greene	Zachariah Merriwether
Jackson	Robert M'Camy
Jefferson	John Brown
Lauderdale	James Jackson
Lawrence	Matthew Clay
Limestone	Nicholas Davis
Madison	Thomas Miller
Monroe and Wilcox	Arthur P. Bagby
Montgomery	James Abercrombie
Morgan	Thomas D. Crabb
Tuskaloosa	Levin Powell

Nicholas Davis was unanimously elected President *viva voce*. Francis S. Lyon was elected Secretary; George W. Crabb, Assistant Clerk; and James A. Bates, Doorkeeper.

Roster of the House of Representatives of the State of Alabama

At the Seventh Annual Session of the General Assembly

At the Town of Cahawba

Begun November 21, 1825—Adjourned January 14, 1826

County of	
Autauga	Robert Broadnax, John McNeill
Baldwin	Edward J. Lambert
Bibb	Jonathon Jones
Blount	Marston Mead
Butler	Nathan Cook
Clarke	John G. Creagh
Conecuh	Samuel W. Oliver, Eldridge S. Greening
Dallas	Walter Crenshaw, Jos. Pickens, James Saffold
Franklin	Peter Martin, James Davis
Greene	J. H. Sims, Robert H. Warren, James C. Neill
Henry	William C. Watson
Jackson	Phillip H. Armbrister, Charles Lewis, John Baxter, Daniel Peyton
Jefferson	John Brown, W. K. Baylor, J. M. Dupuy
Lauderdale	Wm. B. Martin, George Coalter, Jonathan Bailey
Lawrence	John P. Hickman, Joseph Coe, Thomas Coopwood
Limestone	Waddy Tate, Quin Morton, William Edmondson, Joshua L. Martin
Madison	William Kelly, John Vining, Henry King, Harry I. Thornton, William Brandon
Marengo	William Fluker
Marion	George White
Mobile	Thos. I. Hallett, Willoughby Barton
Monroe	James Dellett, John W. Moore
Montgomery	Nimrod E. Benson, John S. Bailey, William McLemore
Morgan	Melcajah Vaughan, Stephen Heard
Perry	George Weissinger, Richard B. Walthall
Pickens	Bowley Conner
Pike	Phillip Fitzpatrick
St. Clair	George Shotwell, Phillip Coleman
Shelby	Samuel W. Mardis
Tuskaloosa	Seth Barton, Richard Inge, John L. Tindall, Marmaduke Williams

Washington	James G. Lyon
Wilcox	John W. Bridges

William Kelly was elected Speaker *viva voce*; Thomas B. Tunstall, Principal Clerk; William B. McClellan, Engrossing Clerk; Rufus K. Anderson, Assistant Clerk; and James Brown, Doorkeeper.

INDEX

Index

References to names occurring in the Census of Madison County (pages 216–223) and the Membership and Organization of the Senate and House of Representatives 1818–1825 (pages 228–245) are not included in this index.